Your Border Collie's Life

Also Available from Prima Pets

KIM D.R. DEARTH

Joanne Howl, D.V.M., Series Editor

Your
BORDER COLLIE'S

Life

Your Complete Guide to Raising
Your Pet from Puppy to Companion

PRIMA PUBLISHING

Published by Prima Publishing, Roseville, California. Member of the Crown Publishing Group, a division of Random House, Inc.

Random House, Inc. New York, Toronto, London, Sydney, Auckland

Interior photos by Kent Lacin Media Services
Color insert photos © Isabelle Français and Tara Darling
Chapter 6 illustrations by Pam Tanzey

Special thanks to the beautiful dogs who appear in this book and their wonderful owners: Tye and Bugsy, owned by Seth A. Linn; Teva, Lori Kavanagh; Rosy, Jason and Michelle Marrone; Spryte, Kim Delkener; Jake, Bill Cuthbertson; and Riley, Mary Lou Stults.

Library of Congress Cataloging-in-Publication Data
Dearth, Kim
    Your border collie's life : your complete guide to raising your pet from puppy to companion / Kim D.R. Dearth.
       p. cm. — (Your pet's life)
    ISBN 0-7615-2536-X
    1. Border collie I. Title. II. Series.
    SF429.B64 D43 2000
    636.737'4—dc21   00-034689

01 02 03 DD 10 9 8 7 6 5 4 3 2
Printed in the United States of America
First Edition

Visit us online at www.primapublishing.com

This book is dedicated to my first two-legged child,
who will be making his or her debut in the world
shortly before this book is published.

Your constant presence kept me company
as I wrote every word, and your gentle kicks
reminded me to get back to work
when my concentration wavered!

Thank you for providing me with daily inspiration.
I can't wait to meet you.

Contents

Acknowledgments

I would like to thank all of the people who helped me with this book, from my husband, Dave, who lived through the writing of every sentence with me, to my family, both biological and in-law, who have always provided encouragement and loving support. I also would like to thank the many Border Collie owners who opened their hearts and shared their special insights into this truly one-of-a-kind breed.

And finally, I'd like to thank Breeze and Brigga, and their human mom, Lynn, for giving me lots of personal glimpses into the greatness that is the Border Collie.

Thank you all!

Introduction

If you are holding this book in your hands, chances are you are a Border Collie owner or are contemplating adding a Border Collie to your life. There is no other breed quite like this, the world's premier sheepdog. Border Collies are loyal, hard working, and love to please their owners. Perhaps you've heard that the breed is smart. In fact, their intelligence is legendary, from their ability to distinguish meaning in the language of a sheep farmer's whistles and tones of voice to their prowess in competitive dog obedience trials and their acting talent demonstrated on television ads and in movies. Maybe you have seen an agility trial on television and were amazed at the speed and responsiveness of this canine athlete. Or, perhaps you've had the unparalleled pleasure of seeing a working Border Collie in action, herding a farmer's flock, as the breed has been bred for centuries to do.

Border Collies also are bundles of ceaseless energy and are highly demanding of an owner's time and attention. The positive qualities of the Border Collie can quickly turn to negatives if they are not fully understood, especially with a novice owner who has not taken the time to research what living with a Border Collie entails. Before you run out and buy the first Border Collie you see, you need to understand all aspects of this breed's character.

An Overview of Border Collie Ownership

First and foremost, Border Collies are working dogs. Typically, this is not the best breed for the first-time dog owner. These dogs have a high demand for both physical and mental exercise, which many new owners find difficult to satisfy. A Border Collie who does not receive enough stimulation through herding or suitable substitutes (such as organized dog sports) or, at the very least, interactive play with his owner for several hours a day, becomes unhappy, and may become hyperactive and destructive.

This is not a latchkey dog. Border Collies fit in best with outdoorsy, athletic owners who view time spent exercising their dogs as a pleasure, not a chore. Border Collies also need to be true members of the family. If they are isolated in the backyard, they become lonely, bored, and depressed.

Border Collies must be socialized early with all types of people, especially children. While they can make wonderful companions for youngsters, adult Border Collies are easily overwhelmed by the antics of children if they aren't used to them, and can become snappish. They also may view kids as little livestock to herd if they haven't been taught differently from puppyhood.

Border Collies are sensitive to harsh corrections, yet will dominate the household if given the opportunity. They need fair, gentle, but strong leadership to show them their place in the family and to teach them the household rules.

What It Means to Have a Border Collie in Your Life

Are you the right owner for a Border Collie? Are you capable of being strong, yet fair and consistent with your dog? Do you have the time to devote to exercising, training, and playing with this dog, who is the canine equivalent of the Energizer Bunny?

Even if you have a fenced yard, don't expect your Border Collie to exercise himself. To provide him with sufficient exercise, you'll need to take long walks, jog, or bike with your Border Collie several times a day, and supplement this with rousing games of fetch or other activities. You also need to realize that the Border Collie's mind is as nimble as his body. Sports such as agility and flyball can work your dog's brain while giving his body a workout as well.

If you don't adequately exercise your dog's mind and body, you'll quickly learn the downside of the Border Collie's intelligence. Your dog will think of all kinds of creative endeavors to pass the time, from redecorating your table legs with artistic chewing to discovering how to scale over, or dig under, your backyard fence.

How Much Thought Have You Given to Having a Border Collie?

Some people want a Border Collie because of the breed's incredible work ethic. This drive to work becomes a negative if it is not given a proper outlet, however. Many people underestimate this breed's need for both exercise and companionship. If you put in much overtime at a demanding job or travel frequently, choose another breed. The Border Collie will not thrive without intense, daily human-canine interaction. Would you buy a Porsche to keep it locked up in the garage? Don't buy the

world's premier herding dog to lay on the couch with you while you watch television.

Dog Ownership: Many Sacrifices, Many Joys

There is nothing more heartwarming than being greeted by a wriggling body and joyous kisses after a particularly rough day. There's no doubt about it—having a dog in your life is a wonderful experience. They are always ecstatic to see you, never judge you, and have an uncanny way of chasing away your blues when you are feeling down. They are always up for anything you suggest, from a jog around the neighborhood to a game of fetch in the park or racing waves at the beach. If you're shy, a dog is a wonderful conversation piece, introducing you to new friends wherever you go. Dogs can make you laugh, they can help you cry—they are the best of companions.

While many people can't imagine a life without pets, you must be realistic about the commitment needed before you bring home a puppy or adopt an older dog. How much time do you have to devote to your dog? While your pet will be grateful for every minute she spends with you, it isn't fair to get a dog if you don't have the time between work, school, or outside activities to give her the companionship she craves. This is especially true in the case of the Border Collie, who languishes without proper exercise and attention. If you are getting a puppy, you'll need to spend extra time housetraining, socializing, and obedience-training your dog.

Are you willing to give your pet the proper exercise? Many people acquire a dog, put up a fence, and think their job is done. Throw a

Border Collie in a fenced yard by herself and your dog will likely respond with a "When are you coming out to play?" stare through the screen door until you join her. As I mentioned above, you need to be prepared to walk, jog, bicycle, swim, play fetch, or engage in canine sports with your dog to provide companionship and much-needed exercise. Once you've experienced the boundless energy of a Border Collie, you'll be happy to take part in some of these activities to help wear your dog out!

You also must be dedicated to obedience-training your Border Collie from the moment you bring her home. She will not hesitate to push her boundaries if you don't teach and enforce proper household manners. You'll need to be a strong and consistent leader to help your pet find her place in the family.

Is everyone in the household excited about obtaining a Border Collie? It's not fair to bring home a dog who one or more members of the family don't truly want. Your dog will need consistent direction from each and every member of the family to understand and obey the rules you set up. If someone in your household doesn't feel up to the challenge of a Border Collie, discuss with your family whether another breed might be better suited to everyone's lifestyle and expectations, or if your family may not be right for a dog after all.

Finally, have you thought about cost? Many people are perfectly willing to shell out the cost of buying a dog, but forget to take into consideration the money needed to keep her healthy and happy. While grooming costs are minimal for a Border Collie, feeding your dog a nutritious diet, taking her in for annual veterinary checkups and vaccinations plus office visits should she get sick or hurt, buying the necessary equipment (crate, bowls, collars, leash, fencing, etc.), and paying for training classes, boarding, and/or pet-sitting services add up to a substantial investment. Figure out these costs spread over the life of your dog and you can see that you will end up paying a small fortune for your Border Collie.

If after carefully and realistically considering all of the above sacrifices involved in dog ownership you still feel your life is incomplete without a loving, loyal, enthusiastic, bundle of canine energy at your side, you may be ready for a Border Collie! As you read on, you'll not only share the personal experiences of many people who have opened their hearts and homes to this breed, you'll also learn everything you need to know about dog ownership, from choosing a puppy and selecting the best food to exercise and health care. So sit back, and let's explore the world of the Border Collie.

So, You Want a Border Collie

In This Chapter

○ What Makes a Border Collie Special?
○ Keys to Your Border Collie's Happiness
○ Where to Find the Perfect Border Collie for You

The Border Collie is known for his superior intelligence, strong work ethic, and incredible loyalty. This is a breed that will work tirelessly for hours at whatever task you ask of him, and attack all duties with unbridled enthusiasm. The Border Collie can also play the clown, inventing goofy games that are sure to bring a smile no matter how difficult your day has been. The Border Collie will bond to you like few other breeds—you will be his life.

These positive attributes can have negative consequences, however. The Border Collie's intelligence and hardworking attitude can easily lead to boredom if he is not given a job to do. If left to his own devices, his creativity can lead to imaginative doggie projects that you may not approve of, such as craters in your flower beds, destuffed living room pillows, and avant garde rips in your kitchen wallpaper.

The Border Collie's unparalleled stamina means this is no couch potato canine. This breed needs intense, daily exercise, no matter what the weather or your mood. You may have heard Border Collies described as hyperactive, obsessive, or neurotic. These are not inevitable Border Collie traits. They usually result from an owner who doesn't provide proper physical and mental stimulation for his or her dog.

Border Collies also need a firm, but gentle hand when being trained, or they will quickly dominate the household. They must be socialized at a very young age with all manner of other pets and people, especially young children, if they are to grow into stable, accepting adults.

> Before acquiring this breed, you must educate yourself about all aspects of the Border Collie's temperament.

Before acquiring this breed, you must educate yourself about all aspects of the Border Collie's temperament, and understand what your Border Collie needs from you in order for him to remain happy. Does your lifestyle allow for the exercise, training, and attention this type of dog not only craves, but also requires? If you conclude that you can provide the proper environment for this breed, your next step is to learn how to find the perfect dog for you by learning all there is to know about this wonderful breed.

What Makes a Border Collie Special?

What makes a Border Collie such a unique and notable breed? All dogs are descendents of wolves, which is more apparent in certain breeds, such as the Alaskan Malamute, than in others, such as the diminutive Chihuahua. Many years ago, man befriended the wolf and decided to harness this animal's considerable talents to suit his needs. Our ancestors then molded wolves into certain types to perform specific jobs, from hunting to guarding, companionship, and herding. If you examine the act of herding, it isn't hard to recognize the wolf's ability to choose specific animals and cut them from the herd. The biggest difference is that, in the herding dog, we have bred out the desire to kill.

A Bit of History

Much of the history of the Border Collie breed, and indeed all breeds more than 100 years old, is not based on fact, but instead is a product of legends, speculation, and bits and pieces of historical evidence. That said, the Border Collie's history possibly stretches to before the time of Christ. Around 55 BC, invading Roman armies introduced large, somewhat fierce herding dogs to Britain. Believed to be the forebears of today's Border Collie, these dogs were used to guard the flock as well as herd.

Invading Vikings in 794 AD introduced smaller, Spitz-type herding dogs who were used to herd reindeer. These dogs were crossed with the Romans' dogs to create a more agile sheep-herding breed that could manage livestock over the rough mountainsides of Scotland and Wales. The introduction of the Spitz dog's black and white or sable and white markings made the resultant dogs easier to see when they were working at night.

Did You Know?

The wolf, from which dogs are descended, was the first animal to be domesticated.

Mention of Border Collie-type dogs are sprinkled throughout early writings. A more detailed description of the "Shepherd's Dog" appeared in Dr. Johannes Caius' *Treatise on English Dogges* in 1576. This book not only gave a physical description of the breed, but also mentioned the trained dog's ability to work from his owner's hand signals and voice commands. *A General History of Quadrupeds,* published in the 1700s, included engravings of dogs who looked remarkably like today's Border Collie.

Border Collie-type dogs gained steadily in popularity as hard-working sheepdogs. As shepherds' flocks grew to keep up with the demand for wool, these "Collies," as they were called at the time, became indispensable helpers and were well established in Britain by the 1800s. Border Collies did not become known by their modern name until 1915 when the secretary of the International Sheepdog Society, formed in 1906, added the word "Border" to their official registered moniker.

Border Collies first entered dog shows in Britain in 1865, in which they were judged against a written standard that sought to establish the ideal "Collie." Although there was a standard, Border Collies ranged greatly in size and color, since British stockmen bred for working ability above any physical characteristics. In time, the Border Collie breed became more uniform; today, a definite type is seen at British dog shows.

> Border Collie-type dogs gained steadily in popularity as hard-working sheepdogs.

In 1873, the first sheepdog trial was held in Bala, Wales, to assess the working ability of this noble canine. A compact, tricolor dog named Tweed won that first trial. Today, sheepdog trials held around the world allow owners to show off their dogs' talent at doing what they were bred to do.

What's the American Kennel Club?

Founded in 1884, the American Kennel Club (AKC) is a non-profit organization dedicated to the protection and advancement of purebred dogs. Composed of over 500 dog clubs from across the nation, the AKC's objectives include maintaining a registry of purebred dogs, promoting responsible dog ownership, and sponsoring events, such as breed shows and field trials, that promote interest in and appreciation of the purebred dog.

To be eligible for AKC registration, a puppy must be the offspring of individually registered AKC parents, and the breeder must obtain the proper paperwork before the puppy's sale. Once registered, a dog is eligible to compete in AKC-sanctioned events and, if bred with another AKC-registered dog, to have his/her offspring registered.

The AKC approves an official breed standard for each of the 147 breeds currently eligible for registration. The standard is written and maintained by each individual breed club. An attempt to describe the "perfect" dog of each breed, the breed standard is the model responsible breeders use in their efforts to produce better dogs. Judges of AKC-sponsored events and competitions use the breed standards as the basis of their evaluations.

Because of the AKC's emphasis on excellence and high standards, it is a common misconception that "AKC registered" or "AKC registrable" is synonymous with quality. While a registration certificate identifies a dog and its progenitors as purebreds, it does not necessarily guarantee the health or quality of a dog. Some breeders breed for show quality, but others breed for profit, with little concern for breed standards. Thus, a potential buyer should not view AKC registration as an indication of a dog's quality.

The Border Collie Controversy

In the United States, the Border Collie's place in the conformation ring has been the source of much controversy and disagreement.

In 1955, the Border Collie was admitted to the American Kennel Club's Miscellaneous Class, which is a sort of holding pen

A Collie by Any Other Name . . .

In the early days of the Border Collie's history, farmers referred to the breed as simply "Collies," which confused Border Collies with the Rough Collie, most often associated with the famous Lassie. Early names given to the Border Collie included the Working Collie, Old-Fashioned Collie, Farm Collie, Scotch Collie, English Collie, and Welsh Collie. Eventually the word "Border" was added to distinguish the breed as the type of dog originating from the border between England and Scotland.

The word "Collie" also has interesting beginnings. It is believed to stem either from the Celtic word "coalley," which means black; the Welsh word "coelius," meaning faithful; or the name for the Scottish breed of sheep, the "colley."

for dog breeds that may eventually seek full AKC recognition. Full recognition allows dogs to compete in conformation shows as well as in the full range of dog sports governed by the AKC. The Border Collie remained in that class in a state of limbo until 1994, when the AKC notified the breed clubs for all breeds in the Miscellaneous Class that they needed to seek full recognition or no longer continue their connection with the organization.

This action caused a rift among Border Collie lovers. While some welcomed full AKC recognition, which would mean the Border Collie could now be shown in all AKC events, from conformation to obedience, tracking, herding, and agility, others felt full AKC recognition would compromise the working heritage of the breed, with dogs being bred more for looks than for working ability. They felt that other organizations, such as the United Kennel Club, offered plenty of competitive dog sports for Border Collies, with conformation showing being unnecessary. In addition, many people feared that the almost inevitable increase in popularity that accompanies AKC recognition would result in overbreeding of the Border Collie, leading to a decline in physical health and stable temperaments. Despite much opposition, the AKC fully recognized the Border Collie in December 1994. In 1996, the AKC chose the Border Collie Society of America (BCSA) to be the official AKC parent club for the breed.

Although it has been a number of years since full recognition occurred, the controversy has not died. There are many people devoted to preserving the Border Collie's working heritage; some refuse to register their dogs with the AKC.

The United States Border Collie Club (USBCC) has been the most vocal in its opposition to AKC recognition. The club is the oldest Border Collie breed club in North America. It does not register dogs or run sheepdog

> There are many people devoted to preserving the Border Collie's working heritage.

trials. Instead, its sole purpose is to protect the heritage of the Border Collie as a traditional working dog. USBCC members register their dogs with working Border Collie registries rather than the American Kennel Club.

There are three established registries for working Border Collies, including the American Border Collie Association (ABCA). This organization registers, maintains, and verifies pedigrees of Border Collies; promotes the breeding, training, and distribution of reliable working Border Collies; and promotes sheepdog trials and exhibitions. Two other registries for working Border Collies are the American-International Border Collie Registry (AIBC) and the North American Sheep Dog Society (NASDS).

On the other side of this controversy are the breed fanciers who insist that beauty and working ability do not have to be mutually exclusive; they are happy to be part of conformation showing. The BCSA maintains that its goal is to protect the breed's herding instinct and ability while supporting the rights of Border Collie owners to pursue any activity they wish, including conformation. It is unlikely that these factions will resolve their differences in the foreseeable future. (For a complete list of Border Collie clubs and registries, see the Resources section at the back of this book.)

Concern Over the Standard

Just as AKC recognition has been a bone of contention, so has the use of a standard for judging and choosing breeding stock. Standards give a detailed description of what a specific breed should look like. They also describe an ideal dog's movement and temperament. While members of the AKC parent club, the BCSA, welcome a standard as a goal breeders should aspire to when breeding their dogs, members of the opposing faction feel physical appearance means little as long as a dog displays good working ability.

In general, Border Collies are medium-size dogs, weighing about 25 to 55 pounds. The coat may be smooth or rough. Although black and white Border Collies are the most common, the breed actually comes in a variety of colors, including tricolor (black, white, and tan), red and white, red tricolor, red merle, blue merle, blue and white, and, although rare, white. Many Border Collies have a white blaze, collar, stockings, and tip of the tail, although these markings are not essential even in the AKC standard. The AKC allows all colors, except pure white, in the show ring.

Working Border Collie clubs don't care what color a dog's eyes are, or even if they match, as long as the dog "has good eye," which means she is able to control livestock with her eyes. The AKC standard recognizes a full range of brown eye color, but only allows blue eyes or partially blue eyes in merles.

> Standards give a detailed description of what a specific breed should look like.

Ear set can also vary quite a bit in both working and AKC Border Collies. Ears can be pricked (erect), semi-pricked or semi-erect, and the tips can fall forward or out to the sides. As with the eyes, working Border Collie fans don't care if the ears match.

The typical stances of a show Border Collie and a working Border Collie are very different. A Border Collie on the job carries her head low to the ground with her hindquarters high and her tail tucked between her legs, ready to change direction in an instant to head off an errant sheep, constantly boring into the flock with her intense gaze. A Border Collie in the show ring adopts a more typical conformation stance, in which the dog is "stacked" by her handler, or enticed to stand square and tall.

The AKC standard stresses that the Border Collie is the world's premier sheep-herding dog and should display characteristics consistent with this vocation. Working Border Collie aficionados stress that herding instinct and ability should supercede all physical characteristics.

Is a Border Collie for You?   Like all dogs and all people, Border Collies are individuals. No two Border Collies have the exact

What Will It Be—Puppy or Adult?

Do you want a puppy Border Collie or an adult Border Collie? They're all so cute! But depending on your lifestyle, one might be a better choice than the other.

Let's face it. Pups are adorable, especially Border Collie pups. Have you ever seen such a face? But the flip side of the cuteness factor is puppies are a lot of work. It takes time to teach puppy the ropes—housetraining, manners, socializing. If you're home a lot—maybe you work from a home office or you're a stay-at-home parent—a puppy could be a good bet. Of course, you also have to be willing to put in time, and not just a few weeks. We're talking years. While extremely intelligent, Border Collies need to be trained as house dogs, and conditioned to not always follow their working dog and herding instincts.

Why not consider adopting an older Border Collie? There are plenty of rescue organizations who can place a wonderful Border Collie in your home. With an older, adult dog, you're past housetraining, crying, jumping (maybe), and chewing.

Don't rule out a puppy or an adult dog: Figure out which might best suit your lifestyle, then decide.

same personality. In general, however, the Border Collie is an intense, energetic, loyal dog who lives to work.

Although some Border Collies are calmer than others, all need lots of attention and exercise to keep them happy. Even given individual differences, there is no such thing as a couch potato Border Collie. These dogs were bred to work and all have an intensity about them that, while admired by some people, can drive others crazy. In fact, some Border Collies develop odd, obsessive behaviors. While this often happens in dogs who aren't given an appropriate outlet for their energy, with others this is just a strange quirk in their personality. You definitely need to have patience and a good sense of humor to live with a Border Collie!

"An important thing to know about Border Collies is that they can be very weird dogs, especially if they don't have a job that keeps them busy, such as herding," says Border Collie owner April Quist, of Livermore, California. "My youngest dog, who is two years old, chases shadows on the wall, flecks of dust floating through the air, and raindrops. My middle dog, who is five, not only watches TV, but tries to actively participate in whatever is going on on the TV. He chases cats and other animals on the screen, biting and licking at them. If he's in another room and there's a commercial on that has an animal in it, he recognizes the sounds—music, voices, etc.—at the start of the commercial and comes running to watch. My eight-year-old dog has odd sound sensitivities—he runs and hides if I put a piece of bread in the toaster, for example. And all three of my dogs are obsessed with the hose outside. I can't water my yard unless my dogs are closed in the house or they'll trample my flowers trying to chase and bite at the water!"

> No two Border Collies have the exact same personality.

Boomer, a Border Collie owned by Mark Miller, also exhibits an odd twist on herding behavior. "When we travel, Boomer rides in the backseat of the van. As long as all the cars are going in the same direction, he's a happy camper. If, however, he sees a car broken down on the side of the road, or a car passing in the opposite direction on a two-lane country road, for example, he lunges and raps his head on the window. It's almost as if he views these cars as stray sheep and wants to get them going in the same direction as everyone else."

Some Border Collie obsessions can be truly comical. While most Border Collies immediately turn serious in the presence of livestock, many often play the clown when they aren't working.

Their intelligence makes it simple to teach them a variety of tricks, and they often invent their own if they find a behavior that makes people laugh. When choosing a Border Collie, it is important to keep in mind what you plan to do with your dog in the future. While all Border Collies need some type of outlet for their energy, some are more intense than others. If, for example, you are looking for a pet who will be happy with jogs around the neighborhood and games of fetch in the yard, you'll want to choose a dog from a more mellow breeding stock. A family with small children should definitely choose a puppy who is calmer and seems more willing to accept the occasional tugs of a toddler. A breeder should work with you to choose the puppy who will best fit your home and family. If, however, your goal is to trial in competitive dog sports such as agility or flyball, a more focused, high-energy dog will be an asset. If you plan to try your hand at competitive sheep-herding trials, you should obtain a dog from a breeder who is active in this pursuit and raises true working dogs.

> When choosing a Border Collie, it is important to keep in mind what you plan to do with your dog in the future.

It is vital that you honestly evaluate your lifestyle and commitment to your future pet before you ever bring your dog home. Deciding on a whim that you would like to become an expert sheepdog handler, then deciding six months down the road that you would rather watch dog sports on television is unfair to your Border Collie and will lead to an unhappy relationship for both of you.

Before purchasing your pet, make sure you spend some time with a number of Border Collies to get a true feel for the work involved in keeping up with this breed. Visit competitive dog sporting events and talk with owners and breeders. Although you'll notice some variety in personality, you'll also get a good feel for the general temperament of the breed.

Temperament   It can't be repeated enough—Border Collies are a high-energy breed. To the novice owner, this energy level can appear to be hyperactivity. With proper exercise of both their minds and bodies, however, Border Collies can make good pets.

In addition to being highly energetic, Border Collies are highly intelligent. While this is an excellent combination in a working dog, it can make a pet Border Collie difficult to live with unless she is given jobs to do, from accompanying you on jogs and bike rides to playing fetch to competitive canine sports. A Border Collie who is not intellectually stimulated quickly grows into a bored "problem child" and may become destructive.

Mark Miller says of Boomer, "He loves to learn new things. We have a toy basket in the den filled with all types of different toys. We often ask him to go get a particular toy—each one has a name—and bring it to us. He digs around until he finds it and then brings it to us. Later we taught him to tidy up, which essentially is where he picks various toys up off the floor and walks over and drops them into the toy basket. When he gets his paws dirty, we ask him to 'clean paws,' which prompts him to walk over and step onto the top step in the swimming pool. He loves to swim, but won't until we give him the 'swim' command."

Lynn Renor, of Madison, Wisconsin, recounts how her Border Collie Breeze taught herself scent discrimination, which is used in higher levels of obedience. "We were playing fetch with apples under an apple tree," says Lynn. "After about the third or fourth time, I realized Breeze was bringing back the same apple. She had used scent discrimination to find the exact apple I had thrown each time. It makes sense, since working Border Collies know the scent of every sheep in the herd.

"She's also done this with bark chips on a playground and even money! I once amazed a group of people by telling them my dog could pick out a dollar bill from a bunch of ones. I had everyone put down theirs and then I put down mine. Of course Breeze picked up the bill with my scent on it!" Border Collies' intelligence also makes them smart enough to figure out how to take over the household if they sense there is no strong leader in their human family. If your dog is demanding attention, forging ahead through doorways, refusing to move from a sleeping spot (especially on furniture), and/or showing any signs of aggression, you may be dealing with a dominance problem. Border Collies need firm, but gentle leadership to help them understand their place in the household "pack." Once they understand their lower-ranking position, they are much happier not having the responsibility of being in charge.

Border Collies form very strong attachments with their families, and actually can become obsessed with their one special person if they spend most of their time with one owner.

Deb Knapp, of Madera Ranchos, California, has two Border Collies. Each has a special person. "Mandy is 'mine' and she goes nearly everywhere with me. I'm lucky I can take her to work, so she is with me all day. The other dog, Boston, is my son's, and since my son is still school-age, Boston stays home most of the day until his boy returns. He is more easygoing than the typical Border Collie, so he can handle it. My husband and I have noticed that when our son goes out the door, Boston turns tail and heads right for his boy's room, where he heaves a great sigh and goes back to sleep, curled in a corner. We've called him out, but as soon as we go on to other things, back he goes.

"Mandy, on the other hand, hates to be left behind. When I'm going out the door and I tell Mandy she has to stay, her head droops, her ears go flat, her legs turn into noodles—she's just a puddle of dejection. If left at home, she appears not to be able to handle the length of time we're usually gone."

Lynn Renor feels that while it's important to spend quality time with your dog, she took it too far with Breeze. "Border Collies will cement a bond with one person and become obsessed with their person. I took Breeze every-

> Border Collies' intelligence also makes them smart enough to figure out how to take over the household if they sense there is no strong leader in their human family.

where when she was young, which made it difficult for her to be left alone when she was older. They can become complete emotional sponges and obsessive codependents!"

As seen in Deb Knapp's dogs, Border Collies can form a strong attachment with people of any age. However, you must be careful when bringing an adult Border Collie around children, especially if she was not socialized with kids from puppyhood.

"Border Collies can be very snappy with children," says April Quist, who has lived with the breed for 15 years. "Sometimes this is out of nervousness, especially if they haven't been well socialized with children, and sometimes out of instinct. My three dogs love children, but I'm careful to supervise them together, because my dogs can switch into herding mode with kids, and will try to control them by nipping at their legs and feet." (For more on Border Collies and children, see Chapter 8, Family Life.)

Cuddles and love are a key point for many Border Collie owners. Says Barbara Thompson of Winston-Salem, North Carolina, "My dogs are always with me when I'm home, and even nap under my desk while I work in my home office. I could not imagine having a household without these sweet, loving creatures."

Life Expectancy   Border Collies live an average of 13 years. If you think your dog will mellow some with age and you'll get a respite from all that exercise, think again! Many of these dogs remain active and energetic well into their senior years. They also are slow to mature and don't really reach adulthood until they are two or three. Of course, many seem puppylike their entire lives, except when they have a job to do.

Keys to Your Border Collie's Happiness

Before bringing a Border Collie home, you need to analyze your lifestyle. Will it complement the needs of your dog? The Border Collie is a highly energetic, demanding breed. To keep your Border Collie happy, you need to provide lots of exercise, training, and attention.

How Much Space Does a Border Collie Need?

The ideal home for many Border Collies is a working sheep ranch with limitless acres for the dog to lord over. If you are dedicated to providing lots of exercise and mental stimulation, however, most Border Collies can adapt to suburban life or even life in the city. The exception to this may be the dog from true stock-dog lines, who has too much herding drive to adapt fully to life off the farm.

If you live in the city or suburbs, don't think you can just let your dog out in an unfenced yard to get some exercise. No dog should ever be allowed to run loose, and Border Collies' herding instinct can be especially dangerous to their health. They are tempted to take off after anything that moves, from squirrels to bikes, roller-bladers, and cars. Car chasing is a serious problem that you must quell from the beginning. Border Collies will try to head off a car and herd it back to their owners, putting them right in the vehicle's path. Most Border Collies don't do well in kennel runs either, where they are likely to nervously pace a path until they are let out. A fenced yard is ideal, but doesn't let you off the exercise hook. You still need to take an active role in your dog's exercise regime, since Border Collies need a partner to play with.

Inside the house, space isn't much of an issue, since your Border Collie is likely to remain stuck to your side, following you from room to room as you go about your business.

How Much Exercise?

If I haven't gotten the point across yet, the answer to this question is a lot! The Border Collie is the consummate canine athlete. At times, you may feel you're living with an Olympic competitor rather than a dog! The Border Collie isn't one to run himself silly in the yard all alone, so you'll need to be an active partner in his exercise plan.

Plan on spending at least one to two hours every day exercising your dog. This can consist of a variety of activities, from jogging, biking, and swimming to playing fetch and participating in organized dog sports. If you live in a city, you'll need to be especially diligent about giving your dog plenty of long walks or playtime in a local dog park to wear him out.

Even human athletes have a hard time keeping up with a Border Collie, so set aside time every day for mental games as well, such as training sessions, which wear your dog out faster than simple exercise.

When exercising your dog, watch for signs that he is overexerting himself. Border Collies can become so focused on the task at hand that they ignore injury or overheating, which can lead to serious consequences. Always provide your dog with breaks in exercise and lots of fresh water, especially in warmer weather.

How Much Training?

All dogs need some obedience training, and the Border Collie is no exception. His intelligence can lead to creative disobedience, so he must be taught the rules of the household from an early age, and these rules must be consistently reinforced throughout his lifetime. Decide from Day One what you will and won't allow your adult Border Collie to do, and then teach those rules to your puppy. For example, if you don't want your adult dog sharing the furniture with you, don't let your eight-week-old puppy sleep on the bed because "he looks so cute!" This will only confuse your dog when you decide he's gotten too big and he needs to stay on the floor. If you have brought a rescue dog into your home, consistency is also key. Don't allow him to get away with certain behaviors in his first several days or weeks because he is "just getting settled in." He will be more confused and unhappy if you change the rules midway through the game than if you set definite household laws from his first day.

Border Collies don't respond well to harsh corrections and they actually shut down emotionally in the face of physical punishment.

A key point to remember when training your Border Collie is that they are extremely sensitive. Use a heavy hand with this dog and you may ruin him for life. Border Collies don't respond well to harsh corrections and they actually shut down emotionally in the face of physical punishment. Some dogs become so afraid of making a mistake that they either lie down and refuse to do anything, manically exhibit a string of behaviors in the hope that one of these is the behavior you're looking for, or roll over on their back in a sign of complete submission. Keep all training as positive as possible, using treats, toys and/or play to motivate your dog to do what you ask. Many Border Collies are so motivated to work that they refuse food treats in favor of a compliment from their owner. A low, growly tone is usually all that's needed to let a Border Collie know he's done something wrong. Even this may be too harsh for some Border Collies!

Although the Border Collie is a sensitive breed, he can also be an opportunist if his owner does not provide clear leadership. As far removed as they may seem from their ancestors, domestic dogs still think like wolves. They live by the code of pack leadership. Every pack has an alpha, and all the other wolves fall into place in the hierarchy from this "top dog" down to the bottom-ranking wolf. In your dog's new human/canine pack, you must function as the alpha. As a matter of fact, every human in your household, including the tiniest infant, must rank above the Border Collie. If your dog spots a weakness in this chain, he may try to move up in rank himself. That is why it is vital that all members of the family agree to and enforce the same household rules consistently from the beginning. While it may be impossible for an infant to enforce household rules, you can convey your child's higher rank to your dog by giving your dog obedience commands while holding your child. Also, insist that your dog treat your child with respect and not as diminutive livestock that should be herded from room to room.

Did You Know?

The Saluki, a hunting dog raised by ancient Egyptians, is the oldest known breed.

That'll Do!

In the tradition of sheepmen and women everywhere, teach your dog this authentic shepherd's command, which means your dog has successfully completed the job he's been doing. Be sure you use the phrase correctly. "That'll do" means the action the dog is doing is okay, but he can stop now, while "No" means the action is not acceptable. For instance, use "That'll do" after your dog has given a warning bark or two that someone is at the door, but use "No" if your dog is chewing on your favorite slippers.

Border Collies' working drive and eagerness to please make them relatively easy to train. If you keep training interesting, your dog will be happy to learn anything you wish to teach, from obedience commands to all manner of tricks and canine sports. Just remember to keep it a positive experience for your Border Collie.

Can My Border Collie Stay Home All Day Without Me?

Ideally, a Border Collie should not be left alone all day, and should instead have opportunities for exercise and playtime throughout the day. For many pet owners, however, this is not a realistic situation. Does this mean owners who work or attend school can never own a Border Collie? Not necessarily, but if you do spend hours at a time outside of the home, you'll need to be especially dedicated to exercising your dog.

If you wear out your dog when you're home, he'll be more likely to accept the times that you're gone. But if you constantly push aside your dog in favor of the other commitments in your life, he is bound to use up his energy with such unacceptable pursuits as chewing, digging, and other destruction.

"Playing Frisbee is Boomer's outlet," says Mark Miller. "He is well behaved at home, because we have taken the approach that a tired dog is a happy dog. We routinely play Frisbee with him in the morning, and when I come home at night. He is more likely to rest and relax in the evenings if he has received a good workout. If he doesn't get exercised, he is more inclined to get toys out of his basket and bother family members to play with him. Rainy days are horrible around the house because he doesn't get his workout, so instead he gets his toys out, tosses them at our feet, and barks until someone throws something to him."

> Border Collies' working drive and eagerness to please make them relatively easy to train.

It's also important for you to give your Border Collie something productive to do while you're gone, such as chewing on a Kong—a hollow rubber toy—stuffed with treats. If you find your dog gets into too much mischief when you're gone, you may need to confine him to his crate until he shows better control.

Although an adult Border Collie should experience no difficulty in waiting until you get home to relieve himself, a puppy is a different matter. Whether your pup stays in a crate or in a blocked-off room, such as a kitchen or laundry room, someone needs to let him out every few hours to do his business. If you can't get home over lunchtime to give your Border Collie a potty break, ask a neighbor or hire a pet sitter to drop by.

Surefire Ways to Make Your Border Collie's Life Unpleasant

We've looked at the things a Border Collie needs to stay happy; now let's look at what is intolerable to the breed.

Things a Border Collie Simply Cannot Live With

A Border Collie cannot live with abuse of any kind. Harsh, haphazard punishment turns this loyal, loving dog into a fearful, depressed animal. Instead, teach your Border Collie what you expect through consistency, positive motivation, and lots of loving praise.

As much as Border Collies can't live with abuse, they also can't live without a clear-cut leader. Be a fair, but firm leader for your dog and she will happily accept her place in your family. Neglect this duty, and she will quickly establish herself as top dog.

Border Collies can't live in isolation. They are very people-oriented and retreat into a shell if they are left alone in a kennel or backyard for hours on end without human interaction. These dogs are happiest when they are by your side, playing, working, or even napping once their energy has been spent.

> Border Collies are happiest when they are by your side, playing, working, or even napping once their energy has been spent.

Things a Border Collie Simply Cannot Live Without

Instead of "Will Work for Food," the Border Collie's motto could easily be "Will Work for Work!" These dogs live to work. While they can live without their traditional vocation of sheepherding, they need some sort of substitute, whether that is an organized dog sport such as flyball or agility, or just accompanying their owners on long, frequent hikes or jogs or high-energy games of fetch.

Along these lines, the Border Collie needs exercise, exercise, exercise! Incorporate lots of active exercise throughout the day to keep your dog fit and happy. Since it is nearly impossible to completely wear out a Border Collie with physical exercise alone, use mental exercise such as obedience or tricks training or games of hide-and-seek to work your dog's mind as well as her body.

Finally, Border Collies can't live without socialization. If a Border Collie is not introduced to all manner of situations and people from puppyhood, she may be shy or fearful as an adult. This is especially important in the case of children; a Border Collie must be taught to tolerate and respect children from a young age or she may never fully adjust to them later in life.

Maybe a Border Collie Isn't the Dog for Me

What if you are buying this book after the fact and already have a Border Collie? What if you either neglected to research the breed or ignored some of the negatives of the breed, and just focused on the positives? What if you now realize that getting a Border Collie wasn't the best choice for you?

If the problem is that your Border Collie is asserting himself and taking over the house, don't give up. This can be easily remedied if you vow to take charge now. Get enrolled in an obedience class right away. Training is the best way for you to regain control and to bond with your dog. If you feel the problem is too out of control to handle in a group setting, find a trainer who offers private lessons or will even come to your home to teach you how to work with your dog. It is imperative that you and your entire family become your Border Collie's leader. Training also teaches you how to curb undesirable Border Collie behavior, such as herding the children or even adults in your family.

If the problem is that you didn't realize a Border Collie would be so energetic, you have some decisions to make. Your first option is to admit your mistake and vow to change your lifestyle to meet your dog's needs. Trying to keep up with an athletic dog will actually prove beneficial to your own health. You may find you enjoy your newly active lifestyle and reap the physical and mental rewards of such a change. On the other hand, you may decide you are not ready to make the commitment a Border Collie demands.

If you decide that you just don't have the fortitude to own a Border Collie, give your dog the best chance possible of finding a new home. Don't turn in your dog to a shelter, where you can't guarantee he will find a home and not be destroyed. First, contact your dog's breeder to see if he or she will take your dog back. If this is not an option, or you didn't get your dog from a breeder, call a local rescue organization and turn your dog over to it. (You can find a Border Collie rescue group through organizations listed in the Resources section at the back of this book.) These groups are experienced in dealing with the breed and will undertake any rehabilitation necessary before placing your dog with a new family.

> If you decide that you just don't have the fortitude to own a Border Collie, give your dog the best chance possible of finding a new home.

Next time, make sure you know all the facts about a breed before you bring a dog home.

Where to Find the Perfect Border Collie for You

If you've decided that indeed the Border Collie is the breed for you, don't make the mistake of rushing out and buying the first one you see. Searching for a dog is an emotional experience, and we too often fall head over heels in love and let our hearts govern our actions without consulting our levelheaded brains. Of course, you want to find a dog with whom you click, but you also must ensure that the dog you pick is truly one you can live with long term. For example, you may like a certain dog's looks and not take the time to ask questions about his parents' health, or you may be so charmed by a certain dog's exuberant personality that you do not realistically consider your ability to handle such a high-energy dog.

Puppies Versus Older Dogs

It might seem that the first step in obtaining a dog consists of finding the right place to purchase one. Before you decide where to get your Border Collie, however, you need to decide whether you want to buy a puppy or adopt an adult dog. Both options have their pros and cons.

Just as parents find it magical to watch their children grow from helpless infants to awkward teenagers to successful adults, so, too, do dog owners' hearts proudly witness their pets' progression from sweet, slightly mischievous puppies to gangly adolescents to self-assured, agile adult Border Collies. If you choose to get a puppy, you'll have the chance to mold that pup from an early age into the dog you would like him to be. You can socialize him with people of all shapes and sizes, as well as with other animals, and know that you are helping him develop into a calm, confident adult. You can feed him the right food from Day One and ensure he gets the proper health care and training.

Along with the joys of puppyhood also come the demands, however. You may spend at least a few sleepless nights trying to ignore a howling puppy who hasn't yet decided to make the crate his home. You'll at least find yourself sleepwalking out into the yard once or several times a night to let your Border Collie relieve himself. You also are likely to become an expert carpet and floor cleaner, and you may find a few household items ripped to unrecognizable shreds, because you weren't keeping an eye on your little darling. Puppies, as cute and loving as they are, also are draining and need lots and lots of attention.

Perhaps you feel you don't have the time and energy to devote to puppy rearing, but you believe you can provide the ideal home for an older dog. An older dog may already be housetrained, and may know basic obedience commands as well. Adopting an older Border Collie also takes the guesswork out of determining your new pet's eventual energy level and need for exercise. Plus, if you obtain a mature Border Collie from a rescue group or a humane society, you'll also secure the added bonus of knowing you are providing a home for a dog who has been given up or abandoned.

Before you decide to adopt, however, you should understand some of the negatives of bringing a grown dog into your home. An adult Border Collie has already established certain behaviors, both good and bad. You certainly can teach an old dog new tricks, but it may take more time and effort to reshape an older pet's ingrained behaviors than it would to teach a puppy what you expect of him. Also, although some dogs are given up through no fault of their own—often because their owners didn't thoroughly research the breed and didn't realize the time and energy commitment required or someone in the family developed an allergy—other dogs end up in shelters or rescue organizations because of serious behavioral problems. Rescue groups and shelters try to evaluate their dogs and to place them in suitable homes; however, a dog's behavioral peculiarities may not fully surface until the dog has settled into his new home. When purchasing an adult dog, try to find out as much as you can about his previous owners and the reason they gave him up. If possible, also try to find out the type of environment in which he was reared, because the first few weeks of a puppy's life play a large part in his personality development and health. Your Border Collie should also be well socialized with people and other dogs, so he knows the proper way to interact in all situations.

> When purchasing an adult dog, try to find out as much as you can about his previous owners and the reason they gave him up.

Pet Shops—Pros and Cons

Now, where should you get your pet? Pet stores rarely have older dogs for sale, but some do sell puppies. For the novice buyer, a pet store may seem like the perfect place to find the puppy of your dreams. A pet store is, after all, the home of instant gratification. An eager potential owner can walk in at any time during business hours, choose the puppy who appeals to her, pay a fee, and take the pup home, expending a minimum of time and effort. Rarely will a pet store ask you questions to determine if the puppy cradled in your arms is right for you or, just as important, if you are right for the puppy. Sounds tempting, doesn't it? But wait! Don't devote a significant amount of your time and energy to researching the Border Collie breed only to choose your puppy in such a haphazard manner.

Most pet stores do not socialize their dogs or care for their mental and physical needs at this crucial developmental stage in their lives. The majority of puppies who end up in pet stores have been taken from their mothers and littermates at too young an age and have suffered the stresses of being shipped to a retail outlet. If they came from a large commercial kennel, they may not have received important socialization and human attention in their early formative weeks.

The pet store may supply you with proof of vaccinations and worming, but it is unlikely to give any information on the puppy's genetics. Border Collies, like all purebred dogs, are susceptible to a number of genetic conditions, and all breeding stock should receive tests for these diseases. Rarely can a pet store produce the documentation of genetic testing that is vital in determining a puppy's health. Although most pet stores offer some sort of health guarantee, often that guarantee is good only until a veterinarian checks the dog, usually within 24 to 48 hours of purchase. Many genetic diseases do not produce symptoms for several years. Finally, pet stores seldom provide ongoing support on housetraining, behavioral problems, and other aspects of raising a healthy, well-adjusted Border Collie.

Breeders—Pros and Cons

Breeders actually comprise several different types of people who breed dogs. The breeder umbrella encompasses commercial breeders, backyard breeders, and hobby breeders. Each type of breeder comes with its own set of pros and cons.

Commercial Breeders Some large-scale breeding operations produce a number of different breeds and generate large quantities of dogs. If you encounter someone who breeds such diverse dogs as

Border Collies, Shih Tzus, and Golden Retrievers, you very likely are dealing with a puppy mill. When a single facility produces many different breeds and an enormous number of dogs, it is unlikely to provide proper genetic screening and health care.

In the interest of making money quickly, many of these breeders sell to pet stores rather than taking the time to place their puppies individually. Again, these puppies often are separated from their mothers too early in their lives and are stressed by the shipping process. Even if you buy directly from them, puppy-mill breeders probably won't provide any ongoing support for owners with questions. They rarely take back a dog past a short window of opportunity, if at all.

> The breeder umbrella encompasses commercial breeders, backyard breeders, and hobby breeders.

Even an extremely large kennel that breeds only Border Collies may not provide the ideal environment for a puppy's formative first few weeks. Excessively large operations are less likely to give puppies the socialization they need to develop into calm, stable, well-adjusted adults who make good family pets.

Backyard Breeders   This category of breeder includes people who breed their dog with the neighbor's, because, "They will make such cute puppies," or so that their children can experience the miracle of birth. Then, they offer the puppies for a discounted price or even "free to a good home." Backyard breeders, like pet stores, may seem like convenient sources for Border Collie puppies. After all, you may think, why should you pay more money for a dog who has a fancy pedigree or whose ancestors excelled at competitive sheepdog trials when all you want is a pet. Once again, the question of genetic health comes into play. Most people who breed once or even occasionally to "recoup the money they paid for their dog" know nothing about the complex genetics of purebred dogs and do not test the mother or father Border Collie for inherited diseases. A backyard breeder typically offers no guarantee of health or any support to the new owner should questions about the dog's care arise later on. These breeders generally live by the credo, "Let the buyer beware." Most backyard breeders refuse to take back a dog who later develops a genetic malady, and few help the owner find a new home for the pet if the dog needs to be given up for some unforeseen reason at some point in his life.

> Being AKC registered means only that a purebred Border Collie mother and a purebred Border Collie father reproduced purebred Border Collie puppies. It does not guarantee good health or temperament.

Don't be fooled by the "but-he's-AKC-registered" sales pitch. Being AKC registered means only that a purebred Border Collie mother and a purebred Border Collie father reproduced purebred Border Collie puppies. It does not guarantee good health or temperament. Also, due to the controversy surrounding AKC registration of Border Collies, there are many wonderful, reputable breeders of Border Collies who do not register their dogs with the AKC. A Border Collie without AKC papers who was bred for sound health and temperament makes a much better pet than one with AKC papers who was the product of breeding on a whim.

Hobby Breeders   People who breed dogs as a hobby or on a limited basis are generally the best sources for purebred puppies. They may only breed one litter a year, but they usually devote much time and energy to ensuring the health and well-being of those puppies. Most hobby breeders know the genetic problems that are specific to Border Collies, and they perform all the necessary tests on breeding stock. Most also test puppies for soundness and give them all the proper vaccinations.

Good hobby breeders raise each and every Border Collie as a member of the family and take great care in finding the right homes for their charges. They can serve as lifelong sources of information on everything from training to nutrition and grooming. In fact, these breeders often pride themselves on the friendships they have developed with their puppy buyers. Most also take a dog back into their home at any time during his life, if the original owner can no longer care for him.

Puppies from hobby breeders usually cost the same or less than those found in pet stores. And, keep in mind that the price of a pup bought from a hobby breeder typically includes genetic testing, socialization, and future support.

Although most people think of buying young puppies from breeders, some breeders occasionally offer older puppies for sale as well. This can happen when a show prospect developed some type of fault as he grew, or when a dog intended for herding or other work does not live up to his earlier promise. These "flaws" usually do nothing to detract from the dog's quality as a wonderful pet. This type of situation provides the advantage of getting a relatively young dog who is probably already housetrained and may also know basic commands, such as "sit" and "come."

Buying from a Breeder

Of course, even though hobby breeders are usually the best possible source for puppies, you still need to thoroughly investigate each breeder to ensure she lives up to your standards. Make sure you get references from each potential breeder, and ask these references if they were satisfied with their

What to Ask a Breeder

○ What are common health problems found in Border Collies?

○ Are your dogs routinely screened for heritable diseases?

○ What health certifications can you show me for parents and grand-parents?

○ What are the most positive and negative characteristics of the breed?

○ What kind of temperament should I expect from a Border Collie?

○ How long have you been breeding dogs?

○ Can you name five other breeders in this breed you'd recommend?

○ What do you expect of potential puppy owners?

○ What type of guarantee do you provide?

○ Will you take back this puppy at any age, for any reason?

○ Do you require limited registration and/or spay/neuter contracts on pet-quality puppies?

puppies and what type of ongoing support they have received from the breeder.

Next, make an appointment to visit the breeder's facilities to personally check them out. If you are looking for a family pet, find a breeder who keeps her Border Collies in the house. Even a breeder who operates a working farm should keep her Border Collies in the home as true members of the family when they are not working. If a breeder keeps her dogs in kennel runs, each dog should receive "house time" every day. The puppies should be whelped (birthed) and brought up in the home, which is impor-tant in acclimating puppies from an early age to the hustle and bustle of family life. Puppies raised in kennels often grow up fearful of normal household noises, such as vacuum cleaners and dishwashers. A breeder also should start to housetrain and crate-train the puppies before releasing them to their new homes; this is impossible to do if a puppy is living in a kennel. In addition, puppies should receive daily handling by humans while they're living at the breeders. Pups who are raised in the house are much more likely to receive this special one-on-one attention than those raised in a kennel.

A breeder should gladly let you see all her dogs, especially the puppies' mother. Although the mom may not run up and lick you in greeting, she should appear friendly. Don't believe a breeder who explains away an aggressive Border Collie mom by saying, "She's just being protective of her puppies" or "She takes a while to warm up to people." A hostile mother is likely to produce hostile puppies.

If you are looking for a family pet, find a breeder who keeps her Border Collies in the house.

If the puppies' dad is on the premises, make sure you meet him as well. Don't be surprised if he is not present; in order to make the best match for their bitches, breeders often use dogs from across the country as studs. If the breeder you are visiting does not own the father, get the name and phone number of the male dog's owner and conduct a phone interview to learn about the dad's personality and health. Ask his owner to ship you a picture or video of the stud and any pertinent health records. The father's photo may even appear on the owner's Web site advertising stud services.

When visiting a breeder, you can expect to answer as many questions as you ask her. In fact, if the breeder doesn't ask any questions at all, don't buy your dog there! A reputable breeder places a puppy as if she were finding an adoptive family for an infant. The breeder will ask whether you have ever owned a dog before and, if so, what happened to him. If you have a history of abandoning dogs, it is unlikely a good breeder will allow you to take home a new pup. Also, a Border Collie may be too much to handle for a first-time dog owner. The breeder also will ask whether you work and how much time you will devote to exercising and socializing your dog. Do you have a fenced yard? Why do you want a Border Collie? What type of training experience do you have? Don't feel insulted or conclude that the breeder is nosy. She is simply trying to guarantee that both you and the puppy find the perfect match.

> When visiting a breeder, you can expect to answer as many questions as you ask her.

By the same token, you should have plenty of questions for the breeder. Find out whether both parents have received health clearances for the genetic diseases common in the Border Collie and request to see the documentation. Ask for the puppies' pedigree. Although a dog with titles or one who has done well in sheepdog trials isn't guaranteed to produce sound puppies, breeders who work with their dogs in some sort of pursuit, whether it be obedience, agility, or herding, usually strive to breed the best Border Collies possible. If you are interested in running your dog in sheepdog trials, you especially want to purchase your dog from someone with expertise in herding. Also, no matter what your plans for your dog, inquire as to what type of training, socialization, and veterinary care the puppies have received.

Finally, ask at what age the puppies will be ready for their new homes. Between eight and ten weeks of age is the ideal time for a pup to bond with his new owner. Don't buy a puppy from anyone who lets puppies go at six weeks or earlier. Pups who are separated from their mothers and littermates at too young an age miss out on important canine socialization and, as adults, may have difficulty reading canine body language and getting along with other dogs.

Conversely, puppies left with their littermates for longer periods of time may bond more with other dogs than they will with their owners. This is why it is unwise to bring home two puppies at the same time. If you would like to eventually own two dogs, wait until you have fully bonded with the first pup before introducing a new one. Another important factor to consider is that the few weeks after the eighth week are considered the puppy's fear imprint period. If you bring home a puppy during these weeks, you must take extra care to ensure the experience is a pleasant one for your new Border Collie. Anything that frightens the puppy during these weeks will remain ingrained for a longer period of time than if the puppy were to encounter the same situation at a younger or older age.

A negative of buying from a hobby breeder is that you may have to wait longer than you would like to get a puppy. Hobby breeders may produce litters infrequently, and demand for their pups is often high. If the breeder places you on a waiting list, keep in mind that six months or a year is well worth the wait for a healthy and even-tempered dog with whom you will live for many years to come.

Signing the Contract

Now, let's address puppy-buying paperwork. A puppy sales contract provides protection for both you and the breeder. It should spell out terms of the sale and any conditions. For example, many breeders require that the owners of pet-quality dogs spay or neuter them. Again, don't take offense at this and feel it is intrusive. The breeder is looking out for the health of your dog and is trying to prevent unwanted puppies from being born in the future.

Another condition frequently included in puppy contracts is the first right of refusal, which means you agree to return your Border Collie to the breeder if you can no longer keep him for any reason during his lifetime.

Animal Shelters—Pros and Cons

Although it is possible to find a purebred Border Collie puppy at an animal shelter, it is highly unlikely. Your chances of finding an adolescent or adult Border Collie at a shelter, however, are much better. Unprepared Border Collie owners may take their pets to shelters when they discover the dog is more than they bargained for, while others may be forced to give up their pets due to extenuating circumstances, such as a family move or illness.

Most shelters do their best to evaluate their dogs and to release them only to homes that are prepared for the responsibility. Some organizations attempt to retrain dogs before placing them, in the hopes of preventing the dogs from being returned in the future. Others offer post-adoption classes for new owners and their dogs. Some shelters, however, are so inundated with homeless dogs and cats that they lack the time and resources to screen the animals as well as they should. If you find a Border Collie in a shelter, find out as much as possible about the dog before making the decision to adopt him. Ask why he was given up and how he has behaved since arriving at the shelter. Also inquire whether he has any health problems and, if so, how they are being treated. Spend some time alone with the dog in a getting-to-know-you room or take him for a walk around the shelter's grounds.

Like a hobby breeder, a shelter asks questions of you to determine if you are a good fit for the dog you are considering. Shelters also require that you spay or neuter the dog you adopt, if they have not already performed the operation.

Shelters offer many wonderful animals for adoption. If you adopt a Border Collie from a humane society, know that you have saved a life.

Rescue Groups—Pros and Cons

If you are looking for an older Border Collie, rescue groups are excellent sources. Rescue groups are organizations that take in dogs of a specific breed and try to rehome them. Like the dogs who end up in animal shelters, rescue dogs may have been given up for a variety of reasons, some of which are not their fault. The advantages of rescue groups are that the people who run them are usually extremely knowledgeable about the Border Collie breed and take the time to retrain Border Collies who are given up because of behavioral problems. Quality rescue organizations also thoroughly check each Border Collie's health and treat any medical problems.

> Rescue groups are organizations that take in dogs of a specific breed and try to rehome them.

Before allowing an adoption, rescue workers ask as many questions of you as you do of them, and may even request an in-home interview to check out your home situation personally. Like the hobby breeder, rescue organizations encourage ongoing contact and make themselves available for follow-up calls or even visits if you encounter any problems after you take your Border Collie home.

Most rescue groups charge a donation for adopting a dog. This fee typically is much less than the cost of a purebred Border Collie pup from a breeder.

What If?

It can and does happen. You've acquired a Border Collie, maybe even done research about the breed beforehand, but after living with the dog for a month or two, you realize maybe it's not the dog you thought you wanted.

Don't panic. And don't immediately see getting rid of the Border Collie as a solution to the problem. Make sure you exhaust all options, such as training or neutering, before you decide to give up your dog.

Know that this can happen no matter what breed you bring home. It's rare for anyone to initially have the "perfect" canine companion. Rather, good companions are partly created, which means they're the result of your efforts. If you put some time, energy, and effort into a puppy or dog, chances are you'll have a suitable companion.

It's true you might not have exactly what you wanted. But who has everything they want, all the time? For example, maybe you've found the Border Collie's intelligence and energy are too much too handle. Border Collies are just that way. You won't change who the dog is. You just need to teach your Border Collie how to control her exuberance. Seek guidance from a professional trainer. Make a list of unwanted behaviors or dislikes about the dog and take the list to someone who can help you work through them.

The answer for solving for the problem is your willingness to work on it, not getting rid of the Border Collie.

One potential con of rescue groups is that they rarely have puppies to place. If you are looking for a puppy, you can try a rescue group, but you will probably end up having to go to a hobby breeder. Even if you are willing to take in an older dog, you may have to wait for quite a while before the rescue organization has a dog with whom you will be compatible. Another potential negative is that no rescue group may exist in your area. If you can locate a rescue group within driving distance, however, it may offer your best bet for finding an older Border Collie who is right for you.

How Do I Choose the Pick of the Litter?

Let's say you've decided to purchase a Border Collie puppy. You have interviewed breeders, checked their references, and visited their homes. You've finally settled on a breeder you feel will provide the ideal puppy for you. Now, you're confronted with a wriggling, licking mass of adorable puppies. How do you choose one?

A good breeder will offer lots of expert advice and help you pick the puppy with whom you are most compatible. He not only will encourage you to visit several times to get to know the puppies before settling on a specific Border Collie, but also will ask you what type of companion you are looking for. Do you want a Border Collie strictly for a pet? Do you want a working dog, or a dog to compete in herding, obedience, agility, or other dog sports? Each of these scenarios calls for a dog with a specific personality type. The breeder knows these puppies inside and out and can guide you toward the pup who will best suit your lifestyle. We will address temperament tests in a moment, but first let's learn how to tell whether a puppy is healthy.

Signs of Good Health

Although it is tempting to take home the runt of the litter or the scrawny pup being bullied by her siblings, you should consider the pup's health before allowing your heart to choose for you. The smallest puppy may be diminutive, but generally healthy, or she may be sickly. You don't want to set yourself up for years of expensive veterinary bills and the possible early demise of your beloved pet.

A healthy puppy has bright, clear eyes. A little clear eye discharge usually is fine, but anything more than that may indicate a health problem. The pup should appear energetic and playful. If the puppy you are interested in seems to want only to sleep, come back and visit at another time to see whether she's perked up. Sleepiness may mean the puppy is merely exhausted from an extended romp with her littermates, or that she is sick. Only a second visit, and an honest evaluation by the breeder, can help you determine which is the case.

A healthy puppy has bright, clear eyes.

Common knowledge has dictated that you should pick a plump puppy. However, we now know excessive weight, even in a pup, is unhealthy. With light pressure, you should be able to feel a puppy's ribs—they should neither protrude nor hide under layers of fat. A protruding belly could also indicate the presence of internal parasites.

Other signs of good health include a clean, soft, and sweet-smelling coat with no signs of fleas; smooth skin that is free of scabs and growths; clean and sweet-smelling ears; strong, white teeth; bubble gum-pink gums; and a cool, moist nose free of discharge.

Temperament Tests

If conducted a number of times by an expert, temperament tests can reveal much about a puppy's personality. A novice who runs a single temperament test on a litter may misinterpret the results or not fully understand the behavior he is seeing. To ensure the accuracy of the readings, therefore, the breeder should test the puppies' temperaments a number of times in different locations. The breeder also should gladly allow you to test the puppies while he is present and can help you put the results in perspective.

What are temperament tests? They are a series of tests that measure a puppy's responses to certain situations and stimuli and that determine her level of dominance, trainability, and interest in people. Most owners will fare well by taking home a puppy who scores in the middle of the road on her temperament tests. A more dominant, strong-willed dog may provide the perfect match for someone who needs a working dog or wishes to compete in an intense canine sport, but probably will prove too much for the average dog owner to handle. Likewise, the extremely shy, hesitant puppy does not make a good prospect for average owners, since puppies with extremely passive personalities can grow into defensive dogs or even fear biters.

Even if you aren't an expert tester, you can get an idea of a pup's temperament. When conducting a temperament test, bring the puppies one at a time to a location with which they are unfamiliar. Tie a different colored ribbon around each puppy's neck to keep track of who is who. Take notes, so you remember how each puppy scored. Although temperament tests do vary, the following basic tests and interpretation guidelines can give you an idea of how these tests work.

○ **Following.** Place the puppy on the ground and take a few steps back, then clap softly and call the puppy. A puppy who follows you right away is people oriented and will train more easily. She will also grow into a more sociable family pet. Avoid the independent puppy who walks away and the fearful pup who runs and hides.

○ **Restraint.** Place the puppy on her back and gently hold her in that position for 30 seconds. The best future family pet will

struggle briefly, then relax. A puppy who remains frozen in fear or who growls or tries to bite is a poor pet choice for the average owner. Pay attention as well to the puppy's eye contact. A polite, easier-to-train puppy will look away. Beware of the dominant puppy who tries to stare you down, even while she's on her back. After you release the puppy, she should recover immediately and may try to lick you or climb in your lap. You should avoid any puppy who runs away and hides or who comes up fighting.

Next, place your hands under the puppy's chest and lift her off the ground for 30 seconds. Once again, the most trainable puppy will briefly struggle, then relax.

o **Pain Sensitivity.** Take the puppy's paw and firmly press between her toes until she reacts. A puppy who immediately yelps or bites at your hand will not adapt well to a household with small children, where she will inevitably get stomped and pulled on now and then. A puppy who responds after several seconds and gently mouths your hand will train with relative ease. Puppies who do not respond have a high pain threshold. These dogs don't respond well during training to gentle physical corrections, such as short, light tugs on the leash when the dog is pulling. Rather, you will need to entice your dog to follow your commands by using positive reinforcement, and if your dog still won't comply, by applying stronger corrections, such as a training collar.

o **Noise Sensitivity.** Stand behind the puppy and throw keys or drop a book. The noise will not startle the ideal family pet, who instead will calmly turn to investigate. An extremely frightened puppy will have a hard time adjusting to the normal chaos of a household. The puppy who doesn't react at all may have a hearing problem. If the puppy appears to not hear, try clapping and calling the puppy from behind her to see whether she is, indeed, deaf. Deaf dogs can make wonderful pets, but they do require extra training.

○ **Curiosity and Retrieving.** Throw a ball across the puppy's path. Does she run after it to investigate and possibly even retrieve the ball? If so, this puppy will be easy to train. Next, tie a rag to a long piece of string. Toss it in front of the puppy and then pull it toward you. Once the puppy chases and catches the rag, let go. A good family pet will seem curious about and follow the moving rag, but should quickly lose interest once the rag stops moving. A puppy who attacks the rag and continues to bite and shake it after the rag stops moving possesses a strong prey drive and may make an excellent working or competitive dog, but is less suited as a family pet. Once again, you should avoid a dog who runs away and hides.

○ **Energy Level.** The average owner should seek a puppy who is neither high-strung nor extremely lethargic.

Your breeder may perform different versions of these temperament checks or may add other tests to the mix. The important thing is to trust the breeder's interpretation of the results and to remember that the results are only the puppy's reactions on this particular day and at this particular moment. A puppy who has been playing all morning or who is feeling slightly under the weather may not react in her usual manner.

Did You Know?

The word for "dog" in the Australian aboriginal language Mbabaran happens to be "dog."

A Boy or a Girl?

Many people hold preconceived notions about male and female dogs. They may contend that males are more protective and females are more affectionate. Males are more aloof, while females are better with children. The myths go on and on but, in reality, every dog is an individual, and many sex-based generalizations about dogs' dispositions are false.

If you plan to breed your dog, however, you should know about some differences between female and male dogs.

Unneutered males tend to mark their property, whether they decide that consists of the backyard fence, trees, and telephone poles encountered during walks or your living room couch. Intact males who smell a female in heat will do anything to get to her, including scaling or digging under the fence you thought was impenetrable. They also may display a willingness to fight anything and everything that gets in their path.

Females, on the other hand, go into heat once or twice a year, which can make quite a mess. Their disposition can change to extremely anxious and restless during these times, and they may drive you to distraction until they mate or their heat cycle ends. If you breed your female, you must also be prepared to deal with her pregnancy as well as the raising and placing of puppies.

If you spay or neuter your Border Collie, you won't have to deal with any of these things. (The advantages of spaying and neutering are discussed further in Chapter 4, Medical Care Every Border Collie Needs.)

2

Welcome Home!

In This Chapter

○ Preparing for Your Border Collie's Arrival
○ Border Collie-Proofing Your House
○ Which Supplies Do You Really Need?
○ Homecoming Day for Your Border Collie Puppy

If, after lots of in-depth research, conversations with Border Collie owners, and heavy-duty soul-searching, you decide you are ready to welcome this whirlwind canine into your life, congratulations! Your life will never be the same, and it will surely never be boring. You are about to meet a new best friend who will be your constant companion. Your dog will introduce you to new experiences you may never have known existed, such as the exciting world of canine sports. He also will teach you the true definition of loyalty. While there's a lot of joy that goes along with such a partnership, there is tremendous responsibility as well.

Before you bring your new puppy or adopted older dog home, there are countless decisions to be made and some shopping to do. You and your family need to discuss and assign dog-care duties, establish physical and behavioral boundaries your dog will adhere to, dog-proof your home and yard, and buy all manner of doggie supplies. You may be tempted to rush your new pet home and work out the details later. But trust me, putting forethought into your Border Collie's substantial physical and emotional needs will ease the adjustment period for both of you and start your relationship out on the right paw!

> Putting forethought into your Border Collie's substantial physical and emotional needs will ease the adjustment period for both of you.

Preparing for Your Border Collie's Arrival

Just as people need laws to understand how to interact in a society, your dog needs household rules to understand how to fit into your family life. These rules must encompass clear-cut behavioral boundaries, as well as indoor and outdoor physical boundaries. In order for these rules to work, everyone in the household must agree on the rules and vow to stick to them. If one family member allows the Border Collie on the couch and another yells at him for the same behavior, your dog will have no idea what is expected of him.

Where will your Border Collie sleep? Where will he stay during the day? Will you limit his access to only certain rooms or areas when you are home, or will you allow him free reign of the house? These questions all require careful consideration and resolution before your dog arrives.

Indoor Boundaries

A crate is an indispensable tool for setting and enforcing your Border Collie's indoor boundaries. Some people mistakenly believe crating is cruel and harshly confines an animal. Nothing could be further from the truth. Like their wild cousin the wolf, dogs instinctively seek out dens. If you don't provide a crate for your dog, he'll actually seek out den-like areas in your house, such as in corners, behind chairs, or under tables. While these areas provide some escape, they still leave your dog exposed to the normal chaos of everyday family life. A crate provides much more security, and is a place he can really call his own. Once your dog is introduced to his crate, he'll seek it out whenever he needs a break.

A crate not only "protects" your dog from the household, it also protects the household from your dog! A Border Collie puppy, or an older dog who has not been trained, quickly finds numerous creative ways to pass his time, from routing through your freshly cleaned clothing still in the laundry basket to creating unique doggie sculptures with his teeth on your dining room table leg. Some Border Collies have been known to dig and chew right through walls as a cure for boredom! Crating your dog also facilitates the housetraining process, since dogs instinctively do not want to soil their dens. (Housetraining is discussed further in Chapter 6, Basic Training for Border Collies.)

Whether you are bringing home a puppy or an adult dog, do not give in to the temptation to immediately give him free run of the house. Remember, your new dog will not know the rules of the household until you teach them to him. And how can you teach your dog if you are not right there with him to correct mistakes and to praise him when he is behaving? Picture this scenario: You are watching television in the family room and your Border Collie is contentedly working on his canine woodworking masterpiece in your dining room. Suddenly, you realize you haven't seen your puppy in a while. You call him to you, and he joyously bounds into the room. You praise him for coming when called and curl up with him on the floor for some more TV watching. An hour later, you get up to get a glass of water. As you wander through the dining room, you discover puppy's disastrous attempts at architecture. Can you punish your Border Collie for this crime against wooden humanity? No! Punish yourself for not keeping a better eye on your puppy.

At this point you may be wondering how you are going to keep a constant watch on this fur-clad bundle of energy. This is where the crate comes in. When you can't watch your puppy, simply place him in his crate. The crate should be located in an area where your Border Collie can be alone, yet still be around his family. A corner of the kitchen is often a good option, since families tend to congregate there. When you can devote your attention to your Border Collie, let him out to explore the house. Hang back at a discreet distance, but be ready to correct any bad behavior with a firm "No!" Don't forget that praise is as important as corrections. When puppy is being good, let him know. These rules also apply to a newly adopted adult dog. Don't assume because a dog is full grown that he automatically knows proper household manners. Take your time, and clearly and consistently teach him the behavior you expect.

As your dog masters the house rules, slowly grant him more freedom. For best results, increase his freedom incrementally. For example, start by gating off the kitchen where your dog's crate is, then perhaps add a hallway, then the family room. Remember to take these steps slowly; wait until you're sure your Border Collie understands how to behave before increasing his roaming space.

In the evening, it's a good idea to either move your dog's crate into your bedroom or have a second crate for this purpose. There is no better way to begin bonding with your Border Collie than to allow him to sleep in your bedroom, where he can take comfort in knowing you are right beside him all night long. There are a lot of new sights, sounds, smells, and noises in your dog's new home. He will feel much calmer and settle in much more quickly if he knows you are nearby. Having a puppy sleep in your room also aids in housetraining by allowing you to hear your pup if he needs to go out to relieve himself during the night. The same goes for older dogs—your adult Border Collie will settle in much more quickly if he can be with you as much as possible.

> If you are leaving your dog alone in any room, you first must make sure all hazards are put away.

Crates are truly wonderful tools. When you are home and can't keep an eye on your new dog, or if you need to leave him alone in the house, a crate provides safety and security for your pet, and peace of mind for you. While crates are indispensable, be careful not to overuse or misuse them. No dog, especially a puppy, should be left in a crate for hours on end. You or a helper, such as a neighbor or pet sitter, should let the dog out every three or four hours—whatever suits the dog best—for exercise and to relieve himself.

As your dog becomes more reliable and you wish to grant more freedom when you are gone, again, take your time. Don't rush from crate to unrestricted freedom, but use gates to confine your dog to a specific room, such as the kitchen. If you are leaving your dog alone in any room, you first must make sure all hazards are put away. (See Border Collie-Proofing Your House, to follow.)

Outdoor Boundaries

Never give your Border Collie unrestricted access to an unfenced area. Your dog might roam off your property, which can result in some harrowing consequences. He could get lost, picked up by the animal welfare department, or hit by a car. He could be stolen, especially if he is very friendly. Plus, you are libel for any mischief your pet gets into, such as deciding to herd your neighbor's children! The bottom line is, don't allow your dog to run loose.

Some misinformed owners believe chaining their dog in the yard is a solution to keeping their Border Collie from straying. No dog should ever be tied up. Tying a dog in the yard can promote aggression in the unlikeliest candidates. Even if your Border Collie is eager to make friends with passersby, being chained can quickly end that desire. When people and animals walk by your yard, your Border Collie naturally advances toward them. When he reaches the end of his chain, he will experience a sharp jerk on his neck, which he will associate with the intruders on the sidewalk. The dog will respond by lunging again more vigorously, resulting in him being jerked back more harshly, which further increases his aggressive behavior.

The best way to keep your Border Collie in your yard and out of trouble is to put up a six-foot-high fence. Your dog will love to run and herd squirrels in his own safe domain. Keep in mind, however, how agile and inventive Border Collies can be. A bored Border Collie quickly figures out that he can scale a six-foot fence or dig under it; he may even attempt to chew through it. Some Border Collies with too much time on their paws have taught themselves how to open latched gates. Never leave your dog in the yard unsupervised for long periods of time.

Some dog owners opt for invisible fencing. These increasingly popular fences consist of a signal-emitting electrical wire that runs through the ground bordering your property and a corresponding receiver on a collar your dog wears. If the dog tries to cross the border, he receives an electrical shock, which usually corrects him against leaving the property. Many Border Collies instinctively want to remain on their territory, and are easily taught to respect boundaries.

This type of containment system presents some problems, however. For one thing, while invisible fences may keep your dog in, they do nothing to keep intruders out, whether those intruders are friend or foe. A stray dog could come onto your property and attack your dog, or a thief could sneak on your property, remove your dog's collar, and steal your pet. Another problem with most invisible fences is that the correction, or electrical jolt, occurs only at the periphery of your property. If your dog is intensely focused on a person or animal walking on the other side of the street, he could break through his boundaries only to find the correction stops once he has cleared the underground wire. The only way to ensure that your dog stays in your yard, and intruders stay out, is to build a sturdy conventional fence, and check it frequently for signs of digging or loose boards that could allow your Border Collie to escape.

Did You Know?

According to the American Animal Hospital Association, over half of all dog and cat owners give their pets human names.

Behavioral Boundaries

As important as physical boundaries are to your Border Collie's well-being and your relationship with him, behavioral boundaries are just as important. Once again, establish rules and stick to them from Day One. If you institute one set of rules when your puppy is an adorable, cuddly eight-week-old, then change the rules as he grows into an agile, active adolescent and adult, he will have no idea what is expected of him. For example, while the Border Collie's penchant for herding is ideal for a working dog, it may need to be curtailed somewhat in a household setting. Although you may think it's cute that your tiny puppy totters after you in the kitchen, chasing the ends of your bathrobe, you will most likely not tolerate a full-grown Border Collie nipping at your children's heels. If you will not appreciate a certain behavior in an adult Border Collie, don't allow it in your puppy. Discourage all bad behaviors now or they will be very difficult to break in the future.

If you are bringing home an adult dog who was rescued, don't allow him to do things you wouldn't otherwise dream of in an effort to make up for his neglectful or abusive past. Your dog will appreciate clear-cut rules and a strong show of leadership by you, his new alpha.

> If you will not appreciate a certain behavior in an adult Border Collie, don't allow it in your puppy.

Setting behavioral boundaries actually reinforces your position as leader. Since the Border Collie can be an independent, headstrong breed, strong leadership is a must. If your dog is especially dominant, you may need to institute certain rules, such as no lying on the furniture, that a more submissive dog might not require. Since in dog culture height directly relates to dominance—a dominant dog will stand over a submissive one—taking

What Do You Mean It's My Turn?

Divvying Up Dog-Care Responsibilities

Often, parents buy a dog "for the kids" and end up taking on all the responsibilities of caring for the pet themselves. Even couples have been known to purchase a puppy with the understanding that they'll share dog-care duties, only to find one spouse doing the majority of the work once the pup arrives. When family members shirk their responsibilities, it not only can cause resentment, it can also prove detrimental to the puppy's care. To avoid these problems, call a family meeting before bringing your new dog home and divide all dog-care duties among family members. Keep in mind that, although children should be given some responsibilities related to puppy care, you may want certain jobs, such as obedience training an adolescent or adult Border Collie or food and water responsibilities, to be handled by an adult. Grooming and games such as fetch are two excellent responsibilities for children. Also, clearly spell out during the meeting the boundaries you expect the dog to follow, so all family members will be consistent in their dealings with your new pet.

Questions you should answer include:

○ Who will feed the dog?

○ Who will walk the dog?

○ Who will clean up after the dog?

○ Who will groom the dog?

○ Who will housetrain the dog?

○ Who will obedience-train the dog?

○ Who will play with the dog to ensure he gets to release his energy and doesn't become bored?

○ What kind of games are okay to play with the new dog and what kind of games should you avoid?

○ Who will take the dog to the veterinarian for his regular checkups and shots, as well as if he becomes sick?

○ Where will the dog sleep at night?

○ Where will the dog stay during the day when people are home? Once he has learned the rules of the household, will he have free run of the house or be confined to a crate or certain rooms?

○ Where will the dog stay during the day when no one is at home?

○ Will the dog be allowed on the furniture?

○ How will the dog be contained in the yard?

○ What kind of treats will you give to the dog? Will you give people food to the dog occasionally, or never?

○ How will you correct the dog when he makes a mistake?

such simple steps as requiring your dog to sleep on the floor automatically tells your dog you are the head of his new pack.

Border Collie-Proofing Your House

Before bringing your new Border Collie home, you need to dog-proof every inch of your house, garage, and property. Puppies, and even adult dogs, have an instinctual need to investigate their surroundings. Just like human toddlers, puppies investigate by placing everything enticing in their mouth. It is your job to make sure there is nothing hazardous within teeth-range of your pet. While you can't barricade your pet from everything in your home unless she is in her crate, you can use some simple precautions. Get on your hands and knees and investigate your house from a dog's-eye view.

> It is your job to make sure there is nothing hazardous within teeth-range of your pet.

Kitchens are filled with many tempting sights and smells. Keep all food items behind closed cupboard doors, at the back of countertops, atop the refrigerator, or on high shelves. Also keep in mind your Border Collie's intelligence and creativity. A Border Collie only needs to watch you reveal the untold treasures of a lazy Susan once or twice before figuring out how beneficial a well-placed paw can be. Install "baby latches" on cabinets to keep out your inquisitive canine, keeping in mind that some foods will make your Border Collie sick if he eats them.

Garbage cans also pose some real dangers. Keep all garbage cans, even those with lids, behind closed doors. A flimsy plastic garbage lid is no match for a foraging Border Collie. Although some garbage is innocuous, other trash, such as tinfoil or poultry bones, can seriously harm your dog. Place a short trashcan under the sink or keep a taller garbage container just outside the door in the garage or an adjoining room with a door you can shut.

Treat your bathrooms in a similar fashion. Cleaning agents may not seem very exciting to us, but their smell and very existence are enough to intrigue a puppy, and many of these supplies are toxic. Keep all cleaning supplies locked up or on high shelves. If you don't want half-chewed cotton swabs, tissue paper, and other doggie delicacies strewn throughout your house, keep your bathroom wastebasket under the sink as well. Keep all makeup, hair products, deodorants, and medications in latched drawers or cabinets. Don't mistakenly assume that bottles and metal or plastic containers will halt a Border Collie onslaught. A determined dog can easily crush a pill vial or hair-spray canister in her teeth and ingest the contents, which may be toxic.

Fluffy bathroom rugs and toilet seat covers may look like the ultimate chew toys to your Border Collie. If ingested by your pet, decorative rugs and linens can cause intestinal blockage. You may need to store these until your pup has gotten past the chewing stage or, if you've adopted an older dog, until you're sure she can be trusted around household accessories. Also, remember to keep the toilet seat down. Although drinking plain toilet water is just a disgusting habit, drinking toilet water that has been treated with a chemical cleaner could be fatal to your pet. A final temptation in the bathroom is the toilet paper roll. While toilet paper won't harm your puppy, you may find it wasteful to have it papering your house, thanks to some creative Border Collie redecorating!

In the laundry room, store laundry detergent, dryer sheets, and toxins such as bleach on high shelves or behind locked cabinets. Keep all your clean and dirty laundry off the ground or you may need to wash clean laundry again, replace a few shredded socks and undergarments, and take your Border Collie to the veterinarian for costly and unpleasant treatment. If you iron in the laundry room, make sure you don't leave the cord from the iron dangling off the side of the ironing board. Not only could your Border Collie chew on the cord and electrocute herself if it is plugged in, she also could accidentally pull the iron down on her.

Carefully examine the room or area of the house where you sew and store your sewing supplies. Store all needles, pins, thread, scissors, and buttons in locked cabinets or sewing kits kept well out of your dog's reach.

In bedrooms, keep closet doors closed to protect your clothing and shoes from chewing disasters. Keep perfumes and colognes on the back side of dressers and shoe polish on a high shelf in the closet. Anything on a nightstand is probably within Border Collie reach, so be careful what you store there.

Home offices, which are becoming more prevalent, present their own dangers. Printer toner can be toxic, and staples, paper clips, thumbtacks, and other office supplies can puncture the stomach or intestine if eaten. Books stored on the bottom of bookshelves can pique a puppy's curiosity. Keep bottom shelves empty of books until you are sure your Border Collie won't devour them.

In the home office and throughout the house, electrical cords and outlets pose a serious threat to a curious dog's health. Insert plastic caps into all outlets not in use, and unplug electrical cords before leaving a puppy in a room alone. If your pup is especially intrigued by wires, bury them under the carpet along the baseboards, or spray them with a "dog-off" product such as Bitter Apple spray or even Tabasco sauce. Never leave cords dangling; your puppy could get tangled and hurt herself.

Houseplants add beauty to your home, but may cause harm to your pup. Consult plant books or speak with someone at your local garden supply store to ensure that none of the plants in your home or yard are poisonous. If your Border Collie loves to dig in dirt, try using large rocks to cover the soil in your indoor planters.

If your basement is a storage disaster, it's probably best to keep your Border Collie out by means of a closed door or doggie gate. If your dog is allowed in the basement, keep all hazards in locked cabinets or on high shelves. It's also a good idea to keep storage boxes up high, since a curious Border Collie can regard a cardboard box as an enticing chew toy. Better yet, invest in durable plastic tubs for storing holiday decorations, old photos, and important papers.

If you have cats, you'll need to keep your Border Collie from getting to the litter box and taste-testing some "kitty crunchies." If you keep the litter box in the bathroom, invest in a litter pan cover to discourage your dog from sampling these unapproved snacks. A determined Border Collie may still poke her head in

> If your basement is a storage disaster, it's probably best to keep your Border Collie out.

the opening and help herself, however. If your cat is a good leaper, another option is to keep the cat box in the basement and block it off with a tall doggie gate. Your cat still has access by leaping the gate, but your Border Collie is kept at bay, unless she is skilled at scaling fences as a result of agility training or mere ingenuity. Other options include putting the litter box in a closet and installing a cat door, installing a cat door to the basement, or making or buying a cat box that has an opening too small for your Border Collie to fit through.

Throughout the house, you and your family need to be diligent about cleaning up. Dirty dishes or glasses left on coffee tables or TV trays are bound to be licked clean if left there for long. Cigarettes can look like tempting chew toys to puppies, but they can cause nicotine/tobacco poisoning. The same goes for cigarette butts left in ashtrays. If you have a party, don't think you can leave the cleanup until morning. It is especially dangerous to leave out glasses with alcohol in them. Your dog not only could get sick from drinking the alcohol, she could knock the glass to the floor and get cut. If you have put out candy and nuts in bowls on tables for your guests, take them up immediately after the guests go home. Chocolate, especially, is toxic to dogs, sometimes fatally so. Make sure your guests understand the dangers of feeding your dog candy. If there are young children present, you may want to keep candy off the coffee table altogether, since they may not understand the grave consequences of giving your Border Collie a nibble.

> If you have children, make sure toys are picked up and stored in toy boxes or in closets behind closed doors.

If you have children, make sure toys are picked up and stored in toy boxes or in closets behind closed doors. A dog can choke or experience intestinal blockage from ingesting tiny toy cars, game pieces, or bitten-off parts of larger toys. Whether or not you have children now, if you plan to have them in the future, consider not introducing your pup to doggie fleece toys. While the difference between a child's stuffed animal and a dog toy may be obvious to us, it's too vague a distinction for most dogs to make. If your Border Collie loves to chew her stuffed toys to unrecognizable shreds, you can be sure she'll do the same to a child's cherished stuffed pal.

When cleaning your home, you may opt to place your Border Collie in her crate, unless another family member can keep an eye on her. Your puppy may decide to take a sip from a bucket filled with your cleaning supply cocktail, and wind up a very sick dog. In fact, most cleaning supplies are hazardous to dogs. Take extra care to keep your puppy away from any type of pest control products, such as ant bait, rat poison, flypaper, and mousetraps.

While holidays bring joy and festive celebrations to your home, they present their own dangers to your dog. Chocolate and rich foods, for example, can be detrimental to her. She might chew, swallow, or choke on ornaments, tinsel, and other decorations. Chewing on a Christmas tree itself or drinking out of the tree stand can make your Border Collie extremely sick as well. After opening gifts, throw away all ribbons and bows since these, too, can cause intestinal blockage. In the spring, grass from an Easter basket can pose the same danger. And when the chill of autumn arrives, protect your pet from Halloween hazards. Don't let your children share their Halloween haul, or you may find yourself making an unplanned trip to the veterinarian.

Border Collie-Proofing Your Yard

Now that you've Border Collie-proofed the inside of your house, it's time to take a look at the outside. Keep your yard cleared of anything that could harm your dog, such as rusty old rakes, nails, wire, and broken glass. Inspect all wooden lawn furniture to make sure no nails protrude and no large splinters are breaking off. If you ever catch your Border Collie chewing on wooden furniture or see telltale teeth marks, spray the wood with a bitter dog-off product from a pet supply store. If you use a clothesline in your yard, hang it high enough to prevent your dog from getting entangled.

Patrol your fence line regularly to ensure there are no weak spots where your dog could break through or areas where your dog has been digging and might escape. Repair or replace any loose pieces of chain-link, since they can hook your dog's collar and choke him. Always securely latch and/or lock the gate to your yard, and make sure neighborhood children understand that they must never open the gate to "let your Border Collie come out and play."

Examine all the plant life in your yard. If you find a plant that could be toxic to your dog, either dig it up and dispose of it or block your Border Collie's access to it with fencing. You'll also need to block your dog from compost piles. The smell of the rotting organic matter will likely attract him. This is potentially dangerous because the bacteria that break down the compost produce toxins. If you occasionally treat your lawn with fertilizers, pesticides, or weed killer, keep your dog off it for 24 to 72 hours after application, until the area is fully dry. Carefully read the labels of any lawn-care products to see if they are hazardous, and keep the labels after you throw away the container, in case your pet becomes poisoned and you need to tell your veterinarian the product's ingredients.

Block your Border Collie's access to swimming pools and hot tubs when you are not around; your dog may decide to take a dip one day only to find that he can't get out of the pool or Jacuzzi. To be on the safe side, teach your dog how to climb the ladder out of the pool in case he gets around your barricade and accidentally falls in one day when you aren't nearby. Also block access to old wells and other potentially dangerous holes in the ground anywhere on your property.

Although your Border Collie enjoys time outside, it is a myth that dogs need to spend hours outside every day unless they are sharing that time with their owners in some type of activity. If your dog will be spending any substantial amount of time outdoors, however, make sure he has access to shade and lots of cool water. Never leave your Border Collie outside for prolonged periods of time in extreme heat or cold. While outdoor exercise is important, your Border Collie wants, and needs, to spend a good portion of his time indoors with you, his family.

Safeguarding Your Yard

While it is essential to protect your dog from any hazards lurking in your yard, you also need to protect your yard from your dog. While pristine rose bushes and succulent tomato gardens may be the picture of perfection to us, they seem incomplete to our dogs. To the canine mind, those roses petals and ripe vegetables would look much better strewn around the yard, and a few potholes and stool piles would surely spruce up the place! The question is, how can you bring your Border Collie around to your point of view?

Even if your dog never agrees with your sense of aesthetics, you can train him to keep your yard relatively free of destruction. If you want certain areas of your yard, such as a flower bed or vegetable garden, to remain intact, block your dog's access to them. Either use interior fences to block off certain areas or keep your dog in a kennel run when you can't supervise him. Teach your dog to defecate in one area of the yard by bringing him there on-leash and praising him when he does his business. Since dogs tend to use the same spot over and over for elimination, this should be relatively easy to do, and will keep your yard free of doggie land mines.

Although digging is a natural behavior for dogs, you can curb this behavior through training. First of all, realize that

Did You Know?

The average cost per year for owning and maintaining a dog in the United States is $1,220.

digging can be a symptom of boredom and excess energy. Dogs who are left unsupervised for hours on end in the backyard often dig out of frustration. A dog who participates in plenty of interactive exercise and play with his family is less likely to dig, bark, or otherwise misbehave. If your dog gets lots of exercise and social time with your family, but still is working on an excavation project in your yard, you need to teach him that this behavior is inappropriate. Watch him discreetly from inside the house whenever you let him out, and immediately interrupt any attempt at digging by rushing outside and sternly telling him "No!" When he stops, praise him. This may take some time, but remember to be consistent and your dog will learn what is expected of him.

> Although digging is a natural behavior for dogs, you can curb this behavior through training.

Border Collie–Proofing Your Garage

Garages and outbuildings usually contain numerous items capable of making your Border Collie sick or even killing him. Many car products, including windshield washer, brake, transmission, and engine fluids, are poisonous to dogs. Due to its sweet taste, antifreeze is especially tempting to dogs and can be fatal. Some new types of antifreeze are safer for pets, but it is still wise to keep your pet away from antifreeze spills and containers.

Puppies especially should never be left alone in a garage, due to these potential dangers. Even if you are going to be in the garage with your Border Collie, store lawn chemicals, car-care products, paint, batteries, gasoline, kerosene, and other hazards on high shelves or in locked cabinets. Make sure you understand

Common Hazards for Dogs

- Household cleaners, laundry detergents, bleach, furniture polish
- Medication
- Suntan lotion
- Poisons (such as ant poison, snail bait, and rat poison)
- Mousetraps
- Human trash (poultry bones, spoiled food)
- Pins, needles, buttons, other sewing accessories
- Ribbons, fabric, or string that can get lodged in the throat or intestine
- Plastic
- Rubber bands, paper clips, twist ties, thumbtacks
- Shoe polish
- Alcohol
- Cigarettes and other tobacco products
- Matches
- Antifreeze, motor oil, brake fluid, windshield-washer fluid
- Paint and paint remover
- Nails, screws, saws

the properties of any chemicals you are dealing with before placing them behind closed doors, however. Some chemicals cannot be safely stored in closed places, especially in hot climates or during the summer, or near hot-water tanks and furnaces, and should be placed up high and out of reach. If your garage contains a workshop, store nails, screws, tools, and other sharp objects in a toolbox or on a high shelf, and cover or hang saw blades where your dog cannot get them. Keep rodenticides, pesticides, and insecticides, all of which can be toxic, high enough that your dog can't reach them when standing on her hind legs.

Common Poisonous Plants

This list contains some, but not all, common plants that can harm your dog. Consult a plant book or a nursery if you have any doubts about a plant in your home or yard.

Alfalfa

Amaryllis

Asparagus (Sperengeri) fern

Azalea

Beech tree

Belladonna

Bird of paradise

Black locust tree

Caladium

Castor bean

Chinaberry

Coriaria

Crown of thorns

Daffodil

Daphne

Datura

Dieffenbachia

Elephant's ear

Euonymus

Foxglove

Henbane

Honeysuckle

Hydrangea

Iris

Ivy (especially English, heart, needlepoint, and ripple)

Jack-in-the-pulpit

Jerusalem cherry

Jessamine

Jimsonweed

Larkspur

Lily-of-the-valley

Mistletoe berries

Monkshood

Moonseed

Morning glory

Mums (spider and pot)

Nightshades

Oak trees (acorns)

Oleander

Periwinkle

Philodendron

Plant bulbs (most)

Poinsettia

Potato (green parts and eyes)

Precatory bean (rosary pea)

Rhododendron

Rhubarb (leaves, upper stem)

Skunk cabbage

Tobacco

Tomato vines

Tulip

Umbrella plant

Water hemlock

Wisteria

Yew tree (Japanese, English, Western, American)

Which Supplies Do You Really Need?

Now that you've Border Collie-proofed your house, yard, and garage, it's time to purchase all the essentials your new dog will need to make your house her home. In addition to basic supplies, such as a food bowl and collar, there are many other fun accessories to be had, from luxurious bedding to fanciful ID tags to myriad doggie toys.

Feeding and Water Dishes

Bowls come in all shapes, sizes, and materials. Although plastic bowls may seem like a bargain, they won't be in the long run. For one thing, plastic bowls look like odd-shaped chew toys to many dogs. Not only are plastic feeders easy to chew, but the food smells and flavors that become embedded in the plastic make them especially tempting. A plastic bowl is no match for a Border Collie's teeth, even a puppy's, and you'll have to replace the bowl often. It can be harmful to your dog, especially a puppy, if he bites off pieces of plastic and swallows them. Another problem with plastic bowls is that teeth marks and scratches in the plastic become a perfect breeding ground for bacteria from your dog's mouth, uneaten food, and other contaminants.

Ceramic bowls are durable and come in a variety of colors and designs. They also are heavy, which keeps them from getting knocked across the kitchen floor by a rambunctious Border Collie. Although some must be hand-washed, others are dishwasher safe. But be warned: Some ceramic bowls have high lead levels which can leach into your Border Collie's food in toxic levels and harm your dog. It is best to use ceramic made in the United States, and avoid antiques. You should even check the lead content of ceramic bowls with a rub-on test kit. While aluminum is a poor choice, stainless steel bowls may be the your best option. They are virtually indestructible and sterilize easily in the dishwasher.

Crate and Bedding

As mentioned previously, a crate serves many purposes. In addition to keeping your Border Collie secure and out of mischief when you can't watch him and aiding in housetraining, a crate provides your dog with "a room of his own." Crates come in two basic varieties: plastic and heavy-duty wire. Both have their advantages and disadvantages. Plastic crates, which are more enclosed and therefore look and feel more like a den, may seem homier to your Border Collie. Many plastic crates are approved for airline use and offer more protection during car travel and from household commotion than do open wire crates. Wire crates, on the other hand, provide better circulation than the plastic variety, which tend to retain more of your pet's body heat. During summer months or in close quarters, the trapped heat of a plastic crate may prove uncomfortable for your pet. If you decide on a wire crate but want to give your dog more privacy, drape a sheet or lightweight towel over the top and partially down the sides.

You may decide to invest in one of each kind. You can use the wire crate for the house and the plastic crate for travel, or keep 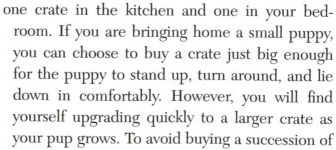 one crate in the kitchen and one in your bedroom. If you are bringing home a small puppy, you can choose to buy a crate just big enough for the puppy to stand up, turn around, and lie down in comfortably. However, you will find yourself upgrading quickly to a larger crate as your pup grows. To avoid buying a succession of crates, buy one big enough for an adult Border Collie, then section it off with a solid, thick piece of wood to make it puppy size. The wood can be shifted incrementally as your Border Collie grows. Remember to spray the wood with a dog-safe repellent to discourage chewing.

Until your puppy is housetrained and past his chewing stage, it is best to leave the floor of the crate bare. If your puppy has an accident in his crate and buries it with a towel, he won't be as bothered by his mess and may be more likely to soil in his crate again. Also, it may take you longer to discover this slip in housetraining. As the puppy gains more control, you can throw in a towel or mat for comfort, but only if you're certain your puppy won't chew on it. If your Border Collie does begin to tear up the towel, remove it until he has gotten past the teething stage, since he could choke on threads or pieces of towel or, worse, suffer intestinal blockage. As your puppy becomes more reliable, or if you have adopted an older Border Collie, you may want to invest in a dog pillow or cushion, or even use old blankets or quilts to soften the floor of the crate. This bedding can be removed from the crate later on and placed beside your own bed once your dog is allowed more freedom in the house.

> Until your puppy is housetrained and past his chewing stage, it is best to leave the floor of the crate bare.

Doggie Gates and Puppy Pens

As you give your pet more freedom, you might still want to block your puppy or adult Border Collie from certain rooms. A doggie gate, or a child's baby gate, works well to keep younger Border Collies in, or out of, certain areas. As mentioned before, however, it may be difficult to contain an adult Border Collie with a gate if he is an experienced jumper. Chewing is another potential problem, especially in puppies. If your pet is a voracious chewer, spray the gate with Bitter Apple. A determined Border Collie can easily chew his way through a plastic gate, although wooden gates generally are sturdier. You can also try wire exercise pens to contain your puppy either in the house or in a certain part of the yard. These aren't as vulnerable to doggie teeth as plastic or wood.

Outdoor Shelter

Once again, I want to stress that no dog should be relegated to live outside. Dogs are pack animals. They need to be with their people, and react to isolation with frustration and loneliness. That being said, if your dog is going to spend any substantial time outside unsupervised, he will need some type of shelter outdoors.

If you purchase a kennel run, make sure it has some type of covering to protect your dog from precipitation and sun. You also may want to buy or build a doghouse. Choosing the size of a doghouse is much like choosing the size of a dog's crate; it should be big enough for your pet to stand up and turn around in, but not so roomy as to lose its den-like quality. A properly sized and constructed doghouse will stay comfortably warm, but not too warm, from your dog's body heat. Make sure the entrance to the house is off center and covered with a flap to allow your Border Collie to escape drafts. Ideally, it will have a solid bottom that is raised off the ground, especially in cold-winter areas. In addition, you'll want a house with a removable roof to make it easier to clean.

> Dogs are pack animals. They need to be with their people, and react to isolation with frustration and loneliness.

Collars and Leads

Your dog, whether a puppy or adult, will need a flat buckle collar to hold his ID tags. (Training collars are discussed in Chapter 6, Basic Training for Border Collies.) Nylon or leather works well, but leather lasts longer. If you are getting a puppy, you will definitely want to purchase an adjustable collar that will grow with your pet. For the first collar, you may want to go with the less-expensive nylon, since you'll probably replace it several times. For a grown Border Collie, a sturdy leather collar is a good investment. Whether your dog is a pup or an adult, the collar should be tightened so that you can fit only two fingers between the collar and your dog's neck. If the collar is too loose, it can get caught on something and choke your pet. Check the size of your Border Collie's collar frequently during his first year.

Leashes, too, come in a variety of materials. Nylon and leather leashes are the most common; as with collars, both work well, but a leather leash is more durable.

One type of leash to avoid is the chain-link leash, because it is difficult to grasp and can hurt you if it gets wrapped around your hand. A six-foot leather leash is ideal for training and taking walks. It is easy to grasp, strong, and durable. Unfortunately, to your puppy it may look and smell like something good to chew. If your puppy insists on trying to walk himself, with leash in teeth apply a

Did You Know?

Researchers are almost positive that dogs dream. If you look at a sleeping dog, sometimes you'll notice his eyes move beneath his eyelid. Because this is what humans do when they dream, researchers believe it is an indication of dreams in dogs, too. No word yet on what they dream about.

bitter dog-safe repellent or Tabasco sauce to the lead. Once your dog is trained to walk properly on a leash, you can also use a flexible, retractable leash to give your dog a little more freedom on walks. Don't use this type of leash if your dog still tends to forge ahead and drag you down the street. Retractable leashes don't allow you the control of a shorter leash and also encourage dogs to pull, since exerting pressure on the leash causes it to expand.

Feeding Your Puppy

To fuel his growth, a puppy needs food that contains high-quality protein. Ask your veterinarian for a recommendation, or look for a food that is specially formulated for puppies. Good sources of protein that you should see on dog food labels include chicken, eggs, and cheese. Be sure that the food you choose is labeled "complete and balanced," and states that feeding trials confirmed the nutritional value of the food. Before taking your puppy home, ask when the puppy last ate and how

> Before taking your puppy home, ask when the puppy last ate and how often and what brand of food he usually eats.

often and what brand of food he usually eats. If you plan on feeding a different brand, introduce it gradually, over a two- to three-week period, or you may bring on diarrhea or vomiting. Check with your veterinarian for a specific answer, but plan on feeding a food formulated for puppies until your Border Collie is 6 to 12 months old.

Puppy Cleanup

If, and when, since you cannot avoid the inevitable, your puppy relieves himself in the house, not just any cleaning solution will do. You'll need an enzyme-based cleaner to remove the scent and stain thoroughly. Many products superficially clean the offending area, but remember, your dog's sense of smell is much keener than yours. An enzyme-based cleaner, available at any pet store, removes all traces of urine, feces, and vomit, which helps to keep your dog from returning to the same spot the next time he needs to relieve himself.

You'll also need some means of picking up your dog's waste on walks and around the yard. You can use anything from store-bought plastic bags to the bags your newspaper arrives in every morning. You also can invest in a pooper-scooper, which allows you to pick up doggie dung without a lot of bending over.

Grooming Equipment

While the Border Collie is an easy breed to keep looking their best, you still need some basic grooming supplies. A pin brush, a slicker brush, and a Greyhound comb work well to remove shedding fur and to stimulate the skin to keep it healthy. Invest in a high-quality dog shampoo and conditioner for baths. Do not use human shampoos and conditioners because they have a different pH factor than do dog products. (Brushing and bathing are covered fully in Chapter 7, Grooming.)

You'll also need a dog toothbrush and some dog toothpaste to keep your Border Collie's teeth clean. Never use human toothpaste, since its foaming agents can make your dog sick if he swallows them. Every dog needs his nails clipped, so you'll want to buy nail clippers, available in a scissors or guillotine style, and start using them on your dog when he's a puppy to get him used to the procedure. In addition, ask your vet if you should purchase cotton balls and ear-cleaning solution. Some dogs need their ears cleaned regularly to prevent infection.

Toys

Now let the really fun shopping begin—it's time to buy toys! There are myriad toys available for pets, in every color, size, and shape imaginable. Some of these toys are fine to leave with your Border Collie when he is alone, and some should only be given to your dog when you are around to supervise.

If you are giving your dog a toy to play with while you are gone, stick with hard toys that can't be chewed apart. Hollow, hard rubber toys such as Kongs are excellent because they can be stuffed with treats to keep your dog occupied for hours. The Buster Cube works on the same principle—you fill it with kibble, and as your dog noses or bats it around, the kibble gradually dribbles out, one piece at a time.

> If you are giving your dog a toy to play with while you are gone, stick with hard toys that can't be chewed apart.

Toys like these not only work off some of your dog's energy, but also give his brain a workout. Hard synthetic bones such as Nylabones are good options, too. These toys keep your Border Collie occupied and also scrape his teeth, which reduces tartar buildup.

Rawhide, however, is not a terribly healthy toy/treat for puppies, since they tend to bite off and swallow pieces that then expand in their stomachs. If you insist on giving your puppy or adult Border Collie rawhide, limit the amount he gets, especially if he seems to be obsessed with the treat, and don't leave him alone with rawhide, or he could eat a small piece and choke on it. Some dogs devour an entire rawhide chew in a matter of minutes, and come back looking for more. If your dog is given unlimited access to rawhide, that makes for a lot of soggy, expanding pulp in his stomach. Take away the rawhide when it has been whittled down near to the end, so your dog doesn't choke on it. If you are going to buy rawhide, read the package carefully to confirm it was made in the United States. Rawhide from other countries often is preserved with chemicals that are unhealthy for your pet. Some American-made rawhide contains harmful preservatives, so if your dog becomes ill after chewing a treat, discontinue using that brand.

Soft rubber toys are fine for when you are playing with your dog, but they are too easy for your dog to rip apart and swallow when he plays alone with them. The same caution applies to fleece toys; many dogs love to destroy these fake fur-balls and eat the insides, which can block their intestines. Never leave a dog alone with a toy that has a squeaker inside; again, your dog can chew a hole in the toy and then swallow the squeaker.

Rope, rubber, or fleece tug toys can be lots of fun for a Border Collie who loves to toss toys in the air and catch them. They also are great for puppies playing together with canine friends. You must be careful how you use these toys, however, when interacting with your Border Collie. If your dog shows any signs of being dominant, playing tug-of-war with him only encourages dominant behavior. Tug-of-war promotes a show of strength on the part of your dog. For tug-of-war to be played correctly, the human must always win. Otherwise, your dog is in a position in which he is stronger or quicker than you, and he is controlling the game. If you have any dominance issues with your dog, avoid playing tug-of-war.

Fleece or other fabric toys are poor choices for a dog who has a penchant for destructive chewing. A Border Collie who is allowed to tear apart a soft stuffed dog toy is every bit as likely to shred a child's stuffed animal or the accent pillows on your living room couch. In the same vein, never give your Border Collie an old shoe

Removing Doggie Stains and Odors

If you have purchased a puppy, you must accept the fact that you will probably encounter a housetraining accident or two, no matter how diligent you are, until your dog is fully trained. Even if you have adopted an adult dog, there may come a time when you find a mess on your carpet, whether that mess is urine, feces, or vomit. Even the best-trained dog may not be able to control himself when he is sick.

Not only must you remove the stain and odor you can smell, but more important, you also need to remove the odor your dog can smell. Remember, a dog's sense of smell is much more acute than ours. Therefore, you'll need to use a product designed specifically for pet-odor removal. Never use ammonia-based products. Since ammonia is present in urine, your dog will actually be more attracted to urinate there again.

If your dog has an accident, first clean up any solid waste that is present. Next, apply an enzyme-based stain and odor remover. Any pet-supply store carries such a product. Follow the directions carefully to ensure the cleaner does its job. If you are applying the cleaner to a carpeted area, test it in an inconspicuous spot first to make sure it won't change the color of your rug.

to chew on; otherwise, you'll need to keep your good shoes under lock and key for the rest of your dog's life.

ID Tags

The traditional collar and tag is the most common form of pet identification. A tag is small but identifiable, and everyone understands the concept of checking a tag for an owner's name and phone number.

Supply Checklist

- ○ Food and water bowls (ceramic or stainless steel)
- ○ Crate (plastic, wire, or both)
- ○ Dog bed or crate cushion, if you are sure he won't chew it
- ○ Doggie/baby gates
- ○ Outdoor kennel or secure perimeter fencing
- ○ Doghouse
- ○ Collar
- ○ Leash
- ○ ID tag
- ○ Enzyme cleaner
- ○ Grooming supplies (pin brush, slicker brush, greyhound comb, shampoo, dental and ear-cleaning supplies)
- ○ Safe toys

While a collar and tag may be crucial to a lost dog being returned to his owner, the collar/tag combination has some drawbacks. A collar and tag are easily removed, either by the dog himself or by unscrupulous people who want the dog for their own ends. Tags must be updated when addresses or phone numbers change, something that often gets relegated to "later" during the hustle and bustle of a move. If a dog wearing outdated tags is lost in an unfamiliar area, the information on the tag may be useless to whoever finds the dog. And tags can be annoyingly noisy, especially when there is more than one on a collar.

Nevertheless, a collar and tag are the first line of defense against loss. An engraved tag should include your name and two phone numbers at which you can be reached. Don't put your dog's name on the tag. This gives leverage to any person who wants to lure your dog—"Come on, Joker, follow me"—or claim ownership.

High-Tech Identification Protection

Identification tags are your dog's first line of defense if she ever gets lost. Many a dog has been quickly reunited with her family because she was wearing a tag with the owner's phone number. However, what if your dog's collar comes off or is removed? How will your Border Collie find her way back home? Two other forms of identification can supplement the ID tag: tattooing and microchip implants.

With tattooing, a series of numbers or letters, or a combination of numbers and letters, is imprinted onto your pet's body, and the code is then recorded in a database. If someone finds your Border Collie, they can call the toll-free number to a tattoo registry, which maintains a database record with your name and phone number, corresponding to your dog's tattoo ID code. The toll-free number usually is provided on a tag that attaches to your dog's collar. Advantages to the tattoo is that it is a permanent and visible means of identification. One disadvantage is that, if your dog loses her collar, whoever finds your pet may not know who to call. If your dog won't let a stranger near her, the person who finds her may not be able to get close enough to read the tattoo. Also, horror stories exist of stolen dogs who have had a tattooed ear removed to keep them from being identified. To prevent this, it is safer to tattoo your dog's inner thigh.

Like tattoos, microchips contain a unique code, which can be read by a hand-held scanner that is passed over the skin of the animal where the chip was inserted. The code corresponds to information in a database, such as the owner's name and phone number. An advantage to microchips is that they, too, are permanent. The microchip itself is composed of non-toxic components sealed in biocompatible glass. The chip, about the size of the lead tip of a pencil or a grain of rice, is fitted into a hypodermic needle and injected under the skin of a dog between her shoulder blades. A disadvantage is that not all scanners read all microchips. Humane societies usually have only enough money to invest in one scanner, at best, and if that scanner can't read the chip in your dog, it's useless. Again, if your dog is uncomfortable with being handled by strangers, she may be hard to scan.

Tattoos and microchips are gaining popularity as permanent means of identifying your pet. However, the standard ID tag that dangles from the collar of your pup remains an invaluable tool for helping return your lost pet to you.

Tags come in a variety of shapes, sizes, and colors. Choose something distinctive, so if your dog gets lost, his tag will stand out to people looking for him. There are a lot of Border Collies and dogs in general in the world, but not all of them wear neon-green, bone-shaped tags.

Plastic and metal tags each have advantages and disadvantages. Plastic is quieter than metal, but it can fade and become brittle with age. Metal is durable, but it can rust. Instead of a tag, a tiny metal or plastic barrel can be attached to the collar. These barrels unscrew to reveal a slip of paper on which you can write important information about your dog such as a phone number, your veterinarian's name, or any medications the dog needs. Engraved metal plates can be attached to collars to reduce not only jingling but also the possibility that the tag could get caught on something. Some nylon collars can be woven or imprinted with a phone number. The important thing to remember is that your dog needs to "carry" identification at all times.

Homecoming Day for Your Border Collie Puppy

The day has finally arrived! It's time to bring home your new puppy and introduce him to his new home and family. If you work outside the home full time, arrange to take off at least a few days to help your puppy adjust. If possible, schedule his arrival for early in the day to give him time to fully investigate his new environment before bedtime.

If you are picking up your puppy, rather than having him delivered to you, prepare for a less-than-smooth ride home.

How Much Is All This Going to Cost Me?

The basic supplies for your new dog can come with a hefty price tag depending on size and quality, and often it's a price you'll be paying more than once. Remember to factor in these costs when making the decision to get a dog. Prices likely will vary depending on where you live, but the following should give you a good idea of what to expect.

Item	Low Price	High Price
Crate	$20.00	$200.00
Food and Water Bowls	3.00	60.00
Collar	4.00	40.00
Leash	4.00	50.00
ID Tag	3.00	15.00
Pet Stain/Odor Remover	4.00	10.00
Brush	4.00	20.00
Toys	1.00	40.00
Food (8 lb. bag)	4.00	9.00
Bed	10.00	200.00
TOTAL	$57.00	$644.00

Unless the breeder has already taken your puppy for short trips, this may be his first car ride. Bring along several old towels in case your pup drools excessively or vomits. The most important thing to do if your puppy whines or cries is to act like nothing is wrong. Don't ooh and ahh over your nervous pup—otherwise, you'll just reinforce his fear of car rides. Instead, act calm and even businesslike. Sing along with the radio, or talk to your puppy in a matter-of-fact tone. The best way to introduce your dog to car rides is discussed further in Chapter 8, Family Life. For now, you'll just want to get through this first car ride as quickly as possible!

As soon as you get home, take your puppy outside to the area you want him to use as his bathroom. Chances are, after his exciting ride, he will need to go right away. Pick a phrase such as "go potty" or "hurry up" and use it when your dog starts to eliminate. Timing is extremely important. If you issue the command before your dog goes, in your dog's mind it may take on the meaning of something else that your dog is doing at the moment, such as "sniff the tree" or "chew on grass." Once your dog understands the command by associating it with the action, you can use the command to elicit the behavior. Each time your puppy eliminates outside, remember to praise, praise, and then praise some more! You must help the puppy realize from the beginning that pottying outdoors is the goal. If he doesn't go right away, bring him inside and put him in his crate for half an hour, then take him out to the designated spot again. Once he has relieved himself, you can bring him inside and let him explore the house. Remember, you'll need to keep a close eye on your pup so that you can correct any mistakes he may make.

> If you work outside the home full time, arrange to take off at least a few days to help your puppy adjust.

Resist the temptation to have all your friends and relatives over to see your new addition; too many people on the first day can be overwhelming for your new dog, whether he's a puppy or an adult. Instead, enjoy a private, getting-to-know-you first day with your pet. Although puppies do need lots of rest, you may want to try to wear your Border Collie out on his first day home to help him sleep through the night! This doesn't mean going on marathon runs around the neighborhood; simply playing with your pup and letting him explore your house and yard should do the trick.

When it is bedtime, take your puppy outside to empty his bladder. Then bring him to his nighttime crate in your room and turn off the lights. Some puppies cry all night during their first night in their new home, while others sleep "like babies" from the beginning. If your puppy begins to cry immediately after you have put him in his crate and you know he doesn't need to relieve himself, ignore him.

> If you make the "potty trip" too fun, you'll find your Border Collie waking you up every few hours to "party"!

It may be tough to do, but he will eventually settle down. If the puppy wakes up whining during the night, however, take him outside and make the trip as quick and businesslike as possible. If you play with your puppy and make the "potty trip" too fun, you'll find your Border Collie waking you up every few hours to "party"! As your puppy gains more control, nightly trips outside become fewer and farther between, and eventually stop altogether.

After the first few days, when life has settled back to normal and you return to work, either come home at lunch to let your puppy out or have a neighbor or friend drop in. Remember, a crate is a wonderful tool that shouldn't be abused. It's a good idea to pick a certain indestructible toy, such as a Kong stuffed with treats, that the puppy gets only when he is crated. This gives your Border Collie something to look forward to when you leave and helps keep him from feeling bored and lonely.

Making an Older Border Collie Feel Welcome

Before you bring an older Border Collie into your home, make sure she has met all the members of your family. Although rescue groups and shelters try to match the right dog with the right family, it is best that you personally ensure that everyone clicks with the older Border Collie before you adopt her. If you already have a dog at home, you may want to bring her to meet the potential adoptee as well. Once you feel comfortable that all your loved ones will get along, it's time to bring your Border Collie to her new home.

The first thing you should do is think of a new name for your Border Collie. Her old name may hold many negative associations for her, so you'll want to start with as clean a slate as possible.

If you have another dog, the initial interaction between the two animals is critical. Have a friend or neighbor meet you at a local park or around the block and leave your new dog with him or her while you go home to get your other dog. Let the dogs meet and sniff on neutral territory, and then go for a walk together, all the while acting calm and positive about the introductions. Bring them into the backyard and watch carefully to be sure your first dog does not become territorial. Once the dogs seem relaxed, you can unleash them.

It is important for you to realize that some tense moments may pass as the dogs establish rank. Do not interfere unless an actual fight breaks out. If a fight does occur, never get in the middle, or you could be bitten. Instead, spray the dogs with a hose to break them apart or throw a blanket over them and try to remove the less-aggressive dog. Once your pets have established who is top dog, things will settle down. While it is understandable to feel protective of your original dog, it is vital that you don't interfere with this process. If your new dog is the natural leader and you keep backing up your first dog, you are merely disrupting pack order and keeping both dogs in a constant state of stress.

Border Collies can get along well with cats if introduced carefully. Begin by letting them sniff each other under a closed door. Next let them in the same room, but keep your Border Collie on-leash so you can pull her back if she lunges at your cat. Discourage any attempts at herding. Practice obedience commands with your dog while you talk to your cat in a soothing voice. Make sure kitty always has areas to escape to and that she has privacy when she eats and uses the litter box.

If you are bringing home an older Border Collie, you may or may not know much about her past. As with a puppy, you must limit her freedom in your home until you have learned her habits. If she is not reliably housetrained, you'll want to keep her crated when you can't keep an eye on her. Once you feel comfortable giving her a little more freedom, block off the kitchen or laundry room with a tall gate. Make sure you still keep your dog's opened crate in the room with her, so she will have a cozy place to rest. Plan on giving your dog at least several days of supervised crate time while you're in the house to help her calmly adjust to her new surroundings and feel confident.

If your Border Collie is a rescued dog, making her feel secure in her new home is crucial. Don't think that just because she is an older dog she would be happier sleeping in the kitchen or laundry room. Make up a special bed in your room. In the beginning, you'll probably want to crate her until you know she can make it through the night without any accidents. After that, a dog bed placed next to your own bed will help your Border Collie bond with you, since she will sense your presence and feel more at ease. This is especially important if you are away from your dog for hours at a time during the day while you work.

If you have taken in a rescue dog, it is important to give the dog a fresh start. If you know your pet was abused, resist the temptation to baby her. Providing lots of praise, love, and firm, consistent leadership will benefit her more than anything else. Grooming and training are excellent ways to bond with your new pet. Practicing obedience also helps you establish from the beginning that you are the alpha of the pack, which helps your dog feel secure.

As with a puppy, you need to establish physical and behavioral boundaries from Day One. Don't fall into the trap of thinking that you can right the wrongs done to your dog by allowing her liberties you wouldn't otherwise dream of granting. Again, firm leadership and lots of love are what your dog craves most of all.

3

Food for Thought

In This Chapter

○ Why Nutrition Matters
○ Choosing the Best Food for Your Border Collie
○ How Often and How Much Do I Feed My Border Collie?
○ Is It Okay to Share My Food?

So, you've chosen bowls, beds, collars, leashes, toys, and other basic doggie necessities. Now, we come to perhaps the toughest, and most important, decision of all when buying essentials for your new pet—what are you going to feed her? Today's dog owner is bombarded with an array of dog food options, ranging from convenient grocery store brands to premium foods at the local pet-supply store to homemade recipes. Then there's the choice of dry versus canned, and the perplexing question: to supplement or not to supplement? Words of advice from well-meaning fellow dog owners are as limitless as the dog food options themselves. How can you make the best choice?

Why Nutrition Matters

First, you need to understand how vital good nutrition is for the health of your Border Collie. Proper nutrition boosts your dog's immune system and helps her fight infections. It keeps her bones and teeth strong, her coat glossy, and her skin smooth and supple.

> You need to understand how vital good nutrition is for the health of your Border Collie.

Not so long ago, people didn't really worry about what they were feeding their dogs. They fed their pets whatever brand was on sale, or just gave them some leftovers, including bones, from the evening meal. As consumers became more savvy about the importance of their own diet, however, they began to be more concerned about what they were feeding their dogs as well.

Changing dog food randomly because a different brand is on sale can give dogs diarrhea or other digestive problems. Feeding trimmed fat or other unhealthy portions of the family meal doesn't give dogs the proper nutritional balance they need for a healthy coat and stable weight. Plus, veterinarians have gotten the word out that bones are dangerous to a dog's health, and can even be lethal if they are swallowed, since they can puncture internal organs.

In order to determine the best food for your Border Collie, you need to understand her nutritional requirements. First, let's dispel a common myth about the dog—she is not a carnivore (strictly a meat eater). Instead, she is an omnivore, which means she needs a small amount of plant material as well as meat for a complete, balanced diet. This stems from the eating habits of her ancestor, the wolf, who consumed the plant matter in her prey's stomach as well as the meat of the prey itself. Therefore, while your Border Collie, in most cases, shouldn't have a purely vegetarian diet (there are vegetarian diets available, but they are very difficult for most dogs to digest), some plant material is important for proper nutritional balance.

Proteins form the major building blocks of your dog's blood, bone, muscle, and immune system. Proteins are made up of amino acids, which are essential in the formation of DNA, as well as for growth, metabolism, the development and repair of body tissues, the digestive system, hormone production, sexual development, the functioning of the immune system, and the transmission of nerve impulses. Of the 22 amino acids, your dog must get ten of them from her food since her body can't manufacture them. These ten essential amino acids are arginine, histidine, isoleucine, leucine, lysine, methionine, phenylalanine, threonine, tryptophan, and valine. Different food sources supply different amounts of these amino acids, resulting in a chemical score for the protein source. For example, eggs, which supply 100 percent of the essential amino acids, have a chemical score of 100, making them an excellent protein source. Proteins are found in meat and meat by-products, including beef, chicken, turkey, lamb, fish, eggs, meat and fish meal, milk, and milk products (whey and cheese). They are also found in plant sources, such as wheat, corn, rice, soy, and barley.

Carbohydrates serve primarily as a source of energy and to help in the digestion of other foods. They are included in most dog foods for taste, added energy, and fiber to aid digestion. If your Border Collie doesn't get enough energy from her diet, her body turns to its own tissues for fuel. An excess of energy fuel in the diet, on the other hand, leads to increased body fat. Carbohydrates are also protein sparing, which means they relieve proteins of some of their duties. When the body takes in enough carbohydrates, it doesn't rely as heavily on proteins to supply energy, freeing those nutrients to perform other necessary functions. Carbohydrates are present in plant sources such as corn, rice, oatmeal, beet pulp, and wheat.

Fats provide about twice the energy per gram than do proteins or carbohydrates. Fats also are extremely efficient, with more than 90 percent digestibility. They supply the essential linoleic, alpha-linolenic, and arachidonic fatty acids to the body, which are needed for healthy skin and coat and, on the cellular level, to make up cell walls. Fatty acids also carry fat-soluble vitamins through the body. Finally, fats make food taste better. Although fats are extremely beneficial, keep in mind that feeding the proper amount of fat is important. Too little fat can result in a dull coat or dry, flaky skin, or it can even slow your dog's growth if the deficiency is extreme. Too much fat can lead to an overweight dog and all the problems that come with obesity. The right amount of fat in your dog's diet, on the other hand, will provide benefits you can see—an energetic dog with a glossy, healthy-looking coat. Fats are in animal products, such as chicken or turkey fat, and in cold-pressed oil, such as linseed, wheat germ, or soybean oil. Fish oil and flaxseed oil are also good sources of certain fats.

Unfortunately, fats are fragile. Heat, light, and oxygen can destroy essential fatty acids, so it's important that they are protected during the dog food manufacturing process. Since fats can easily turn rancid, preservatives must be added to dog food to keep it fresh. There are two main types of preservatives or antioxidants—chemical and natural. Since the early 1900s, manufacturers have used the chemicals ethoxyquin, BHA, and BHT to preserve dog food, and even some human food (ethoxyquin is approved for use in paprika and chili powder, and BHA and BHT are present in bread, for example). There has been some concern over the safety of these chemicals, however. Anecdotal testimonials have blamed these chemicals for everything from allergies to immune system problems to cancer. Yet, to date, no study has proven that these preservatives are harmful in the levels approved for dog food. Still, consumer concern about the long-term effects of these chemicals has led many manufacturers to switch to using natural antioxidants, including vitamins C and E, as preservatives instead. While these natural antioxidants don't have any health concerns associated with them, they are much less efficient preservatives than their chemical cousins, which means the food has a much shorter shelf life. It's critical that you always check the expiration date stamped on dog food bags or cans and don't feed your Border Collie any food that has expired. If you open up a bag that hasn't expired but smells rancid, trust your nose and throw it away.

> While your Border Collie, in most cases, shouldn't have a purely vegetarian diet, some plant material is important for proper nutritional balance.

Vitamins help the body fight diseases and maintain the critical balance between constructive and destructive cellular changes. Vitamins themselves must be properly balanced since excesses or deficiencies of vitamins, or interference between vitamins, can cause serious health problems. The fat-soluble vitamins A, D, K, and E are stored in the liver and fatty tissues. Since they can be maintained in the body, an excess intake of these vitamins can easily become toxic. Water-soluble vitamins, on the other hand, are flushed from the body daily and must constantly be replaced. Both plant and meat sources contain vitamins, plus manufacturers often add vitamins to dog food during processing.

Minerals are needed for the body's metabolic processes and to keep the proper level of salts in the bloodstream. They also are an essential part of your dog's bones and teeth. Canines need seven major minerals and 15 trace minerals. Like vitamins, all minerals, especially trace minerals, need to be properly balanced or they can be toxic. And, as with vitamins, deficiencies or excesses can contribute to myriad health problems, from anemia to hip dysplasia. Minerals are present in both vegetable matter and animal tissues, or are added by the manufacturer during processing.

> Water is necessary for the proper working of every living cell in your pet's body.

Water is the most essential nutrient of them all. It is necessary for the proper working of every living cell in your pet's body. Since water is constantly being used up or excreted through normal body function, dogs need to continually replenish their supply. The best way to keep your dog fully hydrated at all times is to always give her access to plenty of clean, fresh water.

Choosing the Best Food for Your Border Collie

Now you understand the nutrients your Border Collie needs to keep him healthy. But that still doesn't do much to narrow down all the choices bombarding you from the dog food aisle. First, let's address whether a more expensive dog food is really better for your pet.

Premium Food Versus Generic or Store-Brand Food: Is There a Difference?

Perhaps the dog you grew up with was fed generic or store-brand food, and he seemed perfectly healthy. You recognize the big-name manufacturers you find at the grocery store, and who can beat the convenience of buying your dog food while you shop for your own food? Why should you make a special trip to a pet-supply store to buy a premium food that's going to end up costing more money?

First, we need to figure out what makes a food premium. Start by looking at the label. Dog food labels consist of two parts: the main display label and the information panel. The main display label states the brand name, flavor of the food, life stage the food is meant for (puppy or senior, for example), and weight of contents. The information panel is where you need to look to determine the quality of the food. It lists a number of items: the guaranteed analysis (the minimum levels of crude protein and fat and the maximum levels of fiber and water); the ingredient list (listed in descending order by weight); and a statement verifying that the food has undergone feeding trials by the Association of American Feed Control Officials (AAFCO) and provides complete and balanced nutrition. If the label doesn't include this statement, do not buy the dog food, no matter how highly recommended it may be by your breeder or neighbor down the street.

In general, the ingredient list gives you a hint as to whether you are dealing with a premium or lower-quality food. Premium foods tend to list chicken, lamb, turkey, or meat by-products as their first ingredients, while lower-quality foods often have plant sources such as corn as their top ingredient. You must read closely to see if any ingredients were split in their listing, however. For example, a bag that lists several different types of corn scattered throughout its ingredient list may actually contain as high a portion of corn as the "honest" bag that lists corn first and only once. Corn is corn, no matter how you describe it.

This sounds easy—read the ingredient list and choose the one with the better-sounding ingredients near the top. But you need to realize that simply

What's on the Label?

The wide variety of cans, bags, and boxes of pet food shelved in shops throughout the nation has at least one thing in common: labeling. True, the colors, pictures, and words used on individual foods vary, as do the diets within. But all labels must, by law, contain specific information.

Pet food labels give basic information about the ingredient content, nutrient guaranteed analysis, feeding instructions, net weight, the name and address of the manufacturer or distributor, and additional facts about the product. No, pet food labels don't tell everything about a product. But they do give a savvy consumer a good way to begin comparing foods.

At the federal level, pet food labeling and advertising claims are regulated by the Food and Drug Administration, the U.S. Department of Agriculture, and the Federal Trade Commission. State feed control officials determine regulations to which pet food manufacturers in individual states must adhere. Another organization with an important role in labeling pet foods is the Association of American Feed Control Officials (AAFCO). The association is made up of officials from all 50 states, Canada, and Puerto Rico. Although the AAFCO has no regulatory authority (state and federal officials do), it does set forth guidelines, or "models," for feed and pet food regulations that individual states are encouraged to adopt. A large number of states comply with the suggested laws and guidelines. The AAFCO also provides nutritional guidelines for dog and cat foods called nutrient profiles and guidelines for testing foods.

Pet food companies that sell diets that don't meet the label guarantee are subject to a warning, a fine, removal of the product, or cancellation of the product's registration.

Pet food labels contain several elements:

The product name must be placed on the principal display panel, that part of the label most likely to be seen by consumers.

stating an ingredient doesn't verify its quality. Bioavailability, or the ability of a nutrient to be absorbed and used by the body once it's been eaten, is extremely important. This is the main difference between premium and lower-quality dog

Certain nutrient guarantees—guaranteed analysis—are required on all pet food labels: crude protein (minimum percentage), crude fat (minimum percentage), crude fiber (maximum percentage), and moisture (maximum percentage).

The package must include an ingredient listing of all the ingredients used to make the food; they must be listed on the label in descending order of predominance by weight.

Additives must be noted. That includes nutritional additives such as vitamins and minerals, antioxidants such as BHA or BHT, chemical preservatives, flavoring agents, and coloring.

The net weight must be placed on the principal display panel.

Manufacturer information, the name and address of the manufacturer, packer, or distributor, must be included on the label.

The label must state in the nutritional adequacy statement whether or not the product provides complete and balanced nutrition and if it is appropriate for all life stages or one particular life stage.

The amount of food required, or feeding directions, must be printed on the label.

The caloric statement, which is the calorie content of the product, must appear away from the guaranteed analysis and be under the heading "calorie content."

Last, but not least, many pet food packages include a toll-free consumer information number. This isn't mandatory, but it's a good resource for owners wanting to learn more about the product they're feeding their pet.

food. Premium foods are more expensive precisely because they use higher-quality ingredients with greater bioavailability, so nutrients reach your dog's organs and tissues more quickly.

Another quality that sets premium foods apart is that they are manufactured using a fixed recipe, meaning the same exact ingredients are always used and the nutritional quality is consistent. Lower-priced food is often formulated with a variable recipe that uses the least expensive ingredients available at the time of manufacture. These foods may always list the same ingredients, but the exact nature and actual quality of those ingredients may vary dramatically from bag to bag. This change in ingredients can cause digestive problems in your dog and, in extreme cases, can even hinder the proper development of a puppy.

The use of consistent, higher-quality ingredients in premium foods leads to their higher price. The truth is that feeding a premium food may not cost any more money than a lower-quality, lower-priced brand in the long run, and in some cases, may even save you money. How can this be? Since premium foods are more bioavailable, your dog can eat less and get the same amount of nutrients he would receive from consuming a greater amount of a lesser brand. Premium foods also tend to contain less filler. So, although you're spending more money per bag on a premium brand, you might actually spend no more or even less per amount actually consumed by your dog. Another advantage of greater bioavailability is that, as your dog eats less food and absorbs more nutrients from it, he'll produce fewer, and in most cases, firmer stools.

The bottom line when choosing a dog food is to look for a brand from a company with a good reputation, lists better ingredients at the top of its ingredient list and has undergone AAFCO feeding trials. And ask your veterinarian. She sees the results—positive or negative—of most foods. Also, watch your dog. He should get full easily, have healthy, firm stools once or twice a day, and within six to eight weeks of being on a quality diet, should develop a sleek, glossy coat. Watching your dog's behavior is your best indication of whether he is receiving his nutritional requirements.

Canned Versus Dry

Now that you've chosen a brand, you'll need to decide which formula of the brand you want to feed your dog. Most brands of food come in two forms—dry and canned. Both types have their pros and cons.

Dry food is the more popular type, accounting for 80 to 90 percent of the dog-food market in the United States. Proponents argue that dry food aids in dental health by scraping away tartar during the chewing process and by helping maintain healthy gums. Chewing dry food, as opposed to gulping canned, also stimulates salivation and assists in digestion. Dry food also stays fresh longer when left out than canned food, which can turn rancid quickly. Finally, dry food usually is less expensive.

Canned food has the advantage of generally being more palatable. Owners also usually see canned food as a more exciting meal for their pets. On the downside, canned food tends to be more expensive and can't be left out or it will go bad. If your dog doesn't finish his portion, refrigerate the leftovers. You can warm them for a few seconds in the microwave before the next meal to make them more enticing, but stir the food, carefully making sure there aren't any "hot pockets" before feeding them to your dog. Unfortunately, some dogs refuse to eat leftovers regardless of whether they are heated, adding to the expense of canned food.

Some people like to mix canned and dry food for variety. If you are going to do this, make sure you are mixing

Did You Know?

Veterinarians estimate that between 30 percent and 50 percent of today's dog population is overweight.

varieties of the same brand so the nutritional value will be consistent. Also, if you are feeding a senior-formula dry food, for example, don't mix it with an adult-maintenance canned or you negate the effects of the dry food. If you want to spice up your dog's dry food but don't want to spend the money on canned, you also can try adding a little water and microwaving briefly to make a warm doggie stew. Once again, make sure the food is a safe temperature before giving it to your hungry Border Collie.

> If you want to spice up your dog's dry food but don't want to spend the money on canned, you also can try adding a little water and microwaving.

A third category of dog food is semi-moist food. I mention this type solely to warn you not to feed it to your dog. Semi-moist food usually comes in individual bags and is colored and shaped to look like real meat. While this food may look more appealing than dry or canned, this is for your benefit, not your dog's. Don't be fooled by its outward appearance—these foods typically contain high amounts of corn syrup or other sweeteners that are unhealthy for your pet.

In general, dry food is easier to feed, better for your dog's teeth and less expensive than canned (or the to-be-avoided semi-moist variety). If your dog likes his kibble, don't mess with a good thing!

All-Natural Foods

Many people, wanting the best for their pet, go beyond the grocery store versus premium food debate and search for a natural dog food. Unfortunately, there are no standards at the moment to verify what "natural" is. Manufacturers of "natural foods" criticize the general pet food industry, saying that dog food processing depletes ingredients of their nutritional value. Most of these manufacturers advocate using whole grains, whole fresh meats, and organic ingredients. They often sell their food in smaller-portion bags so less food will be exposed to oxidation when opened. Finally, many also offer a line of supplements to be used with their foods. If you want to feed a natural food, make sure you buy from a proven company with a good reputation. Read the ingredient list carefully and question the manufacturer about any ingredient you aren't sure of.

Natural prepared foods can be a more healthful choice for your pet, as long as you research them carefully. However, many all-natural foods have not undergone AAFCO feeding trials and certification, and instead are supported only by customer testimonials. Don't buy food from an unknown manufacturer based purely on its "all-natural" claims, or your dog's nutritional health could suffer.

Preparing Your Border Collie's Meals Yourself

Some owners take the concept of a natural diet even further, by cooking for their dogs themselves or even feeding a raw diet. While in theory this may sound attractive, be aware that it is very difficult to maintain a healthy dog on a home-prepared diet. You will need to find a proven recipe and stick to it 100 percent of the time, or your dog can miss out on essential nutrients. Never begin feeding a homemade diet without first consulting your veterinarian. She may even refer you to a board-certified veterinary nutritionist to ensure you are giving your dog the proper nutrients in the proper amounts. Remember, too much of a certain nutrient can be as dangerous to your dog as too little.

Raw diets present their own perils if not used cautiously. Suddenly switching your dog to a raw diet exposes him to the many disease-causing organisms present in raw meat, which can lead to serious digestive problems. You also must be careful that you handle raw meat carefully so you don't get sick as well.

> Never begin feeding a home-made diet without first consulting your veterinarian.

If preparing your Border Collie's meals still intrigues you, dedicate yourself to finding the best, well-balanced recipes available and carefully monitor your pet's weight and overall health. Cooking for your dog on a whim could spell nutritional disaster for your pet.

Hypoallergenic Diets

Is your dog scratching a lot or chewing at his fur? If he doesn't have fleas, the problem might be a food allergy. But, you say, he's been eating the same food for years. Surprisingly, food allergies take an average of two years to develop. This is because allergies develop due to repeated exposure to a certain substance or ingredient. Mild food allergies can even show up seasonally when a mild inhalant allergy combines forces with the food allergy.

Treating allergies usually begins with a diet trial supervised by a veterinarian. But not just any diet—preferably foods to which the Border Collie hasn't been exposed. Changing from one pet food to another doesn't work because many foods contain similar ingredients. Dietary restriction is the only way to truly determine what food(s) the Border Collie is allergic to. Once the offending agent is pinpointed, an appropriate diet can be started.

Allergies can develop to any protein, whether it is chicken, beef, or lamb, and carbohydrates as well, including wheat and

Food Allergies

It's not common, but some dogs develop food allergies. Digestive upset, itchy skin, or hair loss can be signs that something in the animal's diet is triggering an allergic reaction. What exactly is an allergic reaction? It's an exaggerated response of the immune system to something that's usually harmless; wheat, for example. What the pet is allergic to is called an allergen.

The way the body responds to that allergen is called a hypersensitivity reaction. There are two kinds of hypersensitivity reactions. The immediate type occurs within minutes of exposure and often produces hives, itching, and sometimes, trouble breathing or collapse; anaphylactic shock is an example of this. The delayed reaction produces itching hours or days afterward.

The most common food allergens are wheat, milk, soy, chicken, eggs, beef, fish, and corn. Dyes and preservatives may also trigger allergies.

Should you suspect your Border Collie is suffering from food allergies, discuss the situation with your veterinarian. She can help you determine whether a food allergy is the problem and if so point you and your Border Collie in the right direction to finding a suitable diet. While it can be difficult to pinpoint the allergen that is causing upset in your dog, once you determine it you can avoid the offending ingredient in your dog's kibble.

corn. Lamb used to be thought of as a hypoallergenic ingredient because most dogs had never been exposed to lamb-based food before. Now that lamb and rice foods are increasingly popular, however, dogs are developing allergies to lamb about as often as they are reacting to the old standbys of chicken and beef.

Your veterinarian may try an elimination diet of specially formulated foods made of unusual ingredients such as catfish and rice, or rabbit and potatoes, or may prescribe a homemade diet. As I mentioned before, home-prepared diets are time-consuming and can be expensive. In the case of an elimination diet, your veterinarian must carefully monitor it, since such diets often lack certain nutrients. Another option is to switch to a different commercial diet and hope that gets rid of the problem. Again, consult your veterinarian for your best option. Unfortunately, preservatives, flavoring, or other additives, which many different commercial foods contain, can be the problem.

Food allergies are frustrating to decipher, and only become more frustrating if you change foods randomly without a plan. Work closely with your veterinarian to discover the allergy culprit and relieve your dog of his itchiness.

Prescription Diets

A relative newcomer to dog food options, a prescription diet should be used only on the advice of a veterinarian. There are a variety of brands and a variety of formulas for use with a number of canine conditions, including liver disease, chronic renal failure, diabetes, congestive heart failure, and cancer.

How Often and How Much Do I Feed My Border Collie?

Your dog requires different amounts of food during the different stages of her life. It is up to you to regulate the amount of food your Border Collie gets each day. But before we look at how much you are going to feed your dog, let's determine how you'll feed her.

There are three methods of feeding: free-choice, timed, and portion feeding. Free-choice feeding is exactly what it sounds like—you fill your dog's bowl to the rim and leave it down all day, allowing your pet to eat whenever and how

The Importance of Water

Water is important to every living creature, and your Border Collie is no exception.

Water makes up around 60 percent of your adult dog's body and even more of your puppy's constitution. Dogs need water to help their cells function properly and to aid in proper digestion. Basically, dogs need water to live. Without water, a dog will die within only a few days.

The water in your dog's body needs to be replenished on a regular basis, since it is routinely lost through respiration, digestion, and urination. On hot days or when exercising heavily, your dog needs even more water to keep his body running smoothly.

To keep your Border Collie at optimum health, provide him with constant access to plenty of cool, fresh water.

much she wants. There are several problems with this type of feeding. For one, while some dogs will adjust their intake to the amount of food their body requires, many will not and gorge themselves day after day until they become obese. In addition, leaving down an imprecise amount of food all day long makes it difficult to monitor your dog's eating habits. Chances are, it will take you longer to notice a decrease in appetite in your dog if you are feeding free-choice than if you choose another method. Finally, only dry food can be left down all day without spoiling, so feeding canned or even mixing it with dry is not an option.

The second type of feeding is timed feeding, in which you fill your dog's bowl and put it down for 15 to 20 minutes per feeding, then take up any leftovers. With this method, it is easy to see if your dog's appetite is down, plus you have the freedom to add canned food if you want. You also can add to your pet's food any medication she may need and watch to see that she actually eats it. If you have a dog who tends to overeat, you may again have a problem with this type of feeding. These dogs quickly learn to wolf down their food before you take it away, leading to overeating and increasing their chances of developing bloat, a potentially lethal syndrome in which gasses suddenly accumulate in the stomach, often causing the stomach to twist over on itself. Although bloat is more common in larger, deep-chested dogs, it can occur in the Border Collie as well. (Never allow your dog to eat or to drink a large amount of water right before or after exercising, as this is another suspected cause of the disorder.)

The method of feeding I prefer is the third choice, portion feeding. With portioned feeding, you determine the amount of food your dog needs per day based on age, weight, and recommended feeding guidelines printed on the dog food bag, and divide that amount by the number of times a day you are feeding. If you are feeding dry food, each portion can be left down until the next feeding or can be picked up after 15 minutes or so. This still allows you to see if your dog's appetite is up to par, but gives you greater control over the total amount of food your Border Collie consumes each day.

Puppy Feeding Schedules and Amounts

From the moment you bring home your puppy, you'll want to establish a feeding routine. First, pick a place in your house where your dog can eat undisturbed, but still be close to her "people." The kitchen is usually a good option, and placing your dog's bowl in her kitchen crate can help her feel secure but still be a part of the family goings-on. This also helps your Border Collie associate good things with being in her crate. Secluding your dog in another part of the house, such as the laundry room, to eat can cause her to become overly protective of her food.

In the beginning, continue feeding your dog the food she has been eating at her breeder's home. If she seems to thrive on that brand, don't feel you need to try different foods. Many people mistakenly believe their dog needs variety in her diet, when in fact the opposite is true. Changing your puppy's food too frequently or too quickly can result in digestive problems such as diarrhea. Watching your dog's overall health and appearance is the best way to determine whether she is on the right food. Look for clear shining eyes, a glistening coat, and an alert, playful personality.

> In the beginning, continue feeding your dog the food she has been eating at her breeder's home.

If you feel your Border Collie would do better on a different food, make sure you make the switch gradually. The first week, mix 75 percent of the old food with 25 percent of the new. Make it a 50/50 mix the second week. The third week, decrease the old food to 25 percent and increase the new to 75 percent of the mix. By the fourth week, you should be able to feed your pup 100 percent of the new food without any digestive problems.

Now, what about amount? To determine the amount of food to give your puppy each day, start by consulting the feeding panel on the dog food bag. These instructions usually give an average range of cups to feed per day, based on the weight of your dog. As your puppy gets older, monitor her weight and body condition and adjust her food accordingly.

It's important to remember that the guidelines on dog food bags are simply that—guidelines. Some puppies will need more food, while some will need less. In fact, these guidelines often run on the high end for most dogs, so you need to watch your Border Collie's waistline to determine how much food she really needs.

As mentioned in Chapter 1, people used to think that the pudgy puppy was the healthiest in the litter, but now we know better. In fact, you should be able to feel your puppy's ribs when you run your fingers along her sides. You should have to apply gentle pressure to feel the ribs, and your puppy should not be so skinny as to feel like a washboard with a normal touch. If you stand over your dog and look down, she should have a visible waistline, and her abdomen should "tuck up" from the ribs to the pelvis when you check out your puppy from the side. Signs of an overweight puppy include fat rolls around her neck or the base of her tail, and shortness of breath or a lack of energy when playing. On the opposite side of the spectrum, protruding ribs are signs of a seriously underweight pup. If your puppy seems too fat or too thin, adjust her food accordingly. Don't feel bullied into following the dog food bag's recommendations religiously—your dog's appearance is the best indicator of how much food she needs, and it is best to ask your veterinarian if you have questions.

Puppies need to eat several meals a day for a number of reasons. Since they carry little fat for energy reserves, they need to eat more often. Also, if they don't eat every few hours, their blood sugar levels can drop to a dangerously low level, which can lead to hypoglycemic seizures. Generally, you should feed your puppy three to four times a day until she is five or six months old, at which point you can cut her feeding down to two meals a day.

Always try to feed your puppy at the same time each day. Not only does such a routine ease your dog's mind (she'll know exactly when her next meal is coming), it also helps the housetraining process run more smoothly. Since puppies tend to eliminate soon after each meal, feeding your puppy on a schedule helps you time your trips outside and keep indoor accidents from occurring.

Feeding Your Adult Border Collie

Adult dogs also thrive on routine. While some people feed adult dogs one meal a day, I recommend sticking with the two-meal-a-day regimen throughout the life of your Border Collie. This breed is highly energetic and burns off calories quickly, often leaving them hungry on simply one meal a day.

Dogs, being social animals, really enjoy mealtime around their families. If you've recently adopted an older Border Collie, feeding her on a set schedule in her kitchen crate will help her feel secure and a part of the family, as well as helping with any housetraining problems. However, remember that you are the alpha! Alphas eat first in the pack structure. Dominance problems can arise if you allow your Border Collie to eat first. You should at least start your meal first, and preferably finish it, before your dog begins her meal.

Is It Okay to Share My Food?

Some people live by the rule that a dog is a dog, a person is a person, and their food shall never meet. These folks say feeding table food upsets the balance of the dog's own nutritionally complete dog food. Plus, who wants a dog who begs every time you open the refrigerator door or the snack cupboard?

Did You Know?

Dogs and cats in the United States consume almost $7 billion worth of pet food a year.

Toxic Treats—
Dangerous Foods for Dogs

Certain treats, while they are all right for human consumption, can be dangerous, or even lethal, to your pet.

Certain high-fat meats, such as pork, are difficult for dogs to digest and can trigger pancreatitis, a potentially dangerous inflammation of the pancreas. Also, meats doused in rich sauces, rich gravy, or spices can wreak havoc on your dog's digestive system.

Bones pose a serious danger to your dog. Never feed your dog bones left over from your meal, especially poultry, fish, and pork bones. Pieces can break off and cause constipation, intestinal punctures, or blockage of your dog's digestive tract.

Never be tempted to ease your dog's thirst with anything other than water. Soda contains sugar or artificial sweeteners and unhealthful additives, and alcohol can be harmful or even fatal if consumed in large quantities.

Avoid salty, calorie-laden snacks, such as potato chips. Excessive salt can dehydrate your pet, and extra fat calories will only translate into extra pounds.

Sugary snacks, such as candy and cookies, are also bad for your Border Collie. At the least, they fill him up with empty calories and leave him less interested in his own food, which can result in poor nutrition. At the worst, they can make your dog sick, causing diarrhea and/or vomiting.

Chocolate is especially dangerous for dogs; it can even be deadly. Different types of chocolate pose varying risks. While milk chocolate will probably make your Border Collie ill, baking chocolate could possibly kill him. Be safe and never feed your dog chocolate of any kind.

On the flip side are those owners who acknowledge that, being human, many of us have an unconquerable desire to occasionally give our dog a treat. If you are one of these, it's important that you learn which treats are healthful and which can be dangerous to your dog.

Healthful Treats

The first thing you need to realize is that no matter how healthful treats are, they should never make up more than 5 to 10 percent of your dog's food. The last thing you want is a dog who skips his meals because he is filled up on treats!

There are a number of treat options. Commercial treats range from baked biscuits, which often use the same ingredients as dry dog food but come in fun shapes and colors, to semi-moist treats, which are popular with dogs but tend to be high in sugar and preservatives, to super-creative treats, including a doggie substitute for ice cream. Read the labels of these treats to determine just how nutritious they are and whether you can indulge your dog frequently or give them only on special occasions.

> No matter how healthful treats are, they should never make up more than 5 to 10 percent of your dog's food.

Then there's people food. While some people foods are reasonably healthful for dogs, others are downright dangerous. In general, if you know a treat isn't terribly nutritious for you, it most certainly won't be for your dog. For example, candy, which is a questionable snack for us, is very bad for dogs, and, in the case of chocolate, can even be deadly. Table foods, such as well-cooked meat or unseasoned vegetables, are all right for your Border Collie in moderation, but table scraps, such as the fat you trimmed off your meat, shouldn't be pawned off on your dog. And please, don't feed any people food to a dog with a medical condition that requires him to be on a restricted diet.

Nutritious people food for dogs includes pasta (without the sauce); carrots, celery, and other vegetables; bananas; plain or air-popped popcorn; and well-cooked meat. Some owners use cheese or hot dogs for occasional treats, such as for rewards while training, but again, practice moderation.

Actually, training is an ideal time to dispense treats. Make your dog earn his treats by first requiring him to practice sit or down, or perform some other obedience command. This way you take control of when and why your dog gets a treat instead of the other way around. The last thing you want is a pushy Border Collie who insists you supply treats on his demand!

4

Medical Care Every Border Collie Needs

In This Chapter

○ Your Border Collie's Veterinary Care
○ Preventive Medicine
○ Spaying and Neutering
○ Sick Calls and Emergencies

Ideally, you should select a veterinarian for your Border Collie before you even bring your new dog home. Finding the right doctor for your pet is just as important as finding the best doctor for your family. If you wait until your dog is sick or hurt to choose a veterinarian, you may choose one based on close proximity or convenient hours, and not necessarily on her expertise, compassion, or rapport with animals.

Your Border Collie's Veterinary Care

To choose the right veterinarian from the start, you need to learn what to expect from a veterinarian and what type of medical care your dog needs to maintain his health and to treat any illnesses he might develop.

Selecting the Right Veterinarian

Referrals are a great starting point when choosing a veterinarian. If you live near your dog's breeder, ask him for recommendations. Due to all the hazards of puppy rearing, most breeders put a lot of research into finding a dependable veterinarian. If your dog's breeder lives a distance away, ask other dog owners, such as friends and neighbors, for their recommendations. If you don't get any good leads, page through the phone book. It will list most, if not all, veterinarians in the area, and the display ads can give you some information on their practices, such as services offered and affiliation with professional organizations, including the American Animal Hospital Association (AAHA). But remember, no matter who recommends a veterinarian to you, you'll want to check her out personally to ensure that she is the right veterinarian for you and your Border Collie.

First, make a list of the things you feel are important in a veterinarian and a veterinary hospital. What are the doctor's credentials? Just as a diploma from a well-known, accredited medical school is important when finding a doctor for your family, you should choose a veterinarian with a distinguished academic background. Are the veterinarian and the facility members of the AAHA? Although this isn't necessarily a requirement in choosing a doctor, AAHA members must adhere to certain standards for medical procedures and hospital management.

Does the veterinarian seem to genuinely like animals? And, just as important, does she genuinely like people? While there

Oh, So Special

What's a veterinary specialist? That term can be confusing to owners. A glance under the heading "Veterinarian" in the yellow pages reveals a wide variety of listings under the vets' names: general medicine, specializing in surgery, cancer treatments, cardiology, vaccinations, dentistry, internal medicine. But a veterinary specialist isn't a practitioner who limits her practice to dogs or is interested in a particular area of medicine, such as dentistry. A veterinary specialist is a veterinarian who is board certified by a specialty board approved by the American Veterinary Medical Association (AVMA).

To earn the title of veterinary specialist, the veterinarian must complete a veterinary school program approved by the AVMA, usually extends her education by completing a one-year internship, and completes a two- or three-year residency program in a particular discipline. She must be licensed to practice veterinary medicine in at least one state.

Once the educational requirements are finished, the vet then has to pass battery of rigorous examinations in her field. Only then can she receive official certification by a specialty board, such as the American College of Veterinary Behaviorists or the American College of Zoological Medicine. Certification requirements vary but are governed by the American Board of Veterinary Specialists (ABVS).

The Board has specific guidelines on how specialists may list names or practices. Veterinarians may not imply that they're specialists when they aren't. The terms an owner should look for when seeking out a true specialist are board certified (board eligible or board qualified aren't the same and are considered misleading by the ABVS), diplomate, ACVIM (American College of Veterinary Internal Medicine), and ABVP. The board-certified veterinary specialist's name and title are usually listed like this: Mary Veterinarian, DVM, Diplomate American Board of Veterinary Practitioners, Board Certified in Surgery.

If your Border Collie requires the services of a veterinary specialist, your general practitioner will usually give you a referral. If you want to contact a specialist on your own, contact your local or state veterinary association for a name or call the American Veterinary Medical Association at (800) 248-2862 for a listing of board-certified vets in your area. If you live near a school of veterinary medicine, contact the college. Many specialists work at veterinary colleges.

are many wonderful veterinarians out there who have a special way with animals, the one you choose must be able to communicate with people. It is important that you feel comfortable with your Border Collie's veterinarian and that she is able to explain complex medical information in layperson's terms.

Is the facility small, with just one or two veterinarians, or is it a large multi-doctor practice or even a teaching hospital? Many people want a veterinarian who will get to know them and their dog personally. Seeing the same veterinarian each visit allows her to know the dog's medical history intimately, which can be advantageous when diagnosing ailments. A negative of smaller facilities is that they may lack some of the high-tech equipment found in larger establishments. This may mean you'll be referred to a larger hospital or a hospital for certain procedures during your dog's lifetime. Large practices, on the other hand, often have doctors specializing in certain areas of veterinary medicine and modern equipment and laboratories on-site to conduct tests and interpret the results. You may end up seeing a different doctor each time you visit a larger facility, however, making it difficult to establish an ongoing relationship.

> It is important that you feel comfortable with your Border Collie's veterinarian and that she is able to explain complex medical information in layperson's terms.

Is someone on call 24 hours a day? If not, does the hospital recommend an after-hours facility for emergencies? If so, you need to check out that facility as well.

Where is the hospital located? If you live in a busy household, you may need to choose a hospital close to home. You'll also want a veterinarian who is convenient to get to during an emergency. At the same time, it may be worthwhile to choose one located a few miles away rather than settle for a closer hospital that doesn't meet your other requirements.

For most owners, a hospital's hours are also an important factor. Choose a facility whose hours of operation coincide with your schedule. Most hospitals have evening hours at least one night a week, and/or are open on Saturdays. Although rare, some veterinarians still make house calls; such a doctor may offer the convenience you're seeking.

What kind of services does the veterinarian provide? If you are only looking for medical care from a doctor, then a traditional practice may be right for you. Some hospitals now offer add-on services—such as grooming, boarding, training, pet supplies, and food—for the owner who wants "one-stop shopping." Some veterinarians have their offices in pet-supply stores or obedience schools for the convenience of busy owners.

How much do services cost? Although most veterinarians charge comparable fees to others in the area, some hospitals offer wellness programs or multi-pet discounts that can help you save money. Don't be enticed, however, by a doctor who charges considerably less than the going rate for veterinary care. Someone who charges so little for services may not have the credentials or expertise you are looking for. Quality veterinary care can be expensive—never skimp on your dog's health just to save a few dollars.

Once you've prepared your list of questions, start calling the veterinarians who have been recommended to you or who seem qualified from their phone book ads. Evaluate the call from start to finish. Was the phone picked up quickly or did it ring ten times before someone answered? Was the receptionist friendly and helpful? Even if the person at the front desk doesn't deal directly with the animals, he most likely reflects the overall atmosphere of the hospital. Explain that you are looking for a veterinarian and would like to ask a few questions. Don't be put off if no one can talk to you right at that moment; the hospital might be very busy, and sick animals should be their top priority. The receptionist should gladly take down your name and number, however, and someone should get back to you in a timely manner. If no one returns your call, take your business elsewhere.

Once you've asked your list of questions and narrowed your search, set up a time to personally visit the hospital you are interested in. Again, you should be treated courteously. Ask to see examination rooms, kennel runs, and cages where dogs are kept. Every area, from the waiting room to the kenneling area in the back, should be neat and clean. You'll detect a slight animal odor in any hospital, but other than that, the facility should smell fresh and clean. Make sure you meet at least one of the doctors, even if you have to pay a consultation fee. She should be friendly and a good communicator. The most knowledgeable veterinarian in the world won't be of much help to you if she can't explain how to care for your pet in plain, simple language. Pay attention, as well, to how the staff treats the other clients. A good veterinary hospital treats all clients—human and canine—with courtesy and compassion, whether it is their first visit or they have been coming for years.

When you get home, write down your impressions. Next, contact your state's veterinary medical board. The board can verify that the doctor in question has a license to practice in your state and can tell you if she holds any special certifications. The board also can tell you if any formal disciplinary action has ever been taken against the veterinarian you are interested in.

If you feel you have clicked with the perfect veterinarian, great. But, if you're still not sure, by all means check out another facility. Keep all your notes on each facility in case your first choice doesn't work out.

Your Border Collie's First Visit

From the very first time your Border Collie steps foot (or paw!) in the veterinarian's office, make sure the experience is as pleasant as possible. Believe it or not, some dogs actually look forward to visits to the doctor. Tell your dog in an upbeat tone of voice, "We're going to go visit your buddy, Dr. Bones!" Remain calm and cheerful throughout the car ride and as you enter the hospital. If you are nervous or apprehensive, your dog is sure to pick up on your emotions and act the same. Also, don't baby your dog. If you ooh and aah over him each time he goes to the veterinarian, he'll be convinced a doctor visit is a bad thing, or else you wouldn't be fussing over him! If your Border Collie acts nervous, tell him in an even, businesslike tone of voice that he's being silly. When he calms down, offer him lots of praise and perhaps a treat. You should praise every positive step, from being quiet during the car ride to sitting calmly in the waiting room to standing patiently while he is examined.

If you've adopted an older Border Collie who seems unduly afraid of the veterinarian, don't worry that all is lost. Again, be upbeat and positive and don't indulge inappropriate behavior. With time, patience, and lots of positive reinforcement, even the most fearful dog can learn to tolerate trips to the veterinarian's office.

Did You Know?

Big dogs have larger litters than smaller dogs, but smaller dogs generally live longer.

Questions to Ask Your Veterinarian

Ask questions such as those listed below to evaluate whether a veterinarian is right for you and your dog.

○ What are the credentials of the veterinarian(s)? Is the hospital affiliated with the AAHA?

○ How many veterinarians work at the hospital? Can I request to see the same doctor each time I visit or will I see whoever is available?

○ What type of equipment do you have on-hand at the hospital? If you do not have certain equipment, where would you send my dog to receive treatment? What is that facility's reputation?

○ Do you have an on-site lab or do you send out for test results? How quickly are results available?

○ What are your hospital's hours and where are you located?

○ Do you offer any add-on services such as boarding or grooming?

○ What are the average fees for checkups, spaying/neutering, vaccinations, etc.? Do you offer a wellness program or a multi-pet discount?

○ Do you treat any other Border Collies in your practice? (While much canine medicine applies to all breeds, certain diseases and health concerns apply specifically to Border Collies. You should make sure your veterinarian is knowledgeable about genetic problems that run in the breed.)

Make sure you arrive early for your first appointment so you can fill out any necessary paperwork. Bring a list of questions and concerns, so you remember to bring them up, as well as records of your dog's previous vaccinations and dewormings. To protect your Border Collie, keep him from licking the floor or getting too close to other dogs in the waiting room. Not only could your pet pick up an infection, but he also could get bitten if he intrudes into another dog's space. It's best to keep a puppy on your lap or in his travel crate to keep him out of trouble.

What can you expect from your Border Collie's first veterinary visit? First, the doctor will examine your dog from nose to tail to make sure he is sound. She will check for indications of good health, such as clear, bright eyes; clean-smelling, light pink skin inside the ears; healthy white teeth and pink gums; a shiny coat and smooth, healthy skin; and a normal temperature and heart rate. She will palpate, or feel, your dog's internal organs to ensure they are the proper size and shape, and will listen to your dog's lungs and heart. If your Border Collie is a male, your veterinarian will check that both testes are fully visible. Sometimes one testicle or both are retained inside the body, which can cause health problems down the road and means your dog must be neutered. If your Border Collie is a female, the doctor will check her vaginal area for discharge or other signs of infections. Other general problems the veterinarian looks for during the exam include: watery eyes; infected ears or evidence of ear mites; teeth that do not meet properly; lumps underneath the skin or patches of missing fur; a fever; or symptoms of a congenital problem such as a heart murmur.

Remember to bring a fresh fecal sample, which the hospital will check for intestinal parasites. If you collect the sample several hours before your appointment, wrap it well and store it in your refrigerator until you are ready to go. Puppies especially are susceptible to such parasites, so don't be upset if your Border Collie needs to be dewormed.

The veterinarian will weigh your dog to chart his future growth, or establish a base measurement for an adult dog. She also should address any questions you have about feeding, training, spaying/neutering, and house-training, and discuss proper health care with you. She may even demonstrate how to clip your dog's nails and/or how to brush his teeth.

Questions Your Veterinarian May Ask You

❍ Is this your first dog? Is this your first Border Collie?

❍ What are your feelings on spaying/neutering? (Dogs who are pet quality and are not going to be bred should be spayed or neutered. This helps prevent overpopulation and also is healthier for your dog.)

❍ Have you located a training school for your new dog? (Your veterinarian may offer recommendations, or the hospital itself may hold training classes.)

❍ What type of food are you feeding?

❍ What types of toys does your dog play with? (Some toys should only be played with under supervision, such as toys with squeakers, or toys that are easily chewed apart.)

❍ Are you crate-training your dog?

❍ Do you have any questions concerning housetraining, obedience training, nutrition, etc.?

Next, the veterinarian will administer whatever vaccinations are due, and start your pup on a heartworm preventive, depending on the time of year and whether you live in an area where heartworm is prevalent. She also should discuss fleas and ticks and how to prevent them from infesting your dog. At the end of your visit, be sure to set up a schedule for follow-up visits and shots.

Preventive Medicine

Just as it is important for the human members of your family to have annual checkups, your Border Collie needs to see the veterinarian regularly for wellness exams. Many illnesses are easy to treat if caught early, but can be much more problematic if they are only discovered after serious symptoms begin. Don't wait until your dog is ill—preventive medicine is the best medicine.

Annual Visits

Each year your Border Collie should visit the veterinarian for a complete physical and any booster vaccinations that may be due. The doctor will check your dog thoroughly, both internally and externally, to ensure he is healthy. Examining your dog each year better enables your veterinarian to catch health problems at an earlier stage than if you only bring your pet in when he shows obvious symp-

> Examining your dog each year better enables your veterinarian to catch health problems at an earlier stage.

toms. Also, seeing your veterinarian on a regular basis helps you build a relationship with her and keeps you caught up with the latest information on pet care.

Vaccinations

Vaccines provide an important defense against a number of canine diseases. Since puppies' immune systems are still developing when they are young, they need extra help to prevent them from catching infectious diseases. Your puppy received some immunity from his mother during the first weeks of his life. Female dogs who have been vaccinated or have built immunity by being exposed to and surviving a disease pass on antibodies to their puppies in their first milk. These antibodies remain active in the puppies until they are six to twenty weeks old, depending on the disease. While active, however, antibodies not only protect a puppy against the disease, they also counter the vaccine, which contains a bit of inactivated or killed disease. Since it is difficult to know when a puppy's antibodies have declined enough to accept the vaccine, veterinarians usually recommend a series of vaccinations spaced at three- to four-week intervals during this critical time period.

Most veterinarians give puppies their first vaccinations at eight weeks of age; a vaccine given earlier probably will fail, due to the antibodies in the mother's milk. The series of vaccines usually continues at weeks twelve and sixteen, and possibly longer, with each vaccine taking about two weeks to fully activate. (Note: Your veterinarian may use a slightly different schedule.) Vaccines should be spaced no more than three or four weeks apart, because spacing the vaccines too far apart can leave the puppy vulnerable to the diseases themselves. Conversely, vaccinating more frequently can overload a puppy's immune system.

> Most veterinarians give puppies their first vaccinations at eight weeks of age.

For your Border Collie's health, you should keep your puppy confined to your yard and not let him interact with strange dogs until he is fully immune. For most dogs this is week seventeen or eighteen. Many of the diseases mentioned here are passed by infected dogs in their feces and saliva excretions, leaving the environment, such as the park or even your neighborhood, full of ticking time bombs.

Socialization is vital for young dogs, however. At this point you may be thinking, how can I socialize my Border Collie when he shouldn't go anywhere where he might come in contact with strange dogs? One option is to invite over friends with vaccinated dogs for doggie parties at your house. The danger to your puppy is infected dogs, not all dogs in general, so those that you know have been vaccinated should present no health danger to your pet. Another option is to enroll your pup in a puppy preschool or kindergarten class that requires all owners to show proof that their puppies are being vaccinated. Puppy classes are wonderful, not only for the socialization they provide, but also for important early obedience training.

After the first series of puppy shots, your dog will receive a rabies vaccination at about four months. After that, he will need annual vaccinations for all diseases except rabies, which can be boostered in intervals of one to three years, depending on the law in your area.

Vaccinations against distemper, hepatitis (adenovirus), parvovirus, and parainfluenza are usually given in a combination shot called DHPP. Leptospirosis vaccine may also be added, making a DHLPP vaccine. Rabies, as mentioned above, is a separate vaccination. Other vaccines your veterinarian may recommend fight Lyme disease, coronavirus, and bordetella (kennel cough). Here is a brief explanation to help you better understand the diseases, their symptoms, and treatments, if any.

Distemper   Distemper is a highly contagious virus that attacks the gastrointestinal, respiratory, and nervous systems. It causes symptoms that mimic a cold, such as a cough and eye and nasal discharge, as well as a loss of appetite, vomiting, and diarrhea. Advanced stages can bring weakness, muscle twitches, a lack of coordination, and even seizures. Dogs who develop distemper are treated with fluids and antibiotics to cure secondary infections, but there is no treatment available that will kill the virus. The prognosis is guarded. Some dogs who don't develop neurological signs can get well. Others, however, never fully recover, and for about 50 percent the disease is fatal.

Hepatitis   This disease affects the kidneys, liver, pancreas, and blood-vessel lining. It can cause fever, lack of appetite, abdominal pain, vomiting, hemorrhaging, diarrhea, depression, and prolonged blood-clotting time. Dogs are treated with antibiotics and fluids, and animals with severe cases may require blood transfusions. The prognosis for this disease also varies, with some dogs only experiencing a slight fever, and others succumbing to the disease. Young puppies are especially vulnerable and often die from a bout with hepatitis.

Parvovirus   Parvovirus is extremely dangerous for young puppies. It can cause intestinal inflammation (enteritis) or inflammation of the heart muscle (myocarditis). Symptoms include lack of appetite, lethargy, vomiting, fever, rapid dehydration, and bloody, foul-smelling diarrhea. Parvo is highly contagious. The virus is found in stool, but also can survive in the dirt after the feces have been cleaned up and last in the environment for months. Treatment includes antibiotics, fasting, intravenous fluid therapy, and isolation to prevent spread of the disease. While some puppies recover, the disease is fatal to many. Older dogs may also become ill, but the disease tends to be milder than in puppies.

Parainfluenza   Parainfluenza is a relatively mild virus that is evidenced by a hacking cough, sneezing, and eye and nasal discharge. Often no treatment is necessary as this disease usually clears up on its own.

Rabies   Rabies is perhaps the most feared of all diseases affecting the dog, and with good reason. This always-fatal disease not only is dangerous to canines, but also can infect almost all mammals, including humans. It is transmitted through saliva, usually by a bite. Early symptoms include personality changes (such as depression, aggression, and/or self-imposed isolation), vomiting, fever, and diarrhea. In the final stages, the dog may become vicious, drool, and foam at the mouth. Sadly, there is no treatment, and euthanasia is the only course of action.

Leptospirosis   This disease, which can be caught from water contaminated with infected urine, affects the kidneys, liver, and urinary tract and can be transmitted to humans. Early symptoms include lack of appetite, vomiting, abdominal pain, fever, and weakness. As the disease progresses, the dog becomes extremely thirsty, and his temperature may fall below normal. Treatment with antibiotics and fluids can be very effective if the disease is caught early. Fatal cases are usually due to kidney infection and failure.

Note: Leptospirosis vaccine is associated with allergic reactions more often than other vaccines are. Some veterinarians will avoid vaccinating certain dogs, particularly those with previous reactions, those that are very small, or dogs that are unlikely to be exposed to the disease.

Lyme Disease   This tick-transmitted disease is most prevalent in wooded or grassy areas of Connecticut, Delaware, Maryland, Massachusetts, Michigan, Minnesota, New Jersey, New York, Pennsylvania, Rhode Island, and Wisconsin. Controversy exists over the effectiveness of Lyme disease vaccines, with some veterinarians contending that the vaccine offers inadequate protection. These doctors believe that tick-control products are more effective than vaccination. A dog

Did You Know?

A dog's heart beats between 70 and 120 times per minute, compared with 70 to 80 times per minute for humans.

infected with Lyme disease may exhibit sudden lameness, weakness, fever, and swollen joints. Most dogs fully recover after treatment with antibiotics and fluids, although lameness can last up to several months.

Coronavirus   Coronavirus causes intestinal inflammation and diarrhea. It is particularly severe in puppies, but most older dogs show few or no signs of illness after infection. Many veterinarians also do not vaccinate against this disease, since it is not very prevalent. It occurs most often in dogs who frequently are kenneled or participate in dog shows. Since coronavirus is easily killed by most disinfectants, good sanitation should keep this disease in check. Symptoms of coronavirus include lack of appetite, a single episode of vomiting, orange or yellow-colored diarrhea, fever, and depression. Treatment consists of fluids and antibiotics to control secondary infections. The prognosis usually is good, although rare cases are fatal.

Kennel Cough (Bordetella)   This extremely infectious, but less serious disease, tends to be picked up where large numbers of dogs come in contact with one another, such as at dog shows, boarding kennels, and dog parks. Dogs who will not be in these situations are usually not vaccinated. Often the only symptom is a dry, hacking cough that usually lasts for one to two weeks but can

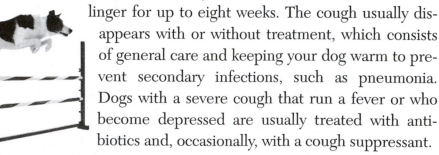

linger for up to eight weeks. The cough usually disappears with or without treatment, which consists of general care and keeping your dog warm to prevent secondary infections, such as pneumonia. Dogs with a severe cough that run a fever or who become depressed are usually treated with antibiotics and, occasionally, with a cough suppressant.

The Vaccine Controversy

Vaccines generally are accepted as the best way to prevent a number of serious illnesses in your dog. Some veterinarians, however, believe dogs are being over-vaccinated, causing immune problems. Some dogs also experience allergic reactions to vaccines, which can range from mild symptoms, such as lethargy and a low-grade fever, to shock, which requires emergency care. To prevent these problems, some practitioners recommend vaccinating against each disease individually instead of using combination vaccines. They also suggest vaccinating less, using safer "killed" versions of vaccines when possible, and even discontinuing regular boosters (except in the case of rabies, which must be vaccinated against by law).

Holistic veterinarians believe boosting a dog's immune system through proper nutrition and exercise and avoiding chemicals, such as certain preservatives in commercial foods and chemically based flea treatments,

> If you and your veterinarian decide that you do not need to booster vaccines every year, but every second or third instead, remember that it is still vital for you to take your dog in for his yearly checkup.

benefit a dog more than vaccinations. This approach may leave your dog susceptible to some potentially dangerous diseases, however. The key is to work with your veterinarian to decide which vaccines your dog needs and which may be unnecessary (such as Lyme disease vaccine, if you and your dog do not live in a tick-infested area). If you and your veterinarian decide that you do not need to booster vaccines every year, but every second or third instead, remember that it is still vital for you to take your dog in for his yearly checkup.

Spaying and Neutering

Some people are resistant to spaying or neutering their pet. Many fall in love with their dog, and reason that if they breed him or her, they will be able to produce another puppy just like their beloved Border Collie. Some decide to breed so their children can witness the miracle of birth right in their home. Still others reason that having a litter or two will recoup some of the money they've spent on their first dog.

None of these is a valid reason to breed your pet.

The truth is, millions of pets are put to death each year because not enough good homes are willing to take them in. Even if you produced a puppy similar to his mother or father (which is unlikely, since puppies are carbon copies of their parents about as often as human children are carbon copies of their moms and dads), can you guarantee you could find good homes for the rest of the puppies in the litter? Anyone who breeds a dog is morally responsible to find each and every puppy a home for life. Are you willing to take on that responsibility?

> Millions of pets are put to death each year because not enough good homes are willing to take them in.

Teaching your children about reproduction is no excuse for producing puppies that may end up homeless or euthanized. Besides, it is not uncommon to lose a puppy during birth. Do you want to expose your children, or yourself, to that heartache? Whelping also can put the mother at risk. Could you ever forgive yourself if your pet died while giving birth?

Purebred dogs are prone to many genetic diseases. (Diseases particular to the Border Collie are discussed in Chapter 5, Common Health Concerns.) To limit these diseases and to ensure the reproduction of healthy dogs, only the best specimens of each

Myths About Spaying and Neutering Your Dog

○ It is unnatural to sterilize a dog.

○ Males are no longer "macho" and become wimps.

○ Females will never calm down.

○ Males will no longer protect their homes and owners.

○ Females will not be as friendly.

○ Both males and females will become fat and lazy.

○ Both males and females will lose their playfulness.

breed should be mated. It takes years of studying pedigrees and genetics to enable a breeder to plan matings that will produce sound, healthy, and temperamentally stable puppies. You may have a beautiful female Border Collie and your neighbor may have a handsome male, but together they may carry genes for some hidden defect that will show up in their puppies. Are you willing to take that chance?

As far as making money by breeding dogs goes, you can pretty much forget it. With all the costs involved, most breeders just about break even. The mother will require various veterinary tests to ensure she is healthy before she is bred and while she is pregnant, and the pups will need to be checked out once they are born. If complications arise during delivery, you may have to pay for emergency veterinary care. The mom will have special nutritional needs while she is pregnant and nursing, and once the puppies are weaned you will need to feed them until they go to their new homes. You also will need to bring the puppies to the veterinarian for their first shots, deworming, and to obtain a health certificate for your legal protection. That's right: If your dog's puppies develop health problems down the road, their new owners could sue you for veterinary expenses. Then there's the cost of finding owners for the puppies, which most likely will require paying for advertising. The truth is, good breeders produce puppies in the hopes of achieving healthier, happier, temperamentally sound Border Collies, rather than to make money.

> It takes years of studying pedigrees and genetics to enable a breeder to plan matings that will produce sound, healthy, and temperamentally stable puppies.

Spaying or neutering not only prevents unwanted puppies, it actually helps your pet stay healthier. Spayed and neutered dogs are less likely to develop a number of health problems, including mammary tumors and pyometra (a disease of the uterus) in females, and testicular cancer, infected prostate glands, and other urogenital diseases in males. Not allowing a dog to mate also protects both males and females from contracting sexually transmitted diseases.

Spaying or neutering can make your dog happier, as well. The desire to mate and the act itself can be stressful for dogs. Some males will refuse to eat if they are around (and for keen-nosed males "around" can mean a half-mile away) a female in heat, and hormonal swings can make females tense and anxious. Sterilization also can prevent some unwanted behaviors in males, such as "marking" of territory (including your furniture), mounting behavior, or aggression against other males. If you own a female, spaying will prevent messy heat cycles and the constant unwanted attention of male dogs in the neighborhood during these times.

Unless you are willing to become a genetics expert and consider breeding a not-for-profit hobby, you should spay or neuter your Border Collie. The procedures are relatively simple and have quick recovery periods. The veterinarian anesthetizes the

Breeding Myths: Common Misconceptions About Breeding Dogs

○ Females need to birth one litter to calm down.

○ "Mother" dogs are sweeter and gentler than females who never have puppies.

○ Children should experience the miracle of birth close up.

○ By breeding my dog, I'll produce a puppy just like him/her.

○ By selling puppies, I'll offset some of the money I've spent on my dog.

dog, and then removes either his testicles (neutering in the male) or her uterus and ovaries (spaying in the female). Most dogs go home the same day or the day after surgery, although you need to restrict their activity for a few days.

There is no truth to the belief that females should be allowed to go into one heat before they are spayed. In fact, dogs should be spayed or neutered before they reach sexual maturity. Maturity traditionally has been defined as six months of age; however, a female may go into heat as early as four months. Some humane societies spay and neuter at a very young age to prevent unwanted pregnancies down the road. Speak with your veterinarian to decide the best time to spay or neuter your Border Collie.

Sick Calls and Emergencies

You know that you need to visit your veterinarian once a year for your dog's wellness exam, but what if your Border Collie is sick or hurt? What types of injuries or illnesses require immediate veterinary care, and what types can you treat yourself at home? This brief overview, below, identifies some signs to help you make that decision. (First aid is discussed further in Chapter 5, Common Health Concerns.)

When to Call the Veterinarian

Certain situations and/or symptoms demand emergency veterinary care. If your dog has been hit by a car, even if she seems okay, see a veterinarian immediately. She should see a doctor if she has been involved in any other type of traumatic event as well, such as a fall from a substantial height, a fight, or even having been a passenger in a car that was involved in an accident. If she loses consciousness, or has trouble breathing or walking, also seek care right away. Other symptoms that need immediate professional attention include uncontrollable bleeding, trauma to the eyes, bloody diarrhea, difficulty urinating, and seizuring. Heat stroke, which is evidenced by excessive panting, difficulty breathing, and an increased heart rate, is an emergency condition. Bloat, as well, demands immediate treatment. If your dog appears restless, drools, attempts to vomit but cannot, and has a swollen, painful abdomen, rush her to the veterinarian—her life may depend on it.

Other symptoms, while still needing veterinary attention, are not emergencies. If your dog experiences the following symptoms, you don't need to rush her to an emergency hospital, but you should see your veterinarian within 24 hours if she doesn't get better or respond to at-home treatment. These symptoms include: straining to defecate; diarrhea (without blood); irritated eyes that are not traumatized; signs of minor discomfort, such as increased scratching; and minor behavioral changes, such as depression or a decreased appetite.

Signs Your Border Collie Is Feeling Under the Weather

Do you suspect your Border Collie is a little under the weather? Below are some signs that may indicate your Border Collie isn't feeling well and needs to see her veterinarian:

○ Acts tired and sluggish and would rather stay in bed. Even refuses fetching a ball;

○ Isn't hungry—refuses several meals in a row;

○ Drinks an excessive amount of water;

○ Throws up several times;

○ Diarrhea or blood in stools;

○ Whimpers when touched;

○ Drooling excessively;

○ Loses weight but isn't on a weight loss program;

○ Gums are very pale or very red;

○ Coat looks dull and feels rough;

○ Tummy looks bloated;

○ Eyes or nose is runny;

○ Scoots or bites or chews at rear end;

○ Coughs and sneezes a lot; or

○ Limps or walks abnormally.

Many symptoms can be caused by a number of problems, ranging from the mild to the severe. One example is limping. If your dog suddenly begins to limp, you'll first want to figure out where the problem lies. Check your Border Collie's pads. A stone or sliver of glass could be embedded there, causing your dog pain. If so, gently remove the foreign object and wash out the wound. If you don't see anything in the pads, check the legs for any signs of swelling or tenderness. In many breeds, including the Border Collie, lameness in the rear can be an early sign of hip dysplasia. In general, if your dog's limping continues for more than a day or two or seems to be getting worse, see your veterinarian.

A lack of appetite is one of the first signs of many illnesses. While your dog may not be particularly hungry on a given day or may just feel a little out of sorts, if your Border Collie skips two or three meals, make an appointment with your veterinarian.

Vomiting should be approached cautiously. If your Border Collie has eaten a lot of grass or had one too many treats, she may just need to clean out her system. If your dog vomits several times during one hour or also has diarrhea and/or a fever (rectal temperature above 103°F), or the vomiting continues, see your veterinarian. Also, as mentioned above, nonproductive vomiting may be a sign of bloat. This is an emergency that requires immediate veterinary care.

> Your veterinarian should always investigate blood in stool, urine, vomit, or nasal discharge.

Diarrhea, too, can result from many causes. First, see if you can clear your dog's system by withholding food for 24 hours. Make sure to provide her with plenty of fresh water to prevent dehydration. After the 24-hour fast, feed meals of cooked rice and boiled, drained hamburger for several days, gradually adding your pet's regular food. If the diarrhea continues, occurs several times during an hour's time, contains blood or mucus, or has a particularly foul odor, it may indicate a more serious cause. Bloody, foul-smelling diarrhea, accompanied by vomiting, is likely to be parvo; see your veterinarian right away. Your veterinarian should always investigate blood in stool, urine, vomit, or nasal discharge.

How to Administer Medication and Pills

Chances are, sometime during your Border Collie's life you will need to medicate her. This is much less traumatic for you and your dog if you proceed calmly and confidently.

If you need to give your dog a pill, you'll want to ensure that your Border Collie swallows the entire tablet, so the medicine can do its work. If your dog usually doesn't investigate her food before eating it, you can try wrapping the pill in a piece of cheese or cooked meat. You'll need to watch your dog carefully to ensure she doesn't eat the treat but spit out the pill. If your dog seems to be on to your tricks, open her mouth and gently place the pill on the back of her tongue near the center. Never haphazardly drop the pill in your dog's mouth or it could lodge in her windpipe. Tilt your dog's head back, shut her mouth, and stroke her throat until she swallows. Carefully open her mouth again to make sure she really has swallowed the pill.

If you need to administer a liquid, your veterinarian should give you a special syringe that measures out the proper amount of medication. Hold back your dog's head at a slight angle, place the syringe between the cheek and back teeth, and slowly dispense the medicine into your dogs mouth, allowing her to swallow every few seconds. Hold her mouth shut until she swallows every last drop. Be prepared: Some medicines taste extremely bitter, and your dog may react by trying to spit as much as possible back out. Be persistent and hang on for dear life! If your dog doesn't get enough medicine down per dose, you may end up having to give even more doses, which won't be fun for you or your Border Collie.

If your dog injures her eye, you may need to apply ointment or drops. Pull down the lower lid and squeeze the ointment in a strip across the length of the eye, then blink the lids once or twice to make sure the medicine distributes

Did You Know?

Tests conducted at the Institute for the Study of Animal Problems in Washington, D.C., revealed that dogs and cats, like humans, are either right- or left-handed.

Emergency Instructions
for the Boarding Kennel/Pet Sitter

What if your dog becomes sick or gets hurt while you are away? Before you leave your dog at a boarding kennel, ask if they have a veterinarian on staff or if they use one in the area for emergencies. In either case, it's a good idea to give them the name and number of your dog's veterinarian, especially if your Border Collie has a specific medical condition. If you have hired a dog sitter, leave an emergency list with your veterinarian's phone number, the phone number of the local emergency hospital, and the phone number for the National Animal Poison Control Center (888-426-4435). Also leave information on any medications your dog needs or any special medical conditions to watch out for. Prepare for the unexpected to ensure that your dog gets the care she needs should an emergency occur.

evenly. To administer drops, hold the eye open and apply the drops directly to the center.

Costs

Some first-time dog owners are shocked at the high cost of veterinary care. Between spaying or neutering, vaccinations, heartworm preventive, flea and tick products, annual checkups, and the occasional visit for a sick or hurt dog, you may be thinking of putting a second mortgage on your house!

Why does it cost so much? First, you must realize veterinarians go through rigorous schooling similar to that of doctors for humans. You are paying for the expertise of a highly skilled and knowledgeable professional. The veterinarian must also cover the

How to Make an Insurance Claim

It's your responsibility as a policyholder to make the best use of your insurance plan. Take these steps to get the most for your money:

1. Designate a file for pet insurance forms.

2. Always take a claim form with you to the veterinarian's office. Many companies require a veterinarian's signature.

3. Make copies of receipts. A receipt must accompany every claim form. Some companies require only copies; others require originals. Keep a copy for your records.

4. Make copies of completed claim forms. If a question or payment issue arises, a copy to review on your end of the phone line will be reassuring.

5. Note an acceptable payment period on your calendar. Reimbursement may slip your mind, and it may be delayed in cases where a problem is encountered and you forget to inquire about the payment's status.

6. Mark claims paid and date received. Leave a paper trail that's easy to understand. Looking back a year later, you'll be glad for the notations.

© 1999 Solveig Fredrickson

overhead costs of running a hospital, including rent or a mortgage for the building, employees' wages, equipment, supplies, insurance, and utilities. These costs add up and are reflected in the price you pay for your veterinarian's services.

What if an emergency happens and you don't think you can afford the veterinary bills? By all means, be up-front about your situation. Some hospitals accept credit cards, while others set up payment plans in dire situations. Do not take advantage of your veterinarian's kindness, however. You should be prepared to pay

Ten Questions to Ask Every Provider

Before choosing a pet insurance or membership plan, be sure to get straightforward answers to all your questions. If it makes you more comfortable, get the answers in writing.

1. Does your policy follow fee/benefits schedules? If so, please send me your detailed coverage limits. In the meantime, please give me examples of coverage limits for three common canine procedures so I can compare them to my current veterinary charges.

2. Does your policy cover basic wellness care, or does it cover only accidents and illnesses? Do you offer a wellness care endorsement that I can purchase on top of my basic plan for an additional fee? What other endorsements do you offer, and how much do they cost?

3. Under your policy's rules, can I continue taking my dog to his current veterinarian, or do I need to switch to another veterinarian?

4. Does your policy cover hereditary conditions, congenital conditions, or pre-existing conditions? Please explain each coverage or exclusion as it pertains specifically to my dog. Is there a feature where pre-existing conditions will be covered if my dog's pre-existing condition requires no treatment after a specified period? What is that period?

5. What happens to my premium and to my dog's policy if your company goes out of business? What guarantees do I have that I won't be throwing my money away?

6. How quickly do you pay claims?

7. What is your policy's deductible? Does the deductible apply per incident or annually? How does the deductible differ per plan?

8. Does the policy have payment limits over a year's period or during my pet's lifetime? How do the payment limits differ per plan?

9. What is the A.M. Best Co. rating of your insurance underwriter, and what does that rating mean?

10. Is there a cancellation period after I receive my policy or membership? How long do I have to review all my materials once I receive them, and what is the cancellation procedure?

for lifelong medical expenses before you buy a Border Collie. Distress over the expense of veterinary services does not provide a legitimate excuse for not paying your bill. Your veterinarian may not offer payment options because of this potential for abuse.

Two options can help you pay for your veterinary bills. The first is the pet insurance plan, which works similarly to the insurance plan you have for yourself and your family. Most pet insurance plans charge a certain yearly fee in exchange for accident and major illness coverage. A deductible may apply and pre-existing conditions may not be covered. Most insurance plans exclude wellness exams and preventive care such as spaying/neutering and vaccinations. Still, if an emergency or major illness strikes your dog, insurance may allow you to seek advanced treatment that you otherwise could not afford.

The second option that is offered by some veterinary hospitals is the savings plan. With this option, you pay a monthly fee, but do not pay for specific routine veterinary visits. Your dog will receive general care, such as vaccinations, checkups, yearly fecal exams, and even nail trimmings, all covered under the plan. Some plans even include office visits when your pet is sick and certain diagnostic tests. These plans allow you to budget payments monthly, instead of contending with a big expense at your dog's annual visit or when your dog is sick, and can end up providing significant savings. Many plans also offer discounts on other products and services available at the hospital, such as prescriptions or grooming.

Veterinary costs can seem overwhelming at times. If you reach a point at which you are unable to afford the care your dog needs, discuss your concerns openly and honestly with your veterinarian. Also, investigate pet insurance and savings plans. One of these options may be right for you.

Common
Health Concerns

5

In This Chapter

○ Parasites, Inside and Out
○ Illnesses and Emergencies
○ Obesity
○ Health Concerns Specific to Border Collies

B y now, you have discovered a nutritious, balanced diet for your Border Collie, and vowed to give him the exhaustive physical and mental exercise he needs to keep him happy and healthy. No matter how diligent you are about preventive care, there will be times your dog will develop some sort of health concern. These concerns can run the gamut from the annoyance of parasites, such as fleas and ticks, to common illnesses, to emergencies and genetic diseases that affect the breed. It is imperative that you know the signs and symptoms of potential health concerns and how to deal with them beforehand to prevent the problems

39

you can and help your pet recover more quickly from the problems you can't.

Parasites, Inside and Out

There's nothing more unsettling than thinking about these creepy, crawly (and in some cases, leaping) insects besieging your dog, and possibly your house and yard as well. Just keep in mind that the best defense is a solid offense. Arm yourself with knowledge about these insidious foes and their battle plans and you and your dog will be able to defeat them.

> No matter how diligent you are about preventive care, there will be times your dog will develop some sort of health concern.

External Parasites

From your puppy's first day in his new home, begin what I like to call the "Puppy Pampering Period." Set aside a few minutes of quiet time, get down on the floor with your dog, and go over his entire body with your hands. This lets you search for any signs of fleas, ticks, or other external parasites, as well as odd lumps or bumps that you may want to have checked out by your veterinarian. Although going over your puppy each and every day might seem excessive, it pays off in the long run by making him comfortable with having his body examined. When he's older, you may only need to check him out once a week or after he's been playing in a field or wooded area. By then, he'll probably look forward to his "doggie massage!" Since your Border Collie will have a long coat when he's an adult, it's especially important that he is comfortable with you examining him down to the skin.

Fleas Fleas have long been the bane of dogdom. They historically have been very difficult to get rid of once you have an infestation. They can cause everything from mild itching to disease. Thankfully, new advances in the flea-fighting arsenal have given us effective weapons against this prevalent parasite. But before we address how to prevent and/or treat fleas, let's take a good look at the enemy.

Fleas are a highly prolific species. At any one time, adult fleas in an environment account for only 1 to 5 percent of the total flea population. At the right temperature and humidity (65 to 80°F with 70 to 80 percent humidity), fleas multiply rapidly.

Fleas jump on a dog and feed for two to three days before they start to lay eggs (up to 40 to 50 per day). These eggs then drop off your pet and land in bedding, furniture, floor cracks, and the lawn outside. Within a day or two, the eggs hatch into larvae. Flea larvae burrow deep into carpet pile and are extremely difficult to destroy. After a larva has fed on debris for five to twelve days, it spins a cocoon. The cocoon is virtually indestructible; no insecticide can kill the flea during this stage. The cocoon can survive up to one year, just waiting for the ideal conditions for the flea to emerge. Vibration, heat, or pressure stimulates the adult to hatch. Depending on the environment, the cycle of the flea from egg to adult can be as short as 21 days or as long as a year.

How can you tell if your dog has fleas? Excessive scratching may provide your first clue. To look for evidence of these parasites on your Border Collie, part his hair along his back and around his tail and hindquarters. Fleas also favor the groin area and armpits. Running a flea comb through your dog's fur in these areas usually catches any adult fleas that are around. Be sure to kill the flea quickly or it will leap into the environment, only to jump back on your dog later. Even if you don't actually see these pests, you may spot their calling cards: white flea eggs or brownish red "flea dirt" (excrement).

Fleas feed on pets, but they live throughout the environment. So, if you end up with an infestation, you'll need to treat not only your dog, but also every part of his environment, from his bed to the carpet, furniture, and yard.

Now, how can you prevent an infestation in the first place? People used to rely on flea collars with very limited success, partly because collars provide the most protection around a dog's head while fleas tend to gather at the other end. If their dog did end up with fleas, they would treat him with a wide variety of products, from shampoos to sprays to dips. While these were helpful, they had to be used again and again over a period of time to be sure all the fleas were killed. Many of these products, because of their chemical content, can be dangerous. If used too often, in an improper amount, or mixed with other products, they can prove harmful to pets.

Fortunately for today's pet owner, new advances in flea-fighting technology offer safer and more effective solutions. You should begin your search for the best product for your Border Collie at your veterinarian's office. She can recommend flea preventive products, or flea treatment if you already have an infestation. In fact, many of the new flea products require a prescription. These tend to be safer than their over-the-counter cousins.

One type of the new breed of flea preventive comes in pill form. These pills contain an ingredient that actually prevents eggs from growing into adults and is harmless to people and dogs. Although this pill can help to control fleas overall, it has drawbacks. For one, it doesn't kill adult fleas. For another, a flea must actually bite your Border Collie in order for the drug to take effect, since it is absorbed into and transmitted to the flea through the dog's bloodstream. In other words, the product won't kill a flea that jumps on and off your dog without feasting.

Topical, spot-on treatments take care of this problem. Squeeze a small amount of the product each month on one spot between the shoulder blades for small dogs, or two spots, between the shoulder blades and along the back by the base of the tail, for larger dogs. The product provides protection over your dog's entire body within a day. These treatments kill, on contact, any flea that dares to jump on your dog, regardless of whether it stops

> Fortunately for today's pet owner, new advances in flea-fighting technology offer safer and more effective solutions.

for a snack. These spot treatments are sold under a number of product names. As mentioned, prescription treatments usually are safer for your dog than those sold over the counter.

What if you haven't tried one of these preventives yet, and your dog is already crawling with these pesky critters? Again, first consult your veterinarian. She will determine whether shampoos, dips, powders, sprays, or a combination are in order. Remember, some of these products can be very dangerous if haphazardly used together, so only combine products on the advice of your veterinarian.

If you already have an infestation, you'll need to treat your dog's environment as well as your dog. First, thoroughly vacuum your house, furniture, and dog's bedding and immediately throw out the vacuum bag, since any adult fleas the vacuum sucked up jump back into the environment the first chance they get. Use a fogger or spray in your house that not only includes an insecticide to kill fleas, but also uses an insect growth regulator (IGR) to keep immature fleas from developing. While both foggers and sprays work effectively, sprays can be useful for getting into hard-to-reach spots, such as deep in carpet pile. Another option is to sprinkle borax or borate powder on your carpet. Read the labels of all products carefully for safety instructions, and keep all people and animals away from the entire treated area until it is completely dry.

In addition to treating your house, you'll need to treat your yard if you have an infestation. Rake up leaves and other debris that fleas thrive on. After that, you have several options. Some owners spray their yards with IGRs to interfere with the flea's life cycle. These compounds are effective and safe for your pet, but they are dangerous to all insects. If you want to make sure you don't kill the "good" bugs with the "bad," there are more natural treatments available. Parasitic worms called nematodes, parasitic wasps, and diatomaceous earth (a fine dirt composed of the cell walls of one-cell algae) can help rid the environment of fleas without harming people, animals, or other insects. If you do still opt to use IGRs or a pyrethrin spray, distribute it sparingly and in limited areas.

Ticks   Ticks, which are found in fields and wooded areas, love to attach to warm-blooded mammals. They latch on for a blood meal and then drop off to lay eggs. As soon as you get home after a long walk in the woods with your Border Collie or a romp through the tall grass by a lake, check him thoroughly for ticks.

Some of the new flea preventives also kill ticks, but if you ever find a live specimen on your pet, you need to remove it immediately. Use tweezers or a special tick remover, never your bare hands (if the tick is carrying a disease, touching it could expose you). Grasp the tick as close to your dog's skin as possible and pull it out quickly. Don't injure the tick while it's attached or it may spit diseased saliva into your dog. For your Border Collie's sake, never try to remove a tick with a lit match—you'll only succeed in burning your dog! Afterwards, flush the tick down the toilet or drop it in alcohol or turpentine to kill it. Flush out the bite area on your pet's skin with warm, soapy water or hydrogen peroxide. If the area swells, try an ice pack and some antibacterial ointment. If the area doesn't clear up after a day or two, see your veterinarian.

Ticks are more than just a nuisance. They also carry a number of diseases, some of which can affect you as well as your dog. Rocky Mountain spotted fever, ehrlichiosis, babesiosis, tick paralysis, and Lyme disease, to name just a few, all are transmitted by tick saliva. That's why it is extremely important that you check your dog regularly; the longer a tick feasts on your pet the more likely it will transmit a disease to him.

All of these diseases are dangerous, but Lyme disease, especially, has been in the news lately because of its effects on both dogs and humans who have encountered an infected tick. Lyme vaccines are available; if you live in or are planning a vacation to an area where ticks are prevalent, talk to your vet about vaccinating your dog.

Skin Mites (Mange)   If your dog scratches intensely but you see no sign of fleas, he may suffer from mites. To diagnose mites, which are much smaller than

> ## Did You Know?
> An average of 800 dogs and cats are euthanized every hour in the United States.

either fleas or ticks, a veterinarian must examine skin scrapings taken from your dog. Several types of mites affect dogs.

The scabies mite digs under the skin to lay its eggs. Although scabies can live anywhere on a dog, they tend to congregate around the earflaps, elbow, hocks, ears, and face. These mites cause a condition called sarcoptic mange. When infected with this mite, your dog will scratch incessantly at his unbearably itchy skin, sometimes causing it to swell and form pus-filled scabs. Treatment usually consists of medicated dips, plus cortisone to relieve the itching. In addition, your veterinarian may give an oral medication such as ivermectin for relief, though probably not for a Border Collie—the breed may be at higher risk for side effects with this drug.

> To diagnose mites, which are much smaller than either fleas or ticks, a veterinarian must examine skin scrapings taken from your dog.

The demodex mite causes demodectic mange, or "red mange." This mite actually lives on virtually all dogs and is passed to puppies by their mothers during nursing. Only a small percentage of dogs are bothered by the demodex mite. Symptoms of the demodex mite often first appear at the skin around the dog's eyes, elbows, and feet, which becomes inflamed and hairless. Puppies with immature immune systems are the usual victims of red mange and often can beat the disease as they grow older. Some dogs who never fully develop their immune system or have defective immune systems may be bothered for life, however. Your veterinarian will treat your dog with medicated dips.

Cheyletiella mange, or walking dandruff, is caused by the cheyletiella mite and, again, is most often seen in puppies. These mites are very active, and tend to move under the flakes of skin they have created when your dog scratches, making it appear he has walking dandruff. See your veterinarian for dipping treatments.

Ringworm   Although ringworm is external, it is not a parasite. Contrary to what its name implies, ringworm actually has nothing to do with worms, but rather is a fungus that can cause a rapidly spreading circle of hair loss surrounded by a red ring. Although it usually isn't itchy, scabs and crusts can form, leading to draining sores. Ringworm is contagious to both dogs and humans, especially children. If your Border Collie has ringworm, don't let any children pet him until the condition is cleared up. Ringworm is diagnosed by flooding the skin with an ultraviolet light (ringworm may glow green), by examining skin scrapings under a microscope, or by running a fungus culture. Your veterinarian will treat the disease by clipping away the infected hair follicles and bathing the skin with a special shampoo. If that doesn't seem to heal the infected area, she will administer antifungal medication.

Internal Parasites

Internal parasites can be even more elusive foes than fleas or ticks, since they are not creeping, crawling, or jumping on your pet. Many types of internal worms are quite common. In fact, most puppies have some type of worm, and adult dogs can also be affected. If you note any of the symptoms below, bring a fresh fecal sample to your veterinarian for diagnosis. You should also have your dog's stool checked during his yearly exam to discover internal parasites that are not producing symptoms.

Roundworms   If your puppy has an especially round pot-belly and dull coat, he may be plagued by roundworms.

Other symptoms of these spaghetti-like worms, which range in size from one to seven inches long, include vomiting, diarrhea, weight loss, and failure to thrive. If your Border Collie is heavily infested, you will even see worms in his stool or vomit; they are white, stringy worms that are either coiled or stretched out. Puppies can get roundworms from their mother while they are still in the uterus or later while nursing, or from an infected environment. It is best to treat all puppies for roundworms by giving deworming medication every two weeks from as early as two weeks of age. If left untreated, an infestation of roundworms can cause stunted growth or even death.

> You should have your dog's stool checked during his yearly exam to discover internal parasites that are not producing symptoms.

Roundworms also can affect adult dogs. Dogs acquire roundworms by eating infected soil and feces. In these older dogs, roundworms may not produce symptoms. But, if a stool sample shows roundworms, your dog needs treatment, for both his health and yours, since on rare occasions roundworms can be transmitted to people who walk on or touch the infective larvae from contaminated soil.

Hookworms   Small, thin worms about a quarter-inch to a half-inch long, hookworms are most prevalent in warm climates. Hookworms live in the small intestine, where they suck blood from the intestinal wall. As they move on to new feeding sites, the old wounds continue to bleed. Puppies usually get hookworms from their mothers while nursing, although the rare puppy acquires them in utero. Hookworm infestation can pose a serious danger, and many pups die soon after exposure. The signs of infestation are anemia (due to intestinal bleeding); dark-colored, thick diarrhea; pale gums; weakness; and emaciation. Puppies with a serious case may need blood transfusions as well as medication to eliminate the worms.

Older dogs can also contract hookworms, although chronic hookworm infections in adults are rare. Adult dogs typically pick up hookworms through contact with contaminated feces or soil. Hookworms can still pose a danger even after it seems that they have been eradicated; dogs who recover from hookworms can develop cysts in their tissue that carry the hookworm larvae. Stress or illness can trigger the release of the larvae, causing a new outbreak. A veterinarian diagnoses hookworms by examining a stool sample and treats them with medication.

Tapeworms   This nasty worm can range in length from less than an inch to several feet. It is made up of a head and a multisegmented body. Each segment contains eggs, and these segments pass out of your dog's body in his feces. When dried out, the segments resemble grains of rice. Sometimes, you can see moving segments attached to the fur around your Border Collie's anus. Other symptoms include mild diarrhea, loss of appetite, and a change in the texture and condition of your dog's coat.

The flea is the main host that transmits tapeworms. If your Border Collie swallows a flea that carries tapeworms, he becomes the tapeworm's host. If you weren't convinced your dog needed flea protection before, this should do the trick!

Your dog also can get tapeworms by eating raw, uncooked meat, rabbits, or certain rodents. If your dog is diagnosed with tapeworms through a stool sample, your veterinarian will prescribe medication.

Heartworm   The heartworm is one of the most dangerous parasites affecting dogs. Carried by the common mosquito, heartworm can kill your pet. When an infected mosquito bites a dog, it imbeds larvae in the dog's skin. Over a period of three to four months, these larvae go through several stages to develop into adult worms. At that point, they find a vein and travel to the right side of the heart and pulmonary artery, where they multiply. One dog plagued by heartworm had 250 worms in his heart. Symptoms include intolerance to exercise, coughing (especially after exertion), weight loss, and general fatigue. Treatment is expensive and complicated. If heartworms are left untreated, dogs can develop severe disabilities or even sudden death.

When dealing with heartworm, prevention is the answer. Dogs older than six months should be blood-tested for heartworm before starting any preventive (puppies less than six months old don't require testing). If they are worm free, they should be placed on a once-a-month preventive for either the mosquito season or year-round, depending on the climate.

Coccidia   Usually found in dogs who are housed in filthy, overcrowded conditions, coccidia are protozoan parasites that are spread through contaminated feces. Puppies are especially vulnerable. Dogs with coccidiosis start out with mild diarrhea that worsens and eventually becomes mucus-like and bloody. If the disease isn't treated promptly, they also can suffer from loss of appetite, weakness, dehydration, and anemia.

Tests run on a stool sample diagnose the problem. Your veterinarian will give your infected dog medication. You must also thoroughly sterilize the dog's housing. Unfortunately, even though the dog recovers, he may carry the disease to other pets and could experience flare-ups in the future when stressed or sick.

Giardia   Another protozoa, giardia is becoming more prevalent. Your dog can catch giardiasis by drinking from puddles or other stagnant, fecal-contaminated water, or even from sharing a water bowl with an infected dog. Mucus-like, blood-tinged diarrhea is the main symptom. Giardia responds well to medication; however, make sure to test and treat all animals in the household that may share water. Pets can also pass giardia to humans through infected water sources, which can make you and your family very sick, though it is often mild in humans.

Illnesses and Emergencies

The best way to be prepared for potential illnesses or emergencies affecting your Border Collie is to expect the unexpected. Prepare yourself ahead of time by knowing what signs to look for, what action to take, and by having a fully stocked first-aid kit handy at all times. Someday, your dog's life may depend on it.

Insect Bites and Stings

Dogs can be curious when it comes to bugs such as bees or spiders, and may get too close for their own good. If your Border Collie ever gets stung, first check to see whether a stinger is still in your pet. If so, brush it out with a firm object, such as a credit card. Don't try to pick it out as you would an ordinary splinter, since squeezing or breaking it could release additional toxins into your dog. Next, apply a paste of baking soda and water directly to the sting, and use ice packs if

Did You Know?

Dogs see color less vividly than humans but are not actually color-blind.

there is swelling. If your dog experiences a severe reaction to the sting, such as extreme swelling, hives spreading over her body, or extreme itchiness, take her to the veterinarian. Facial swelling demands emergency attention, since the swelling can spread to the upper airways and throat and prevent air from reaching the lungs.

Vomiting

Many things cause vomiting, from eating a foreign object to infectious illness, motion sickness, and certain diseases. If your dog is vomiting and she is under a year old, is older than eight or nine, or has a serious medical condition such as diabetes, she should see the veterinarian right away. Also see your doctor the same day if she is running a fever (a temperature greater than 103°F). If your dog is a normal, healthy adult and starts vomiting yet

> Prepare yourself ahead of time by knowing what signs to look for, what action to take, and by having a fully stocked first-aid kit handy at all times.

seems to feel well otherwise, withhold food and water for eight to twelve hours. If she doesn't vomit during the fast, give her a few ice chips to lick every two or three hours. Vomiting or not eating can rapidly lead to dehydration, so it is essential to give your Border Collie fluids. If she is able to keep this liquid down, after a few hours give her about a half-cup of water and repeat this every two or three hours. If she still hasn't vomited after 24 hours, give her a bland diet of two parts boiled rice mixed with one part boiled, drained hamburger, fed a little at a time. If she holds down this food and water, gradually mix her regular food back in over the next 48 to 72 hours. If your dog vomits again at any stage during the treatment, take her to the veterinarian.

Unproductive vomiting demands a different course of action. This may be a symptom of bloat, and requires emergency veterinary attention.

Diarrhea

Like vomiting, diarrhea can stem from many causes. One avoidable precipitator is changing your dog's diet too quickly. Although we enjoy and can tolerate variety in our meals, dogs can't. Don't change dog foods unless your dog isn't thriving on the brand she is eating. If you do decide to change foods, do so gradually or your dog may end up with digestive problems.

Other potential causes of diarrhea include eating something spoiled or toxic, parasites, stress, and disease. If your dog's diarrhea continues for more than 24 hours, contains blood, or is accompanied by vomiting, or if your Border Collie is less than a year old or older than eight years, see your veterinarian. You should also take your dog, regardless of her age, to the doctor when a fever (103°F or greater) or dehydration accompanies the diarrhea or if she looks or acts sick. Check for dehydration by pulling the skin at the back of your dog's neck. If it doesn't spring back into position within a second or two of you letting go, your dog is dehydrated and needs emergency attention.

If your pet has none of the above complications, withhold food for 24 to 48 hours, but supply plenty of water (as long as your Border Collie isn't vomiting). Then, switch to a bland diet of one part boiled, drained hamburger or boiled chicken (with the skin, fat, and bones removed) and two parts boiled rice. If the diarrhea seems to subside after two or three days on this treatment, gradually add your pet's normal food back into her diet.

Taking Your Border Collie's Temperature

The key to taking your Border Collie's temperature is to remain calm; if you're nervous, your dog, too, will become agitated. Use a rectal thermometer, available in traditional glass or digital versions, lubricated with petroleum jelly or a water-based lubricant. Have your dog stand or lie down (whichever seems more comfortable) and insert the thermometer about one inch into the dog's rectum. Leave a glass thermometer in for three minutes and a digital thermometer until it beeps. The normal temperature range for a dog is 100.2 to 102.8°F.

You can give your dog anti-diarrheal medicine, but only at the onset of diarrhea and only after first calling your veterinarian to ask his opinion. He should be able to suggest a medication and dosage over the phone. If your dog doesn't improve, seems to be getting worse, or vomiting or fever accompanies the diarrhea, take your pet in for an examination.

Choking

Choking is a potentially life-threatening situation that must be treated at once. A choking dog might struggle or gasp for breath, paw at her face, act anxious, and her gums may turn blue or white. Choking can be due to a number of factors. Your dog may be choking on vomit, have an upper respiratory disease, her tongue may be swollen due to an allergic reaction, or she may have a foreign object caught in her throat.

Toys are one form of foreign object frequently ingested by dogs. It is very easy for a Border Collie to ingest bitten off parts of toys. Select your pet's toys carefully, and inspect them frequently to make sure she isn't chewing them into dangerous pieces.

Although your dog loves you, she may become distraught when choking, so take care not to get bitten while helping her. If your dog is conscious, don't stick your hands in her mouth. Help her stand on her hind forelegs with her head down or hold her in this position and place your arms around her waist from behind. Your arms should be resting on her last ribs. Give a short, firm, rapid squeeze that brings the ribs in about one inch. This may help expel anything trapped in her airway. Compress the ribs about one inch only—any harder and you risk cracking the ribs or damaging the spleen.

If she is unconscious or lay-ing down, open her mouth and gently sweep your hand from side to side to try to feel any for-eign object. Be careful not to push the object further down her throat and be aware that a

> If (Once) the object comes out, check your pet's vital signs. If she isn't breathing or has no heartbeat, you will have to per-form cardiopulmonary resuscita-tion (CPR). If you are having difficulty getting the object out, don't waste a lot of time trying—get your dog to the veterinarian.

dog's hyoid apparatus—Adam's apple—lies deep in the throat. If you feel a flesh-covered, bone-like structure, don't pull on it—it's almost certainly meant to be there. Pull your Border Collie's tongue forward and remove any obstruction or vomit. If this doesn't work, close your hands together, making a cupped fist, and on one side place your fist just behind and partially covering the last rib. (If the squeeze isn't tempered by the rib, it may rup-ture the spleen or liver. Also, it's easier to move air if the ribs are used). Rapidly push in and up with your cupped fist, moving the chest about one inch each time, repeating as necessary until the object is forced out or until you're convinced nothing is going to come out (about one minute of effort). Remember, if the airway is swollen nothing will come out, ever, so you're just wasting time as the text suggests below.

If (Once) the object comes out, check your pet's vital signs. If she isn't breathing or has no heartbeat, you will have to perform cardiopulmonary resuscitation (CPR).

If you are having difficulty getting the object out, don't waste a lot of time trying—get your dog to the veterinarian. In all instances of choking, a doctor should check your dog anyway to ensure all obstructions have been removed. Your pet also requires immediate veterinary care if the choking did not result from an object and instead indicates symptoms of disease or an allergic reaction.

Bleeding

If your dog is bleeding, hold a piece of gauze or other sterile material over the wound, applying direct pressure. If you don't have anything sterile, grab a clean cloth. If blood soaks the material, add more material on top. Removing the original cloth might prevent a blood clot from forming (blood clots help stop blood flow). Keep applying direct pressure until you can reach your veterinary clinic.

If the bleeding continues and spurts, keep applying direct pressure to the wound while also holding the area just above it (between the wound and the heart) with your hand. If this technique fails, apply a pressure bandage by wrapping gauze around the wound and securing it with tape. Make sure the bandage is tight enough to stop the bleeding, but not so tight that you cut off circulation. If the injury is on a limb, keep checking your Border Collie's toes for swelling and temperature; if her toes start to swell or feel cold, loosen the bandage.

How to Perform CPR on Your Border Collie

If during an emergency you discover your dog is not breathing and/or has no heartbeat, you'll need to administer cardiopulmonary resuscitation (CPR). CPR isn't foolproof, even if performed by a professional. However, it certainly is worth trying when your dog's life is in danger. First, you must be sure a dog is unconscious, or you could be bitten. Never take time out to perform CPR for a dog in this condition if you have transport to a veterinary clinic; rush her to the doctor immediately and perform CPR on the way.

To perform CPR, you need to know your ABCs: airway, breathing, and circulation. First, look into your dog's throat and clear any foreign obstructions. Then, check for breathing. Watch her ribs for the slightest sign of movement, or hold a mirror by her muzzle to see if it fogs up. If the dog is breathing on her own, move on to circulation (heartbeat or pulse). If she is not, place her on her right side and hold her muzzle closed. Then place your mouth over her nose and exhale deeply enough to slightly raise the dog's rib cage, which shows her lungs are inflated. Remove your mouth from the dog's nose and allow the lungs to deflate. Repeat this procedure every three to five seconds, and check for a heartbeat every third time by pressing down with your palm on the left side of the chest just behind the bent elbow or inside the upper thigh of the rear leg. Continue treatment until the dog is breathing on her own. You'll pick up the heartbeat easiest on the down side of the dog: If she is down long the heart will move away from the upper ribs, regardless if she is on the right or left side.

If your pet has a heartbeat, skip the following step. If she has no heartbeat or pulse, lay your dog on her right side and stand or kneel with her back to you. Cup your hands over each other and compress the chest where the left elbow lies when she is in a normal standing position. Compress inward about two to three inches each time, at a rate of 60 to 120 compressions per minute. A higher rate is ideal, but difficult to accomplish. If you are alone, give two quick breaths after every 15 cardiac compressions. If you have an assistant, have one person perform each task and synchronize your procedure so that you are providing one breath per every three to five compressions, followed by a breath, then check for a pulse. Stop CPR every three to five minutes or if you detect movement to see if there is now a heartbeat. Don't stop artificial respiration for more than 30 seconds if the dog is not breathing on her own or she could experience permanent brain damage.

If you still cannot stop the bleeding, you'll need to apply pressure to pressure points in your dog's body that correspond to the injured area. If your dog is bleeding from a front leg, firmly place three fingers up in the armpit on the side of the injury. If your dog is bleeding from a back leg, apply three-finger pressure to the area of the inner thigh where the leg connects to the body on the side of the injury. If your Border Collie is bleeding from her head, place three fingers at the base of the lower jaw, on the same side and below where the bleeding is occurring. If she is bleeding from her neck, place three fingers in the soft groove next to the windpipe on the same side as the wound. Never apply pressure to the windpipe itself, and never apply pressure to your dog's neck if you think she might have a head injury. Note: When using pressure points, you must release pressure for a few seconds at least every ten minutes, or your dog could suffer permanent damage.

> Due to its potential to cause long-term, serious damage, a tourniquet should only be used on an animal who is unconscious and may die without it.

The final resort to staunch a bleeding limb is the tourniquet. Due to its potential to cause long-term, serious damage, a tourniquet should only be used on an animal who is unconscious and may die without it. If you must employ this technique, wrap a two-inch strip of gauze around the limb above the wound, but don't knot it. Wrap each end of the gauze around a stick, then turn the stick slowly and just enough to stop the bleeding. Loosen the tie for several seconds at least every ten minutes. Although you may need to apply this technique to save your dog's life, realize that she could lose a limb because of the interrupted blood flow.

As you can see, bleeding is an extremely dangerous situation that must be handled properly. If your dog is bleeding heavily, the most important thing is to get her to the vet immediately. If possible, ask someone else to drive you and your dog to the clinic, so you can apply the above techniques in the car.

Fractures

If your pet breaks a bone, you'll need to keep her calm and quiet. Check her breathing and pulse and give CPR, if needed. If the bone protrudes through the skin, take your dog to the veterinarian immediately. Loosely place a nonstick pad or gauze sponge on the wound and secure the dressing with tape, taking care not to move the bone or wrap too tightly.

You'll need to keep your dog completely still while you take her to the vet. If you have someone with you, place your dog on a large flat piece of wood used as a makeshift stretcher. If you are alone, try to pick up your dog by placing one arm under and around her neck and the other behind her hind leg or, if her hind leg is injured, under her stomach. If you think she will not lie still in the car, which could cause further injury, you may need to try to splint the fracture.

Splinting, like performing CPR, is very difficult to do correctly and can actually worsen a fracture if done improperly. Place something rigid, such as a rolled up newspaper or a stick, on each side of the fractured limb. Hold the splint in place with lots of tape all along the splint or cloth strips tied up and down the splint. Again, make sure not to move the bone or wrap too tightly. Test the tension by placing two fingers between the cloth and the limb, to guard against tying so tightly that you cut off circulation.

Car Accidents

There is nothing more upsetting than seeing an animal struck by a car. You can do your part to prevent this from

Handling an Injured Border Collie

If your Border Collie is injured, he may growl or snap when you attempt to touch or move him. Don't be offended by this unusual behavior. Your Border Collie is feeling pain, and this is the way he shows it. Remember this before handling your injured Border Collie, and take a few steps to prevent injury to yourself.

First, talk to your dog quietly and calmly. He may be excited or anxious—aren't you when you're injured? Move slowly, and keep talking in a soothing voice.

Next, muzzle your hurt Border Collie. If you don't have a muzzle available, improvise with a man's necktie, a stocking, or a long strip of soft cloth. Loop the cloth over the Border Collie's muzzle and tie a half knot on top of the dog's muzzle, then tie another half knot under the chin. Wrap the material behind and below the ears and tie a full knot at the base of the dog's head. If your dog is having trouble breathing, avoid a muzzle if at all possible.

To transport your severely injured Border Collie to the emergency clinic, use a stretcher. A flat board, a sheet of plywood, for example, works well. If something like that isn't available, use a large towel or blanket. You don't want to injure your Border Collie more seriously, so be very careful moving him onto the makeshift stretcher. Slide one hand under your dog's rear and the other hand under his chest. (You may need a helper if your Border Collie is especially large or you're especially small.) Slowly inch the dog onto the stretcher and cover him with a towel.

Drive carefully but quickly to the veterinary clinic. Have someone ride next to your Border Collie, keeping him calm and still. Call ahead so that the staff expects you, and have them come out to help carry in the dog.

ever happening to your Border Collie by always keeping her on a leash or in a fenced yard.

But as we all know, accidents can happen; someone might inadvertently leave your yard gate open or the leash could break or your dog could pull it out of your hands. If you witness your dog being hit by a car, try to pay attention to what part of the dog's body the vehicle strikes; this is important information for your veterinarian. Wave down traffic and gently get your dog off the road as quickly as possible, being careful not to cause more injury. Many dogs jump up after an accident and try to run off. This is a survival mechanism and shouldn't be misinterpreted as meaning the dog is fine. If your pet can't move at all, she may have a broken back. Place her on a stiff board or on a blanket and get someone to help you carry her carefully to a car, so you can get her to the hospital. Again, have someone else drive, if possible. Check her breathing and pulse and perform CPR, if necessary. Try to control any bleeding. Check for signs of shock and treat accordingly. In all cases, even if your dog seems fine, take her to the veterinarian immediately.

Heat Stroke

Dogs can fall victim to heat stroke when left outside without proper shelter or when exercising excessively in hot, humid conditions. A common cause of heat stroke in dogs is being left in a parked car. Never leave your Border Collie in the car on a warm day. Even if the windows are slightly open, the temperature in your car can quickly reach unbearable levels, which can prove fatal to your pet. Always monitor your Border Collie on a hot (or even warm) day and use your air conditioning if your dog seems uncomfortable.

Signs of heat stroke include excessive panting or difficulty breathing, drooling, an increased heart and respiratory rate, and lethargy. If untreated, your dog could seizure or fall into a coma.

If your dog is suffering from heat stroke, get her away from the heat source immediately. She must receive emergency veterinary care, since delayed treatment could mean death. Complications from heat stroke, such as kidney failure and respiratory arrest, may not show up for hours or even days. Cool your Border Collie down with towels soaked in cold water, put her in an air-conditioned car and rush her to the clinic, where the veterinarian will give her IV fluids and carefully reduce her body temperature.

Never leave your Border Collie in the car on a warm day.

Seizures

Seizures, like many other symptoms and conditions, can result from a variety of causes, from poisoning to diseases, organ failure, and epilepsy. Dogs seem to sense the onset of a seizure, and they may act dazed or anxious, or try to stay by you or hide in a safe place. When the seizure hits, the dog usually loses her balance, falls over, and twitches. She may also drool, urinate, or defecate. Some appear to stare at nothing or to bite at imaginary things. Seizuring dogs often don't recognize their owners. After a seizure, your dog may act normally right away, or she may be disoriented and walk into walls or furniture.

If your dog experiences a seizure, make sure she is in a safe spot (away from sharp objects or the top of stairs, for example). Don't disturb her, and especially don't touch her near her mouth. She may not know who you are and may bite as a reflex. Take note of when the seizure started, how long it lasted, and whether anything seemed to trigger the episode. When the seizure stops, take your pet to your veterinarian as soon as possible. He might place your dog on antiseizure medication, which will not prevent all seizures, but will help reduce their frequency and severity.

Shock

Different causes produce different symptoms of shock. When your dog is in shock, she may be weak and subdued. Her body temperature can range from below normal to normal or above normal (in cases of shock caused by a bacterial infection). Her pulse may be rapid and weak, and her gums may exhibit a delayed capillary refill time. (Test capillary refill time by pressing on your dog's gums, removing your finger, and counting the time it takes the gums to change from white back to pink. Normal is less than two seconds.) If your dog's gums seem to respond normally, but she is acting lethargic and confused, she may be in the early stages of shock.

In all cases of shock, immediate veterinary care is imperative. Control any bleeding, wrap your dog in a blanket, towel, or piece of clothing to keep her warm, and rush her to the veterinary clinic.

Poisoning

Many different substances of varying forms can poison your dog. Some are eaten, while others are inhaled, and still others are absorbed through the skin. Treatment for these toxins varies widely, so it is important not to haphazardly administer antidotes on your own.

Signs of poisoning include: drooling; swollen, irritated skin or eyes; staggering or trembling; seizures; vomiting; and diarrhea. Check your pet's breathing and pulse and begin CPR, if necessary. If you suspect your pet has been poisoned, but you don't know by what, get her to the veterinarian immediately. If you know what poisoned your pet, call your doctor and tell him the exact name of the poison (keep the container or label to bring to his clinic). You must also tell him how long ago your dog was exposed, how much she ate or was exposed to, her vital signs (including temperature and heart rate), and her weight. Your veterinarian vet might prescribe an antidote over the phone that you can administer before bringing in your pet, or he might tell you to rush your dog to the clinic immediately. You also can call the National Animal Poison Control Center 24 hours a day at (888) 426-4435 or (900) 680-0000. The center, which charges a fee, may be able to prescribe an antidote over the phone.

Fish Hooks

If you fish and your Border Collie is your constant companion, you might take her with you on a fishing expedition so you both can enjoy the great outdoors and each other's company. You need to use caution and prevent your pet's access to the fishing equipment, which probably smells like a seafood feast to her. If she gets a fish hook embedded in her mouth or paw, take her to the veterinarian immediately to get the hook removed. If you can't get to a doctor quickly and the hook is in your dog's paw, try to push the hook through the skin until you can see the barb. Cut the barb off with a wire cutter and then pull the hook out backwards where it went in. Wash out the wound with warm water or a solution of one teaspoon salt mixed with a quart of warm water. If your dog embedded the hook in her mouth or swallowed it, never try to remove it yourself.

Even if you have successfully removed the hook, take your dog to the veterinarian in case she needs antibiotics to prevent infection.

Burns

Burns fall into one of three categories: thermal, chemical, or electrical. Examples of thermal burns include

Elizabethan Style

Although wearing an Elizabethan collar may sound stylish, its purpose is medicinal. Hopefully your Border Collie won't need one, but if she suffers an injury, a wound, or a skin problem that mustn't be scratched, bitten, or pawed, the Elizabethan collar will do the job. Named for the high neck ruff popular during the reign of Queen Elizabeth, this lampshade-like collar prevents your Border Collie from turning her head to chew and makes scratching nearly impossible. The size of the collar is tailored to fit the size of the dog.

The Elizabethan collar is effective, but it's not always well received by its wearers. It's a bit bulky, and certainly looks funny. Hopefully your Border Collie will accept this with good humor.

scalding from hot water and getting too close to an open flame. If your dog receives a thermal burn, first check for signs of shock; if she is in shock, rush her to the veterinarian immediately. If she is not showing signs of shock and the wound is medium to small in size, cover the wound with cold compresses, made by soaking rags in ice water then wringing them out. Place a sterile, nonstick gauze pad or a clean, moist cloth over the burn to keep it cool and clean. Then take your dog to the veterinarian. Always forgo home care and immediately take your dog to the vet if the wound covers a large part of the body.

Chemical burns can come from either alkalis or acids. If your dog sustains a chemical burn, again check for signs of shock and seek emergency care if shock is present. Wear protective gloves and clean the wound immediately. If the offending substance was an alkali, wash the wound with equal parts vinegar and water. If it was an acid, wash with one teaspoon of bicarbonate of soda mixed with one pint of lukewarm water. If you do not know what kind of chemical caused the injury, rinse with plain water. Follow the instructions for antidotes that are printed on the chemical's container, if accessible. Get your dog to the veterinarian immediately.

The third type of burn, electrical burn, often brings an additional consequence—electric shock. Wires fascinate some dogs, especially puppies. If your dog chews through a wire, she may experience severe burns and shock. If you see your pet actually bite a wire, turn off the power source or remove the cord with a wooden or plastic broom, to prevent you, too, from being electrocuted. Never touch a dog who is still in contact with a live power source. If you didn't actually witness the incident, your only indication that your dog has been burned may be blisters around her mouth, excessive drooling, or a foul odor coming from her mouth. Check your dog's airway, breathing, and circulation and perform CPR, if needed. Check for shock, and see your veterinarian immediately.

> You can prevent electrocution by covering cords with plastic cord covers or by securing them to the floor with duct tape and covering them with carpet.

You can prevent electrocution by covering cords with plastic cord covers or by securing them to the floor with duct tape and covering them with carpet. Other options are to unplug all appliances not in use and/or rub the cord with Tabasco sauce or a bitter tonic, such as Bitter Apple, from a pet store. Finally, you should never leave puppies unsupervised near live wires.

Allergic Reactions

Any number of things in your Border Collie's environment, including food, grass, bug bites, household cleaning products, or even a new shampoo, can cause allergies. If your dog develops a

First-Aid Kit Essentials

❍ Your veterinarian's phone number

❍ An after-hours emergency clinic's phone number

❍ The National Animal Poison Control Center's hotline number: (888) 426-4435 or (900) 680-0000

❍ Rectal thermometer

❍ Tweezers

❍ Scissors

❍ Penlight flashlight

❍ Rubbing alcohol

❍ Hydrogen peroxide (3 percent)

❍ Syrup of ipecac and activated charcoal liquid or tablets (poisoning antidotes)

❍ Anti-diarrheal medicine

❍ Dosing syringe

❍ Nonstick wound pads, gauze squares, and roll cotton to control bleeding

❍ Adhesive tape

❍ Elastic bandage

❍ Styptic powder (in case nails are cut too short)

❍ Emergency ice pack

❍ First-aid book

❍ Latex examination gloves

sudden, severe allergic reaction, such as facial swelling or trouble breathing, get her emergency care. If the reaction is relatively mild, such as irritated, itchy skin, bathe her with a gentle, hypoallergenic shampoo. Apply cold compresses to any red, itchy areas, followed by a baking soda and water paste. With your veterinarian's recommendation, you may be able to give your allergic dog an over-the-counter antihistamine. (Ask your veterinarian for the proper dosage.)

If this doesn't clear up the problem, take your pet in for an appointment with the veterinarian. Food allergies are common and may require a change in diet. Seasonal allergies are also common;

your veterinarian may be able to prescribe medication to relieve your dog's symptoms.

Eye Injuries

If your Border Collie's eyes are red, swollen, or watery, or if she keeps pawing at them, she may have something in her eye or a condition such as conjunctivitis (a swelling of the pink tissue lining the inside of the eyelids). If you see a foreign object in your dog's eye, flush it out with a sterile saline eyewash or with large amounts of tap water. Even if you remove the object, have your veterinarian examine the eye, in case the cornea was scratched. Take your pet to the veterinarian whenever her eyes are involved. Many eye conditions can be serious if not treated. Your dog's eyesight is too precious to risk.

Obesity

Maintaining the proper weight in your Border Collie is more than a matter of vanity. An overweight dog not only looks less attractive than a thinner dog, but also is less healthy. Extra weight puts strain on every part of a dog's body, from his heart to his lungs and bones.

Maintaining a Healthy Weight

It is important that you monitor your Border Collie's weight throughout his life. Adjust the type and amount of food your dog eats as he moves from puppyhood into adulthood and eventually old age. Make a habit of performing the rib-check test every month or so. Stand above your dog and look down. Does he have a waist? When viewed from the side, does his abdomen tuck up from his ribs to his pelvis or does his belly look like a sagging potato sack? Place your hands along his sides and run them lightly over his ribs. With slight pressure, you should be able to feel each rib. If you have to press hard to find his ribs or you can't find them at all, you have an overweight dog! (For more about the rib-check test and Border Collie nutrition, see Chapter 3, Food for Thought.)

If your dog is overweight, there's a good chance you are at the root of his problem. Although some dogs gain weight because of a medical condition, the number one cause of obesity is overfeeding, and we all know who controls the food bowl! Let's start by examining snacks. No matter how cute and pleading your Border Collie may look, don't allow snacks to make up more than 5 to 10 percent of his diet at the most, and only feed snacks that are healthful. If your dog has a weight problem, also check his daily intake of dog food. Remember that the cups per day listed on the dog food bag are just recommendations, and each dog is different. Feed your dog the amount of food that keeps him trim and healthy.

If your dog is overweight, you first need to consult your veterinarian. She can work up a weight-reduction diet and an exercise plan that will shape up your dog slowly and safely and keep him that way. In general, when dealing with adult dogs, it is better to feed the same amount of a lower calorie food than to cut back the amount of your dog's normal food. If your dog notices he is eating less food, he will feel hungrier than if he eats the same amount of food but with fewer calories. Most premium dog foods come in low-calorie versions, or your veterinarian may put your dog on a prescription weight-reduction diet. Keep in mind, however, that your dog can't do this alone. If you are not diligent in sticking to the diet, and if you keep slipping your Border Collie treats, he'll never lose the weight.

Diet, however, is only half of the equation. Your dog also will need to step up his exercise. Ask your veterinarian to recommend the proper amount and type of exercise to rid your dog of his excess weight. Overweight dogs shouldn't be pushed too hard too fast, or they could sustain injuries. Agility, for instance, is an excellent exercise option for dogs who are already in decent shape, but could be harmful to an overweight dog who could get hurt jumping or navigating obstacles. Instead, your veterinarian might recommend road work. Always start out slowly, gradually walking (or jogging) greater distances with your dog.

Trimming Down a Chubby Puppy

Trimming down overweight puppies requires a slightly different approach. Feeding a low-calorie adult diet to a puppy might deprive him of essential nutrients he needs to grow properly. Instead, feed your pup slightly less of his normal diet and keep monitoring his condition until he reaches an ideal weight. You also don't want to put a puppy on a strictly regimented exercise program. It could do some real damage to his growing bones.

> You don't want to put a puppy on a strictly regimented exercise program. It could do some real damage to his growing bones.

Health Concerns Specific to Border Collies

Sadly, every breed of dog is prone to specific diseases and illnesses. It is important that you educate yourself beforehand about the maladies that can affect the Border Collie, and what kind of tests, prevention, and cures are available for each. If you are educated about the diseases and disorders that run in Border Collies, you'll know what questions to ask a breeder to ensure she is doing everything possible to breed healthy dogs. Not only should you ask a potential breeder if she tests for these disorders, you should ask to see proof. You are making a lifelong emotional investment in your Border Collie; you want to be sure you are buying a healthy dog.

Genetic Diseases and Disorders

Hip dysplasia (HD) is a disorder that affects many breeds, including the Border Collie. This progressive, degenerative joint disease, in which the thigh bone does not fit correctly into the hip joint, ranges from mild, asymptomatic cases to severe cases that cause serious pain and/or debilitation. If your Border Collie experiences difficulty getting up, appears lame, or is reluctant to run and play, have your veterinarian check him for dysplasia. X-rays are necessary for a definite diagnosis. Since this disease can be so devastating, all breeding stock should be evaluated by the Orthopedic Foundation for Animals (OFA), the Institute for Genetic Disease Control in Animals (GDC), or the PennHip system and determined to be free of this condition before a dog produces its first litter. HD is rarely detected before six months of age; accurate diagnosis is not typically possible until the dog is two years old. Diet is believed to affect this genetic problem. That's why it is vital that your Border

> **Did You Know?**
>
> Dogs have extremely sensitive hearing and a sense of smell up to 1,000 times better than humans to compensate for their relatively poor eyesight.

Collie pup grows slowly and doesn't become overweight. Overexercise and injury at a young age may also contribute to this disease. Hip dysplasia is treated with medication and/or surgery, depending on the condition's severity. Some owners also turn to alternative therapies, such as acupuncture.

Osteochondritis dissecans (OCD), abnormal development and growth of joint cartilage, is another genetic malady the Border Collie can develop, although it is more common in larger breeds. The most commonly affected joints are the shoulder, elbow, hock, and knee, in that order. OCD is evidenced by severe lameness, usually manifesting between six and twelve months of age. In mild cases, rest may be all that's needed, while more severe cases may require surgery.

Cerebellar degeneration is an uncommon ailment but does occur as an inherited disease in Border Collies. Puppies appear normal at birth, but signs begin to show at three to five weeks of age: trouble walking, a wide stance, the head bobs or trembles when the pup begins to initiate action. In Border Collies, the disease may continue to be mild and not worsen over time. Dogs often learn to compensate for their tremors, as well. However, these dogs should not be bred, and obviously will not be of working or show quality.

Several eye diseases can affect the Border Collie. Collie eye anomaly (CEA) is an inherited condition that can range in severity from mild sight difficulties to complete blindness. Progressive retinal atrophy (PRA) is even more severe, always resulting in blindness. This increasing degeneration of the cells in the retina usually is not apparent until about two years of age. All dogs should be examined yearly for any eye disorders and certified by the Canine Eye Registration

Foundation before they are bred to be sure no abnormalities are being passed on to future generations.

There are two different forms of epilepsy that can affect the Border Collie. Both cause seizures, ranging from partial to generalized seizures. The first type is primary epilepsy, also known as genetic or true epilepsy. This form of epilepsy usually occurs in dogs one to three years of age, and most likely is caused by a genetic factor. The second form is secondary epilepsy, which is caused by another influence, such as infection, acute injury, ingesting a toxic substance, or a degenerative disease. If a dog experiences one or more seizures per month or tends to have cluster seizures, medication is usually prescribed. This medication must be dispensed faithfully by the owner, with no changes in dose or type of medication without a veterinarian's instructions. Even if you give your dog his medication exactly as prescribed, the seizures may only be lessened, rather than stop altogether. Alternative treatments range from acupuncture to vitamin therapy.

> While Border Collies can be affected by the disorders mentioned here, there are many healthy representatives of the breed just waiting to find a home.

Ceroid lipofuscinosis (storage disease) is extremely serious. Dogs usually are not affected until 18 months of age, at which time an ongoing lipofeescin begins to produce symptoms. Symptoms include unsteadiness, demented behavior, and fear of familiar objects. To date the disease, which is terminal, has been confined to Border Collies from Australian show lines.

You might feel discouraged after reading the above list of health concerns, and wonder how you'll ever find a healthy Border Collie. But remember, while Border Collies can be affected by the disorders mentioned here, there are many healthy representatives of the breed just waiting to find a home. You are better off knowing about potential health problems up front. That way, you can do your best to buy a healthy puppy rather than learn about a disease only when your beloved dog is suffering from it.

Basic Training for Border Collies

By Liz Palika

In This Chapter

○ When to Begin Training
○ The Teaching Process
○ What Every Good Border Collie Needs to Know
○ Housetraining

All dogs, including Border Collies, need training to learn how to behave. When your Border Collie learns to greet people by sitting still, he won't jump up on them. When he learns what the word "stay" means, he will learn to be still and to control his actions. Your Border Collie can learn that chasing the cats is not allowed and that he shouldn't try to herd your children. By learning how to teach your dog, you can then train him so he learns the important rules necessary for good behavior.

Does your Border Collie bark at people outside your yard? If he gets out of the yard, does he refuse to come when you call him? Does he raid the trashcan? Does he jump on your guests? Does he try to herd children and animals? These are not unusual behaviors for a young, untrained dog, but they are unnecessary, potentially dangerous, and annoying behaviors that can be changed (or at least controlled) through training.

> By learning how to teach your dog, you can then train him so he learns the important rules necessary for good behavior.

Your Border Collie tries to herd your children because he was bred to herd sheep and he looks upon your children as his charges; essentially, young things that need protecting. That protective instinct is why he barks at people outside your yard, too. Your Border Collie likes to escape from the yard, so that he can play with the neighborhood kids. He may also try to escape because he's alone; herding dogs are working dogs who need a job to do, and a Border Collie alone without a job is an unhappy dog. He may raid the trashcan because he finds food in it or because it's fun. He jumps on guests because he's excited to see them and they are much taller than he is.

With training, your Border Collie can learn to control himself so that he doesn't react to every impulse. He can learn to sit while greeting people, so he doesn't cover them with muddy paw prints or rip their clothes. He can learn to restrain some of his vocalizations and to ignore the trashcans. Training affects you, too. You will learn why your Border Collie does what he does. You

A well-trained Border Collie will accept your guidance even when he would rather be doing something else.

Basic Commands
Every Dog Should Know

Sit: Your dog's hips move to the ground while his shoulders remain upright.

Down: Your dog lies down on the ground or floor and is still.

Stay: Your dog remains in position (sit or down) while you walk away from him. He holds the stay until you give him permission to move.

Come: Your dog comes to you on the first call despite any distractions.

Walk on the leash: Your dog can walk ahead of you on the leash, but does not pull the leash tight.

Heel: Your dog walks at your left side with his shoulders by your left leg.

will learn to prevent some of these actions, either by changing your routine or preventing the problems from occurring. Training your Border Collie is not something you do to him, but instead is something the two of you do together.

Silly is a Border Collie from Temecula, California. She got her name because as a puppy she was, as her owner, Barbara Wilson says, "A silly whirlwind. She dashed here and there, back and forth, with no reason for her dashing." Barbara and Silly began kindergarten puppy classes when Silly was three months old. They continued with training throughout Silly's first year and when she was under good control, they began herding lessons. "Even though I don't own any sheep and really have no need for a

Start training early in your puppy's life so she learns good behavior instead of bad habits.

What a Trained Dog Knows

A trained dog knows:

❍ The appropriate behaviors allowed with people (no biting, no mouthing, no rough play, and no mounting)

❍ Where to relieve himself and how to ask to go outside

❍ How to greet people properly without jumping on them

❍ To wait for permission to greet people, other dogs, and other pets

❍ How to walk nicely on a leash so that walks are enjoyable

❍ To leave trashcans alone

❍ To leave food alone that is not his (such as on a counter or coffee table)

❍ Not to beg

❍ To chew his toys and not things belonging to people

❍ That destructive behavior is not acceptable

❍ To wait for permission to go through doorways

A trained dog is a happy dog who is secure in his place in the family.

working herding dog, I wanted to give Silly a chance to use her instincts. This is what she was bred to do."

As Barbara and Silly found out, training is an ongoing process. As you learn how to teach your dog, you can apply the training to every aspect of his life, whether he is an active herding dog or simply a family pet. He can learn how to behave at home, to ignore the trashcans, to restrain from chasing the cat, and to chew on his own toys instead of your shoes. He can also learn how to behave while out in public, including greeting people while sitting instead of jumping up. Your dog will learn, through practice and repetition, that training affects his behavior all the time, not just at home and not just during training sessions.

Kindergarten Puppy Class

The ideal time to begin group training is as soon as your Border Collie puppy has had at least two sets of vaccinations; usually between ten and twelve weeks of age. Many veterinarians recommend that you wait even longer. Ask your veterinarian what he thinks. Kindergarten puppy classes introduce the basic obedience commands—sit, down, stay, and come—all geared for the baby puppy's short attention span. Puppy classes also spend time socializing the puppy to other people and other puppies.

When to Begin Training

Ideally, training should begin as soon as you bring home your new Border Collie. If you have an eight- to ten-week-old puppy, that's okay. Your new puppy can begin learning that biting isn't allowed, that she should sit for treats, petting, and meals, and where she should go to relieve herself. By ten weeks of age, you can attach a small leash to her collar and let her drag it around for a few minutes at a time so she gets used to it. Always watch her closely, of course, so that she doesn't get the leash tangled up in something and choke. Young puppies have a very short attention span, but they are capable of learning and are eager students.

Don't let your Border Collie pup do anything now that you don't want her to do later when she is full grown. For example, if you don't want her on your lap when she's 45 pounds of rough paws and hard elbows, don't let her on your lap now. It will be that much harder to change the habit later. Keep in mind as you begin your dog's training that although Border Collies are not large dogs, they are sturdy dogs with an intelligent and forceful personality.

Basic Obedience Class

Most obedience instructors invite puppies to begin the basic obedience class after they have graduated from a puppy class. Dogs (or older puppies) over four months of age who have not attended a puppy class also attend this basic obedience class. This class teaches the traditional obedience commands—sit, down, stay, come, and heel. In addition, most instructors spend time discussing problem behaviors such as jumping on people, barking, digging, chewing, and other destructive activities. A group class is also beneficial for your Border Collie in that it helps her learn to control herself around other dogs and people.

If you have adopted a Border Collie who is an older puppy or an adult, you can still begin training right away. Your new dog will need time to get used to you and her new home; however, training helps your new dog learn what you expect of her and, as a result, makes that adjustment easier. Start teaching the rules to her from the first. If you don't want her on the furniture, never allow her there, and don't make any excuses, such as, "Oh, it's cold tonight, so I'll let her come up and cuddle!" If you aren't consistent, she won't be either!

Is It Ever Too Late?

Although training is most effective when started early in the dog's life and practiced consistently as she grows up, that doesn't mean it's too late to train an adult Border Collie. The downfall to starting training later in the dog's life is that you then have to break bad habits as well as teach new commands. With a young puppy, you're starting with a blank slate and you can teach the new be-

Private Training

Private training is normally recommended for Border Collies with severe behavior problems, such as biting, growling, dog aggression, or uncontrolled behavior. A private trainer works one-on-one with your dog either at your home or at the trainer's facility. This training can usually be tailored to your dog's individual needs.

haviors before she learns bad habits. If you've ever had to break a bad habit (smoking, for example), you know it can be difficult. Nevertheless, in most Border Collies up to about eight years of age, you can, with consistent training and lots of patience and positive reinforcement, control most bad habits.

If your dog is older than eight years of age, your success at changing bad habits will be much more limited. You can teach new commands—sit, down, stay, and heel—and your dog will be able to learn these without too much trouble. However, Border Collies who have not learned to consistently come when called by the time they are eight years old will probably never be reliable.

Sometimes there are behavior problems that are just too severe and are impossible to solve. A habit may be too deeply ingrained or the stimulus causing the behavior is too strong. For example, as you now know, Border Collies like to herd; this is a very strong instinct. The family cats and your children won't appreciate being herded, however, especially since it involves nipping, a common Border Collie technique. Most Border Collies can learn to control this instinct when the kids and cats are not moving quickly, but sometimes a fast-moving cat or playing children is too much stimulation. It is best to protect the cats and kids from your dog's strong instinct. When the kids are outside playing, keep the dog inside. When the family cats are playing with their fishing pole toy in the house, keep the Border Collie outside.

Basic Dog Psychology

Archeologists have found evidence showing that humans and the ancestors of today's dogs, wolves, share a history dating back thousands of years. At some point, for some reason that we don't yet understand, humans and some individual wolves decided to cooperate. Perhaps the wolves, being themselves efficient hunters, aided the human hunters. Perhaps the wolves took advantage of the human's garbage heap. We really don't know why this cooperation occurred, we just know that it did happen and the result was domesticated dogs.

Families and Packs

In the wild, wolves live in packs. The pack is made up of a dominant male, a dominant female, several subordinate adults, a juvenile or two, and the latest litter of pups. Only the two dominant animals breed; the others help protect and provide for the youngsters. This pack has some important social rules—including the no-breeding rule (except for the two leaders)—and these rules are seldom broken. If a youngster breaks a rule inadvertently or on purpose, he is corrected fairly, but firmly. The adult's correction may consist of a growl, posturing over the youngster, or even a physical correction such as pinning the youngster to the ground. If an adult breaks a rule, the dominant male or female gives the correction and it is more forceful than that delivered to the young.

After all, an adult is expected to know the rules and follow them. An adult who continually creates havoc by breaking the rules may be exiled from the pack.

Packs are usually fairly harmonious. Each member knows his or her place and keeps to it. When an adult dies, becomes disabled, or leaves the pack, however, there may be some posturing or fighting until the new pack order is established.

> At some point, for some reason that we don't yet understand, humans and some individual wolves decided to cooperate.

Dogs fit into our family life because they have this pack history. Our family is a social organization similar to a pack, although our families have significant differences from a wolf pack and vary from each other depending upon our culture. We do normally have an adult male and female, although today there may be just one adult. The rules of our family are often quite chaotic. In a wolf pack, the leaders always eat first, but in our families, people often eat any time and in no specific order. These family rules, or lack of rules, can be quite confusing to our dogs.

As herding dogs who take direction and orders from the shepherd, Border Collies need the structure and direction found in the pack. They also need something to take care of, and it doesn't matter whether it's a flock of sheep, the dog's human family, or even another dog. A Border Collie left alone, without direction and without something to take care of, will be an unhappy dog and, potentially, a problem dog.

What Does It Mean to Be Top Dog?

"Top dog" is a slang term for the leader of the pack. In the wolf pack we discussed, the top dog is the dominant male or dominant female, often called the alpha male or alpha female. In your family, there should be no confusion; the top dog should be you, the dog's owner, and your dog should maintain a subordinate position to any additional human family members.

Often during adolescence, a Border Collie with a particularly bold personality may make a bid for leadership of the family. Adolescence typically strikes at sexual maturity, usually between eight and twelve months of age. Luckily, Border Collies tend to be eager to maintain pack harmony and it is normally fairly easy for most owners to maintain leadership

Don't let your dog use his body language to show dominance. Your dog should recognize you (and your children) as above him in the family pack.

of the family pack. Since eating first is the leader's prerogative and is an action the dog readily understands, the owner should always eat before feeding the dog. You should also go through all doorways first and have your dog follow you. Make sure you can roll your Border Collie over to give him a tummy rub without any fussing on the dog's part. A dog who takes over the leadership of the home can make life miserable for all concerned—this is when growling, barking, biting, and mounting behaviors become apparent—so make sure you maintain your position as the dog's leader.

Although it is very important that your dog regard you as the leader or top dog, don't look upon every action your dog makes as a dominance challenge. Most of the time your Border Collie won't care about his position in the family pack; he knows you're in charge. During adolescence, and for more dominant personalities, training is very important, however.

You Are the Top Dog!

There are several behaviors that in dog language say, "I am the boss!" It is important to send the right signals to you Border Collie, and by using the following tips, you should be able to avoid any confusion and create a good relationship with your dog.

○ Always eat first!

○ Go through doors and openings first; block your dog from charging through ahead of you.

○ Go up stairs first; don't let him charge ahead of you and then look down at you.

○ Give your dog permission to do things, even if he was going to do it anyway. If he picks up his ball,

tell him, "Get your ball! Good boy to get your ball!"

○ Practice your training regularly.

○ Have your dog roll over for a tummy rub daily.

○ Do not play rough games with your Border Collie; no wrestling, no tug-of-war.

○ Never let your dog stand above you or put his paws on your shoulders. These are dominant positions.

The Teaching Process

Teaching your dog is not a difficult project, although at times it may seem to be nearly impossible. Most dogs, especially most Border Collies, want to be good—they just need to learn what you want them to do and what you don't. Therefore, most of the teaching process consists of communication. You need to reward the behaviors you want your dog to continue doing, and you need to interrupt the behaviors you wish to stop. Let's use the herding behavior as an example again. Should you see your Border Collie lower her head and stare at your cat (that stare, called "eye," is the first step in herding behavior), you can interrupt that behavior by telling her, "Sweetie, no!" in a firm, no-nonsense tone of voice. When she lifts her head, looks at you and sits, praise her in a higher than normal tone of voice, "Good girl!"

Did you notice I emphasized two different tones of voice? Like us, dogs are verbal animals and are very aware of different tones of voice. When the leader of a wolf pack lets a subordinate know that she made a mistake, the leader uses a deep growl to convey that message. When things are fine, the pack has hunted, and all is well with the world, the leader may convey that with higher pitched barks or yelps. When you copy this technique—using a deep, growling voice for letting the dog know she's made a mistake and a higher pitched tone of voice to reinforce good behavior—your dog doesn't have to stop and translate that information. She just understands.

> Most dogs, especially most Border Collies, want to be good—they just need to learn what you want them to do and what you don't.

Don't confuse high and low tones of voice with volume, though. Your dog can hear very well—much better than you can—and it's not necessary to yell at her. Instead, simply sound like you mean what you say.

As you begin teaching your dog, remember that human words have no meaning to your dog until she's taught that they do. She's probably already begun learning some words, though. She may know: treat, cookie, ball, toy, walk, car, and bed. She may have already learned: leash, outside, go potty, inside, and no bite! But other words are just sounds, just so much meaningless gobbledygook. During training, you are teaching her that words like sit, down, come, and heel have meanings that are important to her.

So how can you teach your Border Collie that these sounds have meanings? First, repeat the word as you help your dog perform the act. As you help her sit, say, "Sweetie, sit!" You can reinforce it after she has done as you asked by praising her, "Good girl to sit!" By using the word, your dog will learn that the word has meaning, she should pay attention when she hears that word, and she should do whatever the word requires her to.

A treat can be a wonderful training tool to help teach your dog to pay attention to you. When he looks at you, praise him, give him the treat, and then follow through with other training.

Just as communication is a big part of the training process, so is your timing. You must use your voice to praise your dog as she is doing something right—AS she is doing it, not after the fact. The same thing applies to letting your dog know that she's doing something you don't want her to be doing. Use your voice to let her know she's making a mistake AS she begins to stare at the cat. Don't wait until she's already in motion. Then, when she stops or decides not to herd (or stare), praise her for making the right choice. When your timing is correct, there is no misunderstanding; your dog knows exactly what message you are trying to convey.

Don't rely on corrections (verbal or otherwise) to train your dog. We all, dogs and people alike, learn just as much from our successes as we do from our mistakes, and we are more likely to repeat our successes! Don't hesitate to set your dog up for success, so you can praise and reward her. If you want to keep your Border Collie off the furniture, have her lie down at your feet

Training Vocabulary

Listed below are terms you may encounter while training your Border Collie.

Positive reinforcement: Anything your dog likes that you can use to reward good behavior, including treats, praise, toys, tennis balls, and petting.

Praise: Words spoken in a higher than normal tone of voice to reward your dog for something she did right; part of positive reinforcement.

Lure: A food treat or toy used to help position the dog as you want her, or to gain her cooperation as you teach her.

Interruption: The moment when you catch your dog in the act of doing something and you stop her. This can be verbal, in a deeper than normal tone of voice, or it can be a sharp sound, such as the sound made by dropping a book on the floor. An interruption stops the behavior as it is happening.

Correction: Usually a deep, growly verbal sound or words to let your dog know that she has made a mistake, as she is doing it. A correction can serve as an interruption, but you can also let your dog know that you dislike what she is doing. It should be firm enough to get your dog's attention and stop the behavior at that moment, and that's all, no firmer. Another form of correction is a snap and release of the leash.

and hand her a toy to keep her busy BEFORE she jumps up on the furniture. You can then reward her for good behavior instead of correcting her for bad.

A properly timed correction lets your dog know when she's making a mistake, but doesn't tell her what to do instead. Let's say your Border Collie is chewing on your leather shoes. If you simply correct her, you are conveying to her that chewing on your shoes is wrong, but you aren't teaching her what she can chew on. And since chewing is important for dogs, that's an im-

Corrections should be given as the dog is making the mistake, not after the fact.

portant message. So instead of just correcting her, you can correct her (to show her what is wrong), then take her to her toys and show her something of hers to chew on (to show her what is right), and, finally, praise her when she picks up one of her toys (to reinforce a good choice).

Teaching Your Border Collie to Be Handled

Your Border Collie is a very intelligent dog, but he still needs help caring for himself. You must be able to brush him, comb him, bathe him, trim his toenails, and clean his ears. When he's sick or hurt, you must be able to administer to him, whether it's cleaning when he has an infection, caring for his stitches after an injury, or washing out his eyes if dirt gets in them.

It's important to teach your Border Collie to accept handling of his body before there's an emergency. If you teach him this early (as a puppy or as soon as you bring him home), then when he has a problem that requires special care, you will have built that bond of trust already and he will know to relax and let you care for him.

You can do this with the following exercise. Sit on the floor and invite your Border Collie to lie down on the floor between your legs, on your lap, or in front of you. Start by giving him a tummy rub to relax him. When he's relaxed, progress to giving him a full-body massage. Begin the massage at his muzzle, rubbing your

The Training Process

To teach a new command:

❍ Show the dog what to do with a lure, your hands, or your voice.

❍ Praise him for doing it and reward him with the lure, if you used one.

❍ Correct him for mistakes only when he knows and understands the command and chooses not to do it.

To correct problem behavior:

❍ Prevent the problem from happening when possible.

❍ Set the dog up for success by teaching him to do something else and then rewarding it.

❍ Interrupt the behavior when you catch the dog in the act. Let him know he made a mistake.

❍ Show him the appropriate behavior and then reward or praise him for doing it.

fingers gently over the skin and checking his teeth. Move up his head, touching the skin around his eyes, then go on to his ears. Handle each ear flap, look in each ear, and massage around the base of each ear. As you massage, look for any problems. Look for discharge from the eyes or nose. Look for dirt, excess wax, or redness in the ears. Let your fingers feel for lumps, bumps, or bruises on his skin.

Continue in this same manner over your Border Collie's whole body. If he protests at any time, go back to the tummy rub for a moment, let him relax, and then continue. Do not let him turn this into a wrestling match; instead, keep it calm, relaxing, and gentle.

Do this exercise daily and incorporate your grooming regime into it. Even though Border Collie's have a silky, easy-to-care-for coat, they still need daily grooming. A daily brushing can greatly lessen the hair shed in the house. In addition, if you groom him daily, you can find things, such as fleas or ticks, before they become major problems. If your dog needs medication or first-aid treatments, you can deliver those while massaging, too. Simply make it part of the massage and don't let it turn into a fight.

A tummy rub can help relax your dog if he's over-stimulated. You can also follow through with any needed grooming. In addition, this is a wonderful time for bonding with your dog.

There is a side effect of this massage you will enjoy. When you're finished, your Border Collie will be totally relaxed, like a limp noodle. So plan ahead and do it when you want him to be quiet and relaxed. If he's hyper and overstimulated in the evening when you would like to watch a favorite television show, sit on the floor, massage him, and then let him sleep while you watch your show!

The Importance of Good Socialization

Socialization is a vital part of raising a healthy, mentally sound Border Collie. A young Border Collie who has been introduced to a variety of people of different ages and ethnic backgrounds will be a social dog, one who is happy to meet people and is unafraid. A Border Collie who has been kept in the backyard too much will be fearful. He may grow up afraid of children, or of senior citizens. A dog who has never met people of a different ethnic background than his owners may be afraid of different people. A Border Collie who is afraid can become aggressive out of fear; these so-called "fear biters" are dangerous. A dog who

Introduce your dog to other friendly, well–behaved, healthy dogs. Avoid rowdy, poorly behaved, aggressive dogs; they could scare your dog and ruin the socialization you've done so far.

bites out of fear often doesn't think before he acts. Most of these fear biters have to be destroyed eventually because of their danger to people.

Socialization also refers to meeting other dogs and pets. Your Border Collie should have opportunities to play with well-behaved dogs, so he learns what it is to be well-behaved and how to act around other dogs. Ideally, your Border Collie should also meet friendly cats, rabbits, ferrets, and other pets. Always protect your Border Collie by introducing him to pets that are known to be friendly to dogs, and protect those pets from your Border Collie. Don't let him chase them.

Socialization also includes helping your Border Collie to be comfortable with the sights, sounds, and smells of the world around him. Let him see and hear the trash truck that comes each week. If he's afraid of it, have him on-leash when the truck comes and let the driver offer him a dog treat. Let him watch the neighborhood kids go by on in-line skates; just don't let him bark or chase them. Walk your Border Collie past the construction crew mending the potholes in the road. Let him watch the men work and smell the hot asphalt. Take him to lots of different places, so he can smell new smells and see new sights. The more he sees, hears, and smells, the better his coping skills.

Don't overload your Border Collie, though, by trying to introduce him to everything all at once. You can start socialization when your puppy is nine to ten weeks of age by introducing him to calm, friendly family members and neighbors. Keep in mind that behaviorists suggest that imprinting should be done before

12 weeks of age, so it is important your Border Collie be introduced to and act nice toward kids, cats, or others early in life. Let these people pet him and cuddle him, but don't allow rough games; keep the experiences very positive. Week by week, you can introduce your puppy to more people and different things.

Should your Border Collie puppy be frightened of something, don't hug him, pet him, and try to reassure him. Your puppy will assume those comforting words are praise for being afraid. Instead, use a happy tone of voice, "What was that?" and walk up to whatever scared him. Don't force him to walk up to it, just let him see you do it. For example, if your puppy sees a trashcan rolling in the street after the wind has blown it over, and he appears worried by it, hold on to his leash (to keep him from running away) and walk up to the trashcan. Ask your puppy (in an upbeat tone of voice), "What's this?" Touch the trashcan. Pat it several times so your puppy can see you touch it. If he walks up to it, praise him for his bravery!

> You can start socialization when your puppy is nine to ten weeks of age by introducing him to calm, friendly family members and neighbors.

A Crate Can Help Your Training

Originally designed as travel cages, crates have become very popular training tools for a variety of reasons.

Using a crate to confine your baby Border Collie during the night and for short periods during the day helps him learn and develop more bowel and bladder control since his instincts tell him to keep his bed clean. He is not going to want to relieve himself in his crate.

A crate helps your puppy develop bowel and bladder control, prevents accidents from happening, and becomes your puppy's special place.

Using the crate to confine your Border Collie when you cannot supervise him prevents him from doing something you don't want him to. Your Border Collie can't chew up your shoes, raid the trashcan, or shred the sofa cushions if he's confined to the crate. By preventing undesirable actions from occurring, you are also preventing bad habits from developing. As he grows up, you can gradually give him more freedom; but not until he's mentally mature—about two years old for most Border Collies.

Many first-time dog owners resist the idea of a crate, saying it's too much like a jail. But dogs like small, secure spaces, especially when sleeping. Most dogs quickly learn to like their crate and it becomes a very special place. My dogs continue to use their crates (voluntarily) into old age because the individual crates are each dog's personal space where they can retreat to when tired, overwhelmed, or when they don't feel well.

Introduce the crate by opening the door and tossing a treat or toy inside. As the dog goes in, say the command phrase you wish to use, such as "Sweetie, go to bed!" or "Sweetie, kennel!" When he grabs the treat or toy, praise him, "Good boy to go to bed! Yeah!" Repeat this phrase several times. When mealtime comes around, feed your dog his next meal in the crate, placing the food to the back of the crate, but don't close the door yet. Let him go in and come out on his own.

At night, put the crate in your bedroom next to your bed so your Border Collie can smell you, hear you, and know that you

Choosing the Right Crate

Crates come in two basic types. A plastic crate gives the dog more security because of its solid sides, but the solid sides make these crates bulky and they don't break down much when you need to store them. The wire-sided cages usually fold down into a smaller, flat package, although they are still quite heavy. The wire sides provide more ventilation for the dog, but are open and don't provide much security. To choose the right kind of crate, consider your needs. Are you going to have to move the crate much? Are you short of storage space? Consider your dog as well—does he need more air flow or more security? Choose a crate that gives your Border Collie room to stand up, move around, lie down, and stretch out.

are close by. He will be less apt to fuss during the night when he's close to you. You will also be able to hear him if he needs to go outside during the night. In addition, by being close to you, your dog gets to spend eight hours with you. In these busy times, this is precious time!

Let your Border Collie spend the night in his crate and a few hours here and there in it during the day. Other than at night, your Border Collie should spend no more than three to four hours at a time in the crate; he needs time to run and play during the day.

What Every Good Border Collie Needs to Know

Dogs together have their own rules for social behavior. Unfortunately, those rules are not necessarily the same as your own. In a dog pack, it's normal to sniff each other's rear end, for example, whereas we (people) consider that extremely poor manners—even when a dog does it! Your Border Collie needs to learn the social rules you will require of her, so life with her is enjoyable rather than embarrassing.

No Jumping

Border Collies are not big dogs, but they are very athletic. Although a Border Collie jumping up on an adult is probably not going to knock anyone over, the dog's muddy paws will not be appreciated. A Border Collie jumping on a child or a senior citizen with poor balance could cause harm. Therefore, it's usually a good idea to teach your Border Collie not to jump on people when she greets them.

> There are several different ways you can use the sit to stop the jumping up.

If you teach your Border Collie to sit each time she greets people (anyone, including you, your family, guests, and people on the street), you get rid of the jumping behavior; she cannot jump on them and sit at the same time. Sit becomes a replacement action for jumping up. We'll talk about the mechanics of teaching the sit later in this chapter.

There are several different ways you can use the sit to stop the jumping up. First, if your dog doesn't have her leash on, as when you come home from work, make sure you greet her with empty hands. As your dog dashes up to you, grab her buckle collar (which she should be wearing with her ID tags), tell her, "Sweetie, no jump! Sit!" and with your hand on her collar help her sit. Keep your hands on her as you praise her for sitting. If she tries to jump up, your hands are on her to prevent it and you can continue to teach her.

The leash is also a good training tool to help you control your dog. When guests come over, ask them to wait outside for a moment (weather permitting, of course!) while you leash your dog. Once your Border Collie is leashed, let your guests in. Make sure your dog sits before your guests pet her. If they pet your Border Collie before she sits, they are essentially rewarding her for bad behavior. If she jumps up, correct her, "No jump!" and have her sit again.

You can do the same thing when you and your dog are out in public. Have her sit before anyone pets her. If she's too excited and cannot hold still, don't let people pet her until you make her sit. If people protest, "Oh, I don't mind if she jumps!" explain that you are trying to teach her good social manners.

To Bark or Not to Bark

All dogs bark; it's their way of communicating. However, most neighbors do not appreciate a dog who barks excessively. The first thing you need to do is teach your Border Collie a command that means "quiet" and enforce it while you're at home. Ask a neighbor to help you. Have him come over to your house and ring the doorbell. When your dog goes dashing to the door, making noise, tell her, "Sweetie, quiet!" as you grab her collar. If she stops making noise, praise her, "Good girl to be quiet!" If she continues making noise, gently close her muzzle with your hand as you tell her to be quiet. When she stops, praise her. If she barks again, repeat this process.

Many Border Collies will learn this command with repeated training. However, some are a little more persistent about making noise. With these dogs, the correction needs to be a little stronger. Fill a spray bottle with a vinegar-water mix (one ounce of vinegar to seven ounces of water). There should be just

Anti-Bark Collars

Several different types of bark-control collars are available to dog owners. Some give the dog an electric shock or jolt when she barks, some make a high-pitched sound, and one gives off a squirt of citronella. The citronella works on the same principle as the vinegar/water squirt bottle: The smell disrupts the dog's concentration and is annoying enough that she stops barking. This is the collar I recommend for most Border Collies; it is very effective for the majority of dogs and is a humane training tool.

enough vinegar to smell. If it smells too strong (to your nose), dilute it a little more.

Then, when your Border Collie charges to the door barking, follow her and quietly tell her, "Sweetie, quiet!" If she stops, praise her. If she doesn't, use a narrow of water and vinegar and aim it at her nose, making sure to avoid her eyes and mouth. Your dog will find the vinegar smell disgusting and stop barking to think about it. As soon as she stops barking, praise her. The squirt bottle works as an interruption because your dog has a very sensitive sense of smell and won't like the smell of the vinegar. It can stop the bad behavior (the barking) without giving an overly harsh correction. Be careful, though, to keep the spray out of your dog's eyes. If you do accidentally spray the solution into her eyes and redness or pain occurs, a visit to the veterinarian is warranted.

Use the same training techniques (verbal correction, collar, closing the muzzle, or the squirt bottle) to teach your Border Collie to be quiet around the house. When she is reliable in the house, move the training outside. If she barks at the gate when kids are playing out front, go outside the gate, and correct her with a verbal command and a squirt from the bottle if necessary. Always, of course, praise her when she's quiet.

No Begging

Border Collies are quick to pick up on a person who is an easy mark; and with those large soulful brown eyes, who can resist a Border Collie? You should! There is no reason any Border Collie should beg for food from people who are eating. Begging is a bad habit and one that usually escalates to worse behavior. Your dog may start by picking up food that has fallen to floor, then progress to pawing at a hand or leg, trying to solicit a handout. Eventually, your dog actively begs and makes a nuisance of herself. Sometimes it goes so far that she steals food from the kids' hands or off the table.

Fortunately, this is an easy habit to break, although it requires consistency from all family members. Later in this chapter you will learn how to teach the down/stay command. When your Border Collie has learned the down/stay, simply have her down/stay in a particular spot away from the table (or where people are eating) and make her hold her position while people are eating. By teaching her to lie down and stay in a corner of the room, so that she's not underfoot and can't beg under the table, you are breaking the bad

Teach your dog to hold a down/stay while you're eating. He will learn that he gets to eat when you are finished, so he must be patient.

habit. When everyone has finished eating, the dog can then be given her meal or a treat in her bowl away from the table.

No Exile

I don't like to exile dogs to the backyard while people are eating. Although this is much easier than training your dog—just put the dog outside and close the door—it has a tendency to build frustration in her. She knows you're eating and she knows she's been exiled. That is enough right there to cause frustration. When you let your dog in the house later, she's going to be wild!

If you allow your dog to remain in the house, however, and require her to behave, she learns self-control. She knows she will get something to eat after the people are finished, so she learns to wait.

When you begin teaching this new rule, use the leash and collar on your Border Collie. That way, if she makes a mistake and tries to beg (and she will initially!), you can use the leash to take her back to the spot where you want her to lie down and stay. Correct her as many times as you must until she holds the position or, in a worst case scenario, the meal is over.

No Biting

All it takes is one bite and your Border Collie could be taken from you and euthanized. All dogs owners must take this issue seriously because right now the legal system works against dogs, not for them. There have been far too many serious dog-bite incidents in which people, especially children, have been severely mauled or killed.

A dog bite is legally defined as the dog's open mouth touching skin. Puncture wounds or broken skin are not required to qualify it as a bite. Vicious intent is not necessary either. If your Border Collie is in the backyard and decides to grab the neighbor's son (who has the dog's toy), that is a bite, even if the skin is not bro-

No Rough Games!

Border Collies are not large dogs, but they are tough, athletic dogs who like to play and love to play rough. Unfortunately, some rough games, such as wrestling and tug-of-war, give your dog the wrong message about how she should regard or treat people. Wrestling teaches her to use her strength against you, to fight you, and to protest when you hold her tight. Tug-of-war teaches her to use the strength of her jaws and her body against you. Neither game teaches her to respect you or be gentle with you.

After too many of these rough-and-tumble games, every time you try to trim her toenails, a wrestling game will ensue. Or when you want her to hold still, she will fight you. When you try to take something out of her mouth, she may decide to play tug-of-war with it. Bad behavior!

Instead of playing these detrimental games, play hide-and-seek or retrieving games.

ken. Or even if your Border Collie decides to play cow-dog, and gives a nip in an effort to herd the child, he has technically bitten and may be considered a vicious dog.

It's important to teach all dogs that teeth are not allowed to touch skin—ever! That means your dog is not to grab your hands when she wants you to do something. Nor should she use her mouth to protest when you're taking a toy away from her. To keep your dog safe, never allow her to use her mouth in such a way that her teeth or her mouth itself touch skin.

It's easy to teach young puppies that they should not use their mouth. Take your hand away as you correct your puppy verbally. A consistent "No bite!" in a deep, growly tone of voice is usually all that is needed. If your Border Collie puppy tries to use her mouth during playtime, tell her "No bite!" and get up and walk away— end the game. If she bites hard, say "Ouch!!!" in a high-pitched,

Time Out!

Sometimes when puppies are corrected for what is natural behavior to them (such as mouthing), they throw a temper tantrum. If your puppy should throw herself around, flail, and act like a cornered wild animal, don't mess with her or try to stop it. Instead, simply put her in her kennel crate for a time out. Don't yell at her, scold her, or try and reassure her—just put her in her crate, close the door, and walk away. In 15 or 20 minutes, if she's quiet and calm, let her out, but don't make a big fuss over her—just open the door and let her out.

Just like most human children, most puppies will throw one or two tantrums sometime during puppyhood. If you give in to it, your puppy will learn that this horrible behavior works. If you give her a time out, however, she'll learn that this behavior doesn't work and is not rewarding.

hurt tone of voice, followed by a deep growly "No bite!" If the puppy is persistent about using her mouth, grab hold of her collar with one hand while you close her mouth with the other hand as you tell her "No bite!"

If you have trouble teaching your Border Collie to stop using her mouth, if she seems intent on mouthing you, or if you have a gut feeling that you may be bitten by her one day, call a professional trainer or behaviorist to help you. Don't wait until a bite occurs.

Digging

Dogs dig for a number of reasons, all of which are very natural to them. As pack denning animals, Border Collies like a tight, close, snug place to cuddle up in and a hole in the ground is just right. As digging is so natural, you should offer your Border Collie a spot where she can dig to her heart's content—maybe out behind

Too Many Toys?

If your dog is a chewer, don't try to change his behavior by giving him lots of toys. Too many toys will give him the idea that he can chew on anything and everything because virtually everything is his! Instead, give him just two or three toys at a time. If he likes toys, you can buy him new ones, but rotate the toys so he has only two or three at a time. On Monday, you could give him a rawhide, a squeaky toy, and a Kong toy. On Tuesday, substitute a new rawhide, a rope tug toy, and a tennis ball. By rotating the toys, you can keep him interested in them without overwhelming him.

When your dog picks up one of his toys, rather than something of yours, praise him! Tell him what a smart dog he is and how proud you are of him! Really go overboard. When he learns this is a good choice, he'll be more likely to repeat the behavior later.

Remember that if you find he's chewed something up earlier, don't punish him. After-the-fact corrections don't work.

the garage where it won't be too obvious to you. Dig up this area and make the dirt soft. Bury a few dog toys and treats and invite your dog to dig there.

In the rest of the yard, fill in any holes she has made and spread some grass seed. If she goes back to one or two holes and re-digs them, crumple up some hardware cloth (wire mesh) and put that in the hole. Then fill it in with dirt. When she tries to re-dig that hole, the wire mesh will prevent her from doing so and will not feel at all comfortable on her paws.

Destructive Chewing

As with many other undesirable activities, destructive chewing is a natural behavior for puppies. Most Border Collie puppies begin to chew when they're teething—losing the baby teeth and getting in their adult teeth. The gums are sore and chewing seems to help relieve the discomfort. Unfortunately, at this point many puppies learn that chewing is fun. While it may be fun for the puppy, chewing can be incredibly destructive and costly. In addition, the puppy who chews things will inevitably swallow something she shouldn't, so chewing also is dangerous. Therefore, you need to control this bad habit.

You can prevent a lot of bad behavior by keeping your puppy close to you when she's in the house. Close doors or put up baby gates; don't let her have free run of the house. If she's under your supervision, you can teach her what is right to chew on and what is wrong. When she picks up one of her toys, praise, "Good girl to have a toy! Good toy!"

> If you are unable to solve a problem yourself, don't hesitate to call a professional trainer or behaviorist for help.

When she picks up something she shouldn't, correct her by taking it away, walking her to one of her toys, and saying, "Here. This is yours." When she picks up her toy, praise her.

As with many other problem behaviors, prevention is very important. Keep your Border Collie close to you, close closet doors, keep the dirty clothes picked up, and empty the trashcans. If you can prevent her from getting into trouble as a puppy, when she grows up, she won't have any bad habits and won't be tempted to try these destructive behaviors.

Other Bad Habits

Border Collies are usually pretty good dogs. Their biggest problems are generally herding kids and cats, jumping on people, and not coming when called. Training can help all three of these problems if you are consistent with it.

If your Border Collie has some other behavior problems, you can approach them in the same manner we did these. What is your dog doing? Why is she doing it? When does she do it? Can you use your training to teach her? Can you prevent it?

If you are unable to solve a problem yourself, don't hesitate to call a professional trainer or behaviorist for help. Ask your veterinarian for a recommendation. Effectively correcting a problem will only enhance the bond between you and your Border Collie.

Housetraining

Housetraining your Border Collie is primarily a matter of taking him outside when he needs to go, making sure he relieves himself while out there, teaching him a phrase that tells him to try to go, and then restricting his freedom until he is reliably trained.

Using a Crate to Housetrain

When I introduced the crate earlier, I said that a crate is a wonderful tool to help you housetrain your Border Collie. Since dogs are born with an instinct to keep their bed clean and will toddle away from their bed as soon as their legs can support them, the crate helps the puppy develop bowel and bladder control. Of course, you must never leave your dog in the crate too long; if you do, he will have to relieve himself and will be upset at doing so in such a confined space.

Housetraining Guidelines

Using a crate is not all you need to do to housetrain a baby puppy, older puppy, or adult Border Collie. You need to teach him to go outside and to relieve himself outside where you want him to. Your dog also needs to learn your phrase for telling him to do his business.

Just sending your dog outside won't work. If you just send him out there alone, how do you know whether or not he's relieved himself before you let him back in? He may have spent the time watching the birds at the feeder rather than relieving himself and, once you let him in, he may remember his bladder is full and then—whoosh, it's all over your floor!

> Do not consider your Border Collie reliably housetrained until he's eight or nine months of age and hasn't had an accident in months!

You need to go outside with your dog. When he's sniffing and circling, tell him quietly, "Go potty!" (Use whatever word or phrase works for you.) When he does what he needs to do, praise him, "Good boy to go potty!" Once he's done what he needs to do, bring him inside with you, but still restrict his freedom. Close doors or put up baby gates to keep him close. Do not consider him reliably housetrained until he's eight or nine months of age and hasn't had an accident in months! If he's younger and hasn't had any accidents, it just means you're doing everything right!

When Accidents Happen

If you catch your puppy in the act of relieving himself inside, you can let him know he's making a mistake, "Oh, no! Bad boy!" and take him outside. If you find a puddle and he's already moved away, however, don't correct him. It's already too late.

Housetraining Timetable

Your Border Collie will need to relieve himself after:

- Waking up
- Eating
- Drinking
- Playtime
- Every two to three hours in between

Be alert; when your puppy is sniffing the floor and circling, grab him quick and take him outside!

Keep in mind that your Border Collie must relieve himself; the act of urination or defecation is not wrong. Instead, when there is an accident, it is because the place he did it was wrong. If you correct him after the fact, he could easily misunderstand you and think that the act of urination or defection is what you're angry about. Then you'll have a dog who sneaks off behind the furniture to relieve himself.

Go outside with him, praise him when he does it outside, and then supervise him in the house. Correct only those accidents that you catch happening.

Asking to Go Outside

Because so many dogs have a hard time controlling their barking or howling, I do not like to teach any dog to bark to go outside. Why emphasize a behavior that might already be a problem? Your dog needs a way to let you know he has to go outside, however, so we'll teach him to ring some bells instead.

Go to a craft store and get two or three bells (each one to two inches across). Hang them from the doorknob or handle of the door where the dog goes in and out. Make sure they hang at your dog's nose level. Cut a hot dog into tiny pieces and rub one piece on the bells. Invite your dog to sniff it. When the bell rings, praise him, take him outside, and give him a tiny piece of hot dog outside.

Repeat this three or four times per session for a few days. When he starts ringing the bells on his own, praise him enthusiastically and let him outside!

Five Basic Obedience Commands

Every dog should know these five basic obedience commands. These are the foundation for good behavior; with these commands, your Border Collie learns self-control and how to behave well at home and in public.

Sit

The sit exercise teaches your Border Collie to hold still—a hard concept for many young Border Collies! When he sits, he isn't jumping on people; you can feed him without him knocking the bowl out of your hands; and you can get his attention so that he can do other things. This is an important lesson in self-control.

There are several different ways to teach your dog to sit; as long as the method is humane and works, it's all right to use it. One of the easiest methods relies on a

Hold a treat in your hand and let your dog sniff it. Then take the treat up and back over his head. As his head comes up, his hips will go down.

treat as a lure. Tell your Border Collie, "Sweetie, sit!" as you take a treat and hold it above his nose. Move that hand back toward his tail, over his head. As his head goes up to follow the treat, his hips will go

When your dog sits and his hips are on the ground, praise him.

down. As he sits, praise him, "Good boy to sit!"

Another easy method involves shaping the dog into position. With your Border Collie close to you, tell him, Sweetie, sit!" as you place one hand on his chest under his neck and push gently up and back as the other hand slides down his hips and tucks them under. Think of a teeter-totter—up and back at the front and down and under at the rear. As you position your Border Collie in the sit, praise him, "Good boy to sit!"

With one hand on the front of the dog's chest under his neck, push gently up and back as you slide the other hand down his hips. At the same time, tell your dog to sit. Praise him when he does.

Down

When combined with the stay command (to follow), the down teaches your Border Collie to be still for gradually increased periods of time. You can have him lie down and stay while people are eating, so he isn't begging under the table. You can have him lie at your feet while you're watching television in the evening; or you can have him stay quietly while guests are visiting. The down/stay is a very useful command.

Have your dog sit and then show him a treat. Tell him to lie down as you take the treat from his nose down to the ground in front of his paws.

Start by having your Border Collie sit. Once he's sitting, show him a treat in your right hand. As you tell him, "Sweetie, down!" move the treat from his nose to the floor right in front of his

As your dog lies down, praise him.

front paws. Lead his nose to the floor. As his head follows the treat, your left hand can be resting on his shoulders to help him lie down. If he tries to pop back up, your left hand can keep him down. Once he's down, praise him and give him the treat. If he doesn't follow the treat down, gently pull his front legs forward and shape his body into the down position. Try to help him do the command himself rather than physically positioning him.

If your dog doesn't lie down for the treat, just scoop his front legs out from under him and gently lay him down. Praise him even though you're helping him do it.

Stay

You want your Border Collie to understand that stay means hold still. You can use this command with both the sit and the down, but you should never ask him to sit/stay for nearly as long as you ask him to hold a down/stay; the down/stay is an easier position to hold for longer periods of time. In either position, he should hold it until you give him permission to move.

Start by having your Border Collie sit. With an open palm toward his nose, tell him, "Sweetie, stay!" At the same time, exert a little pressure backward (toward his tail) with the leash, so he won't be as apt to follow you when you take a step away from him. When he seems to be holding still, release the pressure of the leash. After a few seconds, go back to your dog and praise him.

As he learns the command (in both the sit and down positions), you can gradually increase the time and distance away from him. For example, for the first few days, take one step away and have him hold the stay for ten seconds. Later that week, have him hold the stay while you take three steps away and have him be still for 20 seconds. Increase it gradually, though; if your Border Collie makes a few mistakes, you're moving too fast.

The signal for stay is an open–palmed gesture right in front of the dog's face.

Walking Nicely on the Leash

A dog who chokes himself on the leash and pulls so hard your shoulder hurts is no fun to take on a walk. That's torture, not fun! When your dog learns to walk nicely, without pulling, and pays attention to you when you talk to him, then walks are fun!

Hook the leash to your Border Collie's collar and hold the leash in one hand. Have some good dog treats in your other hand. Show your dog the treats and then back away from him so that it appears you are leading your dog by his nose. When he follows you, praise him. When he's following you

Use a treat and your happy verbal praise to encourage the dog to follow you on the leash as you back away from him. Praise him when he follows you.

nicely, turn so that he ends up on your left side and you're both walking forward together. You can still use the treat to encourage him to pay attention to you. Stop, have him sit, and praise him! Practice this often and keep the walking distances very short, with lots of sits and praise. If, while you're walking, your dog gets distracted, simply back away from him again and start all over.

When your dog is following you nicely, turn so that the both of you are walking forward together. Keep a treat handy to pop in front of his nose should he get distracted. Praise him.

Come

It is very important that your Border Collie understands that "come" means he should come directly to you, on the first call, every time you call him. He isn't to come just when he wants to, or when nothing else is very interesting, but instead is to come all the time, every time.

Have your Border Collie on the leash and hold the leash in one hand. In the other hand, have a box of dog treats. Shake the dog treats and, as you back away from your dog (so he can chase you), call him to come, "Sweetie, come!" Let him catch up to you, have him sit, and then give him a treat as you praise him, "Good boy to come!"

The box of dog treats is a sound stimulus that makes your verbal command much

Make sure your dog will come to you reliably all the time before you try it off-leash.

Training Collars

There are many training collars to choose from. Which one is right for your Border Collie?

Buckle collar: This collar is used to keep identification on the dog and is often the first collar worn by puppies. This collar does not give the dog any correction at all and is useful simply for ID or for holding the dog.

Chain collar: Often called a choke chain, this collar works by constriction. When used properly in correction, it is snapped tight and then released. This gives the dog a quick snap and release (tight and then loose) correction and he understands you are trying to get his attention. When used incorrectly, the collar can tighten and constrict the dog's neck, possibly causing neck damage. As the collar works by constriction, it can choke the dog and should never be left on an unsupervised dog.

Prong or pinch collar: This collar looks like a medieval torture device, with its inward pointing prongs. The prongs are flat, however, and do not threaten the dog's skin. This collar does not choke the dog and works by making corrections feel uncomfortable. If you put it around your leg and give a snap and release correction, you can feel that it's uncomfortable but not painful. This collar works for strong, powerful dogs who are trying to overpower their owners.

Head halters: This collar is good for many breeds because it gives the owner more control without giving a hard correction.

Each of these training tools has pros and cons. You may want to try a couple of different tools and see what works best for you and your dog.

more exciting. Since the come command is so important, use the sound stimulus (shaking the box of treats) often during your training.

When your dog is responding well on the leash, make up a long leash (20 to 30 feet in length) and repeat the training with the long leash. Continue using the box of treats, too. Don't be in a hurry to take the leash off your Border Collie. Most Border Collies aren't mentally mature and ready for off-leash training until they are at least two years old. Some aren't ready for off-leash training even then. Your training on-leash must be very, very good with few mistakes before you try it off-leash, and then do so only in a fenced, secure area.

Training Is an Ongoing Process

Training your Border Collie can be a lot of work. You need to pay attention to your dog, respond to her, and teach her right from wrong. You may also need to make some changes around the house and other family members will have to cooperate.

A well-behaved dog is a joy to own and a pleasure to spend time with.

The rewards are worth it, though. Silly's owner, Barbara, says that Silly is a joy to spend time with. "Now I even wish I'd given her a different name because she is such a sweet, obedient dog." She adds, "But she can still be pretty silly come playtime, so I guess the name still fits!"

7

Grooming

In This Chapter

○ Home Grooming Versus Professional Grooming
○ Routine Care Every Border Collie Needs

Border Collies are the natural beauties of the dog world. They don't require a lot of primping and preening to keep them looking their best. They do need to be brushed frequently to keep their skin healthy and coat gleaming, however, and to keep mats (tangled fur) at bay. The occasional bath also is necessary to keep your Border Collie smelling fresh and clean. And, as with all breeds, their teeth, ears, and nails need regular upkeep.

Whether you choose to do all your dog's grooming yourself or opt to take her to a professional groomer, you still need to learn the basics of grooming. Unless you plan on paying a professional to brush your dog every week, or even every day during the shedding season, you should acquire that skill. You also need to become comfortable with cleaning your dog's teeth, ears, and eyes and clipping her nails to keep her looking and feeling her best.

Home Grooming
Versus Professional Grooming

It's important that you help your Border Collie puppy or adult dog get used to being handled from the first day you bring him home. This will make him comfortable with the entire grooming process and will make grooming go smoothly in the future for you and/or a professional groomer. Take five minutes every day to sit on the floor with your Border Collie and examine his entire body, all the while keeping up a running monologue of praise. Look in his eyes, and check his ears. Open his mouth and examine his teeth, lightly massaging your finger along his gum line. Next, run your hands along his body, paying extra attention to his feet. Pick up each paw and massage it, gently parting the toes and touching the nails. Many dogs become anxious when their nails are trimmed; with some, anxious doesn't even begin to describe their disdain for the process. Ease your dog's fears, and make your job easier, by getting your pet comfortable with the procedure from the start. This daily "Puppy Pampering Period" also helps you catch coat or skin problems, such as fleas or suspicious lumps, early on.

> Whether you choose to do all your dog's grooming yourself or opt to take her to a professional groomer, you still need to learn the basics of grooming.

If your puppy or adult dog was not handled often from birth (if he was a rescue dog, for example), you may need to work harder at getting him used to being touched. Gently manipulate any part of his body he seems sensitive about. The minute your dog calms down and stops resisting, praise him.

If you feel at ease grooming your Border Collie on the floor, then stick with it. If you prefer to use a grooming table or plan to take your dog to a professional (who will definitely use a table), you'll want to accustom your dog to being up off the ground. A grooming table allows you to sit or stand while you are brushing your dog, thereby preventing strain on your back. If you don't want to invest in a grooming table, you can put a rubber mat on top of a table that is a comfortable height.

To begin, first simply hold out the brush and allow your pup to sniff it. If he seems calm, you can try running the brush lightly through his fur. Although young puppies require little grooming, brushing for a few minutes each day acquaints them with the process. Your puppy may initially react to this strange sensation by biting at the brush. If you realize you are pulling or tugging his fur, then, of course you should stop what you're doing and proceed in a gentler manner. If you know you're not hurting the puppy and he's merely trying to assert himself, however, don't give in. Otherwise, he'll quickly learn that biting is a means of getting his own way. Instead, ignore the behavior and continue brushing.

If your Border Collie continues to mouth the brush, calmly but firmly command "Off" or "Leave it." Don't shout; you don't want to scare the puppy into compliance. Although your puppy may be too young to know any commands yet, it is never too early to begin training. Your voice usually will distract your Border Collie, so he stops what he's doing. As soon as he lets go of the brush, praise him. You also can offer him a treat for behaving, but don't over-reward, since that creates its own problems (he'll expect a treat every time he does what he's supposed to do).

Some owners inadvertently make grooming difficult by trying too hard to make the experience fun for the dog. While grooming should be enjoyable, turning it into a play session is a mistake. Don't let your Border Collie play with the grooming equipment, or he'll never hold still for future grooming sessions.

Even if you usually groom your Border Collie, there may come a day when you want a professional to groom him. How do you go about finding a groomer?

First, ask other dog owners or canine professionals for their recommendations. Your breeder, veterinarian, or pet sitter may know of good groomers in the area. Once you have a few names, visit the shops personally. Ask what kind of training the groomers received. Did they graduate from a grooming course and/or apprentice with an experienced groomer? Pay attention to how the staff treats the dogs. Are they confident, yet gentle, when they are working with difficult dogs? Are they patient with puppies or dogs who have never been groomed? If the groomers enjoy their job, chances are their upbeat attitude will rub off on their clients' dogs.

> While grooming should be enjoyable, turning it into a play session is a mistake.

Check out the facility carefully. While the reception area will most likely be neat and tidy, you need to ensure that the grooming area is clean and sterile. The staff should wash out and sanitize tubs after each dog's bath, as well as sterilize crates between dogs.

If you must leave your dog for several hours beyond the time it takes to groom him (for example, if you leave him at the groomer's for the day, while you're at work), ask how often the groomer will take your Border Collie out to relieve himself. A dog who is left in this new environment for hours on end may have an accident in his crate, making him more stressed and anxious.

What to Look for in a Groomer

The groomer you select for your Border Collie should:

❍ Possess certifiable knowledge and hands-on experience

❍ Treat clients with courtesy and listen to their concerns

❍ Handle each dog firmly, but gently

❍ Show a genuine love of dogs

❍ Never allow puppies who are not fully vaccinated to be around older dogs

The grooming facility should:

❍ Be sterile and clean

❍ Have an adequate number of crates in all sizes to house clients' dogs

❍ Have a special outside area for potty breaks

Once you decide on a shop, take your pet for an introductory appointment. Inform the groomer that this is your Border Collie's first visit, and ask if he will spend a little extra time making sure your dog has a pleasant experience. If you have done your homework and spent time preparing your dog at home, this first grooming session and any to follow should be pleasurable for everyone. After all, what dog wouldn't like an occasional day at the spa?

Routine Care Every Border Collie Needs

Let's get down to the basics. How often will your Border Collie need to be groomed? What equipment do you need? And just how do you go about convincing a Border Collie he needs a bath when he has other ideas in mind?

Brushing

Border Collie coats can actually be divided into two types. Both have a weather-resistant double coat, the undercoat of which is short, dense, soft fur. The outer coat is where the two types diverge. One has a medium to long, flat or slightly wavy outer coat, while the other type has a short, smooth outer coat. Dogs with the first coat type, a rough coat, have shorter hair on their faces and longer featherings on their front legs. Smooth-coated Border Collies may have some feathering on their forelegs and a fuller coat on their chest.

You should brush your Border Collie at least once a week year-round. And, unless you want to chase Border Collie-fur dust bunnies around your house, you should brush your pet more frequently during the spring and fall, when Border Collies tend to "blow," or shed, their undercoats.

Remember, however, that no matter how often you brush your Border Collie, you'll never be able to keep your home free of hair. Sharing your life with a Border Collie (as with most breeds) means not getting upset over a stray hair floating across your kitchen table, and learning to coordinate your clothing—and your furniture—with the color of your dog. In the case of a black and white Border Collie, this may be difficult, unless you're a fan of faux zebra print!

To brush your Border Collie, you need several different pieces of equipment. First, use a pin brush, which has long bristles, often with rounded tips, set in a rubber base. Brush the entire coat down to the skin. By thoroughly brushing the coat, you are not only removing dead undercoat and preventing mats, you're also spreading the oils of the skin evenly across the entire coat to keep it glistening. Next, use a slicker brush, which is a stiffer brush with angled bristles. The slicker removes even more undercoat, plus it is perfect for grooming the shorter hair behind the ears. Shedding blades or rakes also are wonderful for removing dead coat during shedding season. These tools really dig down into the coat, leaving only the live hairs behind. Finish up with a greyhound comb, which has both fine- and wider-spaced teeth. Run the wider-toothed end through your dog's entire coat, then the fine-toothed end to ensure that your Border Collie is free of mats. If you see any evidence of fleas, run a flea comb through your dog's coat as well.

If you encounter a tangle, don't tug at it. Hold the mat tightly in your fingers and carefully work at it with the tip of a comb. You also can spray the mat with diluted creme rinse to make it more pliable. If the mat still won't budge, you may need to cut it out. Use blunt-tipped scissors to cut it away from your dog, and be careful not to nick the skin. You can also use scissors to trim the hocks lightly and the feathering on the front legs and the tail to neaten them up.

Bathing

I mentioned brushing before bathing for two reasons. First, you'll brush your dog more often than you'll bathe him, so you need to feel comfortable with the different brushing tools and techniques your Border Collie will require. In addition, you should always thoroughly brush your dog before you bathe him. If your dog is matted before he goes into the bath, the mats will only grow tighter into an impenetrable mass.

Did You Know?

Human bites are usually more dangerous than dog bites because a dog's mouth has fewer germs and bacteria.

Border Collie Grooming Essentials

- ○ Pin brush
- ○ Slicker brush
- ○ Shedding blade or rake
- ○ Greyhound comb
- ○ Flea comb
- ○ Blunt-tipped scissors
- ○ Quality dog shampoo and conditioner

- ○ Nail clippers or grinder
- ○ Styptic powder
- ○ Cotton balls
- ○ Ear cleaner
- ○ Dog toothbrush or thimble brush
- ○ Dog toothpaste

Where are you going to bathe your dog? Although a tub inside is the best place for a bath, some people like to bathe their Border Collie outside during the summer. While you can opt for outdoor bathing on a warm day, if you use a garden hose, run it through a window and attach it to an inside faucet that enables you to control the water temperature. Even on a hot day, icy cold water is too shocking for a bath.

Another option, which more and more grooming salons are offering, is a do-it-yourself grooming tub. You pay a nominal fee to bathe your dog at the salon in a large, waist-high tub. Not only does this arrangement save you from an aching back, but it also typically includes use of a quality shampoo, conditioner, towels, and a professional dryer at no extra cost.

If you don't live near a do-it-yourself grooming salon, your best option is your own bathtub. Before corralling your dog, gather all your supplies, including shampoo, conditioner, cotton balls, and lots of towels. Cover the bottom of your tub with a rubber mat and then put your dog in the tub. He may resist at first, so it is important that you remain calm, but assertive. If you are upbeat, but show you won't stand for any nonsense, he'll realize you mean business and that baths are nothing to fear. If you're bathing your dog in the tub, ignore ringing doorbells, jangling phones, family squabbles, and other distractions. You must never leave your dog unattended; he could get hurt trying to jump out.

Clean out your Border Collie's ears (see the section on ear cleaning to follow) and then put a cotton ball in each ear to keep out water. Rinse his coat with lukewarm water, starting at the rump and working backward to his head. Cups of water just don't do the trick; invest in a spray attachment for your shower. Hold the nozzle close to his body to penetrate the fur and to keep the water from spraying and frightening him. Thoroughly soak him before applying shampoo.

Once your dog is wet, lather him well, working the shampoo deep into the coat. Use only a high-quality canine shampoo. People shampoos contain a different pH factor than dog shampoos and can strip your Border Collie's coat of essential oils. Make sure you lather every inch of your dog. Some owners forget their dog is three-dimensional and only shampoo the dog's back and the outside of the legs. Take extra care to clean the easy-to-miss groin, armpit, and anal areas. When washing your dog's head, be careful around his eyes. If you get shampoo in them, flush them out immediately with clean water.

After giving your dog a sound lathering, rinse him well. Residual shampoo in your dog's coat can make his skin itchy and irritated. After he is fully rinsed, lather him up again. Two full shampoos will get him squeaky clean. Follow the final shampoo with a canine conditioner. Read the instructions to determine how long to leave in the conditioner. Many conditioners are applied like shampoos, while some can be sprayed in and left.

Once you are convinced you have removed all traces of shampoo and conditioner, turn off the water and grab a large towel. Towel-dry your Border Collie by squeezing out excess water; never rub him dry or you could tangle his coat. Keep toweling until your dog is just damp. You can let your Border Collie air-dry as long as he is kept inside in a warm, draft-free area. A dog can become chilled even on a hot day if a breeze is blowing. Blow-drying your Border Collie helps him dry faster and gives his coat a more finished look. It is best to use a professional canine blow-dryer, which you can buy or use at a do-it-yourself salon. If you decide to blow-dry your dog with your own hair dryer, be sure to use the cool setting, since human dryers can easily burn a dog's skin. Brush as you dry to prevent the hair from tangling.

How often should you bathe your dog? Don't believe the old wives' tale that dogs should only be bathed once or twice a year. As long as you use a high-quality shampoo, dogs can be bathed regularly without losing essential oils. Border Collies, in general, require a bath every two to three months, or more often if they get dirty or develop doggie odor.

Nail Clipping

While it is true that exercising on hard surfaces, such as long walks on pavement, wears down a dog's nails, all dogs still need their nails cut occasionally. You will need to clip your adult Border Collie's nails every few weeks or whenever you hear them clicking on hard surfaces, such as the kitchen floor. Puppies' nails grow even more quickly and need to be trimmed every week. Long nails are not only unsightly, they can actually interfere with your dog's movement. Nails that are allowed to grow unchecked can cause the toes to splay and can even begin to curl under and cut into a dog's pads. You should keep your dog's nails short, so that they rest just above the ground when he stands.

There are two basic types of nail clippers: the scissors and the guillotine. You also can use a nail grinder, but it may take some time to get your dog used to the noise. Grinding also is more time consuming, and the friction of the grinder can burn your dog's nails if you keep it on a nail too long. However, the advantages of a nail grinder are that it leaves the nails smoother and prevents you from cutting into the quick—the blood vessel that runs through your dog's nails.

If you use scissors or guillotine clippers, keep them sharp and clean. Dull clippers won't make a clean cut, and rusty, dirty ones can infect your dog if you cut the quick and your pet bleeds. The objective when clipping nails is to trim as close to the quick as possible without accidentally nicking it. Dark nails are more difficult to cut than light-colored ones, since it is impossible to see the pink vein. Remove the dry-looking hook at the tip of the nail, cutting off small bits of nail at a time. As you cut the nail shorter, you'll notice it becomes softer and you'll see a small grayish-white dot under the nail, which is the end of the quick. When you reach this point, the nail is short enough; you can now move on to the next one. Keep in mind that the more often you trim, the shorter you can get the nail,

Did You Know?

The pompon cut used on Poodles was originally developed to increase the breed's swimming abilities as a retriever. The short haircut allowed for faster swimming but the pom-poms were left to keep the joints warm.

since the quick actually recedes with frequent trimming. Cut each nail as quickly and cleanly as possible; cutting slowly tends to pinch the nail and cause your dog discomfort.

If you accidentally cut the quick, don't panic. Apply a styptic powder to staunch the bleeding and continue clipping the other nails. Don't stop and make a big fuss over your mistake, as it may make your dog even more apprehensive the next time you attempt to clip his nails.

When clipping your dog's nails, also check the pads of his feet and remove any pebbles or other small debris that may be lodged there, and also be sure to clip and remove any matted fur between the toes. Check your dog's feet frequently during winter to make sure they're not irritated from road salt or ice. Canine booties or petroleum jelly applied to the pads can protect your Border Collie's feet during cold months. If you notice your dog excessively biting at his paws, wash them off thoroughly to keep him from ingesting road salt.

Ears

You (or your groomer) should check your Border Collie's ears for irritations, such as mites or ear infections, during each grooming session. The ear should be pale pink and relatively odorless; a red, smelly ear or one with yellow, brown, or black debris usually indicates a problem. If you suspect your dog has an ear infection, see your veterinarian.

To maintain a healthy ear, wipe it out regularly with a cotton ball soaked with 3 percent hydrogen peroxide, light mineral oil, or a canine ear wash to remove any wax buildup. Clean only the outer part of the ear—never reach into the ear canal or you could damage it. You also should carefully trim or pluck any stray hairs you find

Conquering Grooming Disasters

Here are some of the more common grooming problems you may encounter and the best ways to handle them.

Burrs: Although romps through fields or wooded areas offer wonderful exercise for your dog, you may pay the price of burrs, seeds, twigs, or other things sticking to your dog. Border Collies' leg featherings are especially attractive to these hangers-on. Try to remove them immediately with a fine-toothed comb. Mink oil conditioners, available at grooming shops or supply stores, can make the coat sleek, which makes it easier to remove burrs.

Skunk Spray: You may have heard that tomato juice takes out the smell of skunk. This is not true. It leaves you with a pinkish, sticky dog! Instead, use a high-quality skunk shampoo; your pet-supply store or groomer should be able to recommend one. Remember to brush your dog thoroughly before bathing him since any dead, loose fur just retains the smell and prevents the shampoo from penetrating all the way down to the skin.

Another option that comes highly recommended is a special "recipe" you can easily prepare at home. Include in your dog's bath one quart bottle of 3 percent hydrogen peroxide, 1/4 cup of baking soda (sodium bicarbonate), and one teaspoon of liquid soap. Follow the bath with a tap-water rinse.

No matter what you use, though, your dog may continue to smell slightly skunky every time he gets wet for several weeks or even months.

Paint: Before it hardens, immediately wash out any latex paint your dog brushes against or rolls in. This paint, which is toxic, thankfully is water soluble. If your dog gets into oil paint, you'll have to cut away the fur with paint on it. Never use varsol or turpentine, and never let your dog chew at the paint.

Gum: You discover a bright pink wad of bubble gum stuck to your Border Collie's fur—don't rush for the scissors yet. Try rubbing the gum with ice cubes to make it brittle. If the gum is stuck only to the ends of the hairs, try to break or lift it off. If it's down in the coat, however, try using peanut butter as a solvent. If your dog steps in gum, try rubbing it with ice and then peeling it off the pads. If the gum is attached to the hair on the paw, cut it away.

Tar: Hot tar can scald your dog. If your pet has come in contact with hot tar, apply cold water immediately and see your veterinarian. If your Border Collie has a too-close encounter with cooled, sticky tar, apply ice cubes to harden the tar and then cut it away with scissors.

growing inside your Border Collie's ears, as they can tickle and cause your dog to scratch and possibly injure his ear.

Tooth Care

One area of grooming that tends to be overlooked is dental care. Unhealthy teeth in dogs can lead to inflamed gums and tooth loss, which, in turn, can make it painful or even impossible for a dog to eat. Long-neglected teeth can even cause serious conditions, such as heart or digestive problems. Your dog requires both at-home teeth brushing and veterinary dental care. Although you'll need to periodically take your dog to the veterinarian for dental scalings and cleanings, brushing his teeth regularly will reduce the plaque buildup and help keep your pet healthy. Ideally, you should brush your dog's teeth every day or two, but even brushing only once a week or once a month will provide some benefits.

Your dog should already be used to you massaging his gums from your daily puppy pampering sessions. To prepare him for his first teeth brushing, put some canine toothpaste on your finger, push back your dog's lips, and massage the teeth and gums. Once your dog accepts this, you can graduate to using a finger brush (which looks like a rubber thimble) or a dog toothbrush. Never use human toothpaste; many brands contain foaming detergents that can irritate a dog's stomach if he swallows them.

8

Family Life

In This Chapter

○ Playtime
○ Playing Nicely with Children
○ Making Your Border Collie a Good Neighbor
○ Traveling with and Boarding Your Border Collie

Now let's get to the heart and soul of owning a Border Collie—incorporating your dog into your household. While it is vital that your dog receives proper nutrition, training, and veterinary care, her day-to-day life with you holds the key to her happiness. Countless Border Collies are given up because owners didn't fully consider the enormous emotional and physical needs of the breed before bringing one into their home.

How can you help your Border Collie fit into your family? What are the best ways to expend some of her intense energy, while at the same time strengthening the bond between you? What's the truth about mixing Border Collies with kids? How about other pets? Ill-behaved dogs are a leading cause of tension between neighbors. How can you ensure that your Border Collie will be welcomed by your neighborhood, instead of being viewed as a nuisance? What about when you leave home to go on vacation? Should you bring your dog along? Should you find someone to watch your pet and, if so, how do you locate a suitable kennel or pet sitter? By now your head may be spinning from all these vital questions. Don't worry—you'll find the answers here! By the end of this chapter, you'll know the best ways to make your Border Collie a full-fledged member of the family.

> While it is vital that your dog receives proper nutrition, training, and veterinary care, her day-to-day life with you holds the key to her happiness.

Playtime

Every dog needs to play, for a number of reasons. Playing with her owner keeps a Border Collie both physically and mentally fit, and bonds her more closely to her special person. You can "play" with your Border Collie in many different ways, from taking long walks to making up creative games and joining a competitive canine sport. Whatever you choose to do, you'll reap the rewards of a happy, healthy dog.

Exercise

To owners, it may seem there is no such thing as a tired Border Collie. If you keep in mind that these dogs were bred to herd all day, every day, in all types of weather conditions, you will be less likely to become frustrated with your dog's tireless energy. Learning to work with your dog's exercise needs instead of fighting them will lead to a much happier dog, and owner.

Even if you have a fenced yard, realize that many Border Collies won't exercise without human interaction. Don't view this time as a chore—cherish it as quality bonding time with your pet and a time to get some exercise yourself!

Border Collies are consummate ball-lovers. They will play fetch for hours, or until your arm can't possibly throw one more time. Some owners with large yards hit a tennis ball with a bat to get extra distance, and expend extra Border Collie energy, with each throw. Throwing a Frisbee or kicking around a soccer ball are other pastimes most Border Collies take to immediately. When playing soccer with your dog, however, teach her the command "Leave it," or she may control the ball so obsessively that no one else can get near it, especially children. If you own two or more Border Collies, teach them to play fetch separately, or you'll find that one dog is fetching and the others are herding the dog with the ball!

Many Border Collies invent their own rules to tried-and-true games. Lynn Renor, of Madison, Wisconsin, says her one Border Collie, Brigga, figured out a way to play ball even when no one else wants to play with her. "The house we live in is old and the floor slants," Lynn explains. "Brigga realized that if she drops a ball by the couch it will roll across the room all by itself. She then retrieves it and starts the game all over. She'll play this for hours by herself."

If your dog gets along well with others, invite a friend or two to visit with their dogs and hold an impromptu doggie party. There's nothing like canine companionship to wear out, or at least wear down, a wound-up Border Collie.

While backyards are wonderful for exercise, your dog will also need opportunities to exercise off your property (on-leash, of course). If you live in the city and don't have access to a backyard, you'll need to be especially diligent about getting out and about with your pet. Long, brisk walks and hikes are great forms of exercise. Border Collies also make great jogging or biking companions. Take care to train your Border Collie how to run next to a bike, however, or she may try to herd the bike, setting the two of you up for a collision course! Be careful that your dog is not overexerting herself, especially on hot days. Border Collies' obsessive, hard-working nature and willingness to do whatever we ask of them often causes them to work themselves to the point of exhaustion. It is up to you to put some limits on exercise and know when your dog has had enough. Also check your dog's pads frequently to be sure they aren't injured. Most Border Collies become so focused on whatever they are doing that they won't limp until they get home.

Swimming is a great alternative for hot days when you don't want to risk a brisk jog. To ensure that your Border Collie enjoys her first dip, introduce her to water slowly. If she's forced to dive right in, she may get frightened and in the future avoid water altogether. Instead, try to entice her with a flotation toy, by throwing a stick into the water, or by wading into the water and calling her to you. Beware; once you get your Border Collie into the wet stuff, you might have a hard time getting her out! After your dog spends time in the water, always hose her off thoroughly to wash away chlorine from a pool or bacteria from a lake. Also, wipe her ears dry to ward off an ear infection.

If you are like most Border Collie owners, you'll quickly notice that what seems like a lot of exercise to you barely causes your dog to break into a pant. If your

Border Collie comes home from a five-mile jog only to grab her ball from her toy box for a frenzied game of fetch, try incorporating some mental work into her physical play. Games such as hide-and-seek, teaching tricks, or even practicing obedience commands will work your dog's mind as well as her body and wear her out more effectively.

Obedience

Obedience work is a more structured means of "play" than fetch or hide-and-seek. Of course, all Border Collies must receive at least a minimum of basic obedience training to teach them proper manners and to enforce the pack structure of your household. Perhaps, however, after attending a class or two with your Border Collie, you've found yourself practicing a little more than you thought you would. Perhaps you've started to show up early for class and hang around afterwards, asking the instructor for extra pointers. Maybe you even felt a little depressed on graduation night, wondering what you were going to do without your weekly obedience fix. Face it, you've been bitten by the obedience bug!

If you decide you'd like to try competitive obedience, you can pursue this sport at as low or as high a level as you wish. A good way to introduce both yourself and your dog to a low-key judging situation is to sign up your Border Collie for a Canine Good Citizen (CGC) test. Sponsored by the AKC and hosted by dog clubs around the country, this test measures your dog's reactions to ten real-life situations and results in a pass/needs-more-training grade. Don't be upset if

Did You Know?

According to the American Animal Hospital Association, more than 40 percent of pet owners talk to their pets on the phone or through the answering machine.

your dog doesn't pass the first time; your Border Collie hasn't "failed," she simply needs more training in the areas marked. There are books devoted to the CGC test, and many dog training clubs offer classes designed to ready your dog for the test.

The ten parts of the test are:

- **Accepting a friendly stranger.** Demonstrates the dog will allow a friendly stranger to approach and speak to the dog's handler in a natural, everyday situation.
- **Sitting politely for petting.** Demonstrates the dog will allow a friendly stranger to touch her while she is out with her handler.
- **Appearance and grooming.** Demonstrates the dog will welcome being groomed and examined and will permit a stranger, such as a veterinarian, groomer, or a friend of the owner, to do so.
- **Out for a walk (walking on a loose leash).** Demonstrates the handler is in control of the dog.
- **Walking through a crowd.** Demonstrates the dog can move about politely in pedestrian traffic and is under control in public places.
- **Sit and down on command/staying in place.** Demonstrates the dog has received training and will respond to the handler's sit and down commands, and will remain in the place ordered by the handler.
- **Come when called.** Demonstrates the dog will come when summoned by the handler.
- **Reaction to another dog.** Demonstrates the dog can behave politely around other dogs.
- **Reaction to distractions.** Demonstrates the dog always remains confident when faced with common distracting situations, such as the sudden closing of a door or the clatter of a dropped pan.
- **Supervised separation.** Demonstrates the dog will maintain her training and good manners when left in the presence of a trusted person other than her handler.

If your dog passes the CGC test, she will receive a certificate stating she is a Canine Good Citizen. While this certificate makes a wonderful addition to your pet's scrapbook and/or can be framed and added to your Border Collie brag wall (along with her puppy pictures, pedigree, etc.), it also can be used as a selling point when trying to rent an apartment or stay in a hotel room with your dog.

If you enjoyed the CGC test, just wait until you try a real obedience trial! Dogs can earn a number of obedience titles through the AKC, with each title progressively more difficult to obtain. AKC obedience is open to Border Collies registered with the AKC or those who have obtained an Indefinite Listing Privilege, which allows dogs to compete in certain performance events but not conformation shows. If you do not wish to show in AKC obedience, an alternative is offered by the United Kennel Club, which does not recognize Border Collies for conformation purposes but does allow them to compete in performance events. (Below are the rules for AKC obedience trials; contact the UKC, listed in the Resources section at the back of this book, for a complete list of their rules and regulations.)

The first level of AKC obedience is called Novice. This program requires your dog to demonstrate her prowess in heeling both on- and off-leash at different speeds through a particular pattern, coming when called (Recall), and holding a sit for one minute and a down for three. In addition, during the Stand For Examination exercise, your Border Collie needs to stand still and remain calm while the judge approaches and runs a hand over her. Each dog starts with a perfect score of 200 and loses points

> A good way to introduce both yourself and your dog to a low-key judging situation is to sign up your Border Collie for a Canine Good Citizen (CGC) test.

for flaws in her performance. To earn the title of Companion Dog (CD), your Border Collie must earn a qualifying score of 170 points or more and at least 50 percent of the points available in each exercise during three different trials under three different judges. Top-placing dogs receive award ribbons. Dogs who fail to earn a top score but obtain qualifying scores still earn a leg toward the CD and take home a qualifying score ribbon. Although obedience trials are competitive, the greatest competition your dog faces is herself.

The exercises for the second level of obedience, called Open, are slightly harder than those of novice training. An open trial requires the dog to perform off-lead heeling and long sits and downs with the handler out of sight. It also includes new exercises such as navigating a broad jump and two retrieves, including one over a jump. Dogs who obtain three qualifying scores under three different judges earn a Companion Dog Excellent (CDX) title.

The next obedience level, the Utility level, is even more difficult. The dog performs drills of increased complexity, such as the signal exercise, in which she responds to sit, stand, down, and come commands at a distance from her handler, who can use only hand signals. In another Utility exercise, scent discrimination, the dog must pick an article with her handler's scent out of ten similar articles. Other tests in this category include a directed retrieve, in which the dog must pick up one of three cotton gloves under her handler's direction, and a directed jump, in which she must leap both a solid jump and a bar jump at a distance and under her handler's command. Dogs earn a Utility Dog (UD) title at this level.

Once a dog obtains the Utility level of obedience prowess, she can go on to compete for Utility Dog Excellent (UDX) and Obedience Trial Championship (OTCH) titles. A dog who qualifies in both an Open and Utility class on the same day and repeats this feat ten times is awarded a UDX. To earn an OTCH, a dog must place first in both Open and Utility, and then place first again in either Open or Utility. In addition, the dog must accumulate 100 points (with points based on the number of dogs competing), either by winning or placing second in Open or Utility.

Due to their intelligence and eagerness to please, Border Collies frequently are top winners in obedience competitions. Be sure to keep training interesting, and your dog will be happy to practice obedience sits and downs until they're tuned to perfection. Border Collies thrive on repetition as long as they gain some reward from it, whether that reward is food, play, or even simple praise. You'll need to vary your exercises, however, or your Border Collie will quickly catch on to the pattern and begin to anticipate your next move, which could cost you points, or even disqualify you, in the obedience ring. Also practice your "poker face" when training obedience. Any subtle change in your facial expression or body posture could lead your dog to believe the exercise is over and it's time to go home!

> Border Collies thrive on repetition as long as they gain some reward from it, whether that reward is food, play, or even simple praise.

Another problem Border Collie owners encounter is their dog's love of an appreciative audience. If your dog clowns around in the ring and gets reinforced by laughter or even applause, you're going to have a hard time stifling this comic streak.

Sometimes, if you can find that right balance of obedience and Border Collie creativity and penchant for performance, you can wind up with a true performer. If you find that your Border Collie really craves the limelight of going in the ring, there is one final area of obedience that can use this showmanship to its best advantage. If you'd like to try obedience with a little flair, you might find that freestyle is for you and your canine performer. This relatively new addition to the world of competitive obedience requires dog/handler teams to perform intricately choreographed maneuvers set to music. Freestyle obedience resembles a canine-human dance—complete with costumed partners!

Canine Sports

What if advanced obedience isn't for you, and you're looking for a different outlet for your dog's inquisitive mind and high energy? What if you enjoy obedience, but would like to add another dimension to your dog's play? You can always try one of the many canine sports in which Border Collies can compete and excel.

One such sport, agility, is a fast-paced and exciting activity that tests your Border Collie's ability to navigate various obstacles, including tunnels, jumps, weave poles, A-frames, and teetertotters. The Border Collie's speed and flexibility make her a natural for this sport, and, as is the case at obedience trials, Border Collies often are the top winners at agility trials. Agility is a progressive sport, in which each level requires the dog to conquer additional obstacles at a higher speed within an increasingly narrow time frame. If intense competition isn't for you, you can simply take an agility class for some great canine (and human!) exercise without ever competing in a trial. Several different organizations offer competitive agility events, each with their own rules and titles. The AKC, UKC, North American Dog Agility Council (NADAC), and the

> The sport of flyball seems to have been designed for tennis ball-obsessed Border Collies.

United States Dog Agility Association (USDAA) all offer agility competitions.

The sport of flyball seems to have been designed for tennis ball-obsessed Border Collies. This fun, fast-paced canine sport pits two teams of dogs against each other as they compete side by side in a type of relay race. The first dog from each team races over four hurdles to a box at the end of her team's row. Each dog hits her respective box with her paw, which releases a tennis ball into the air. The dog must catch the ball, turn, and race back over the hurdles to the rest of her team. When she crosses the starting line, the next dog from her team is immediately released, and the race continues until all dogs from one team successfully complete the drill. Two teams usually compete in best three-out-of-five heats. Tournament competition can consist of double elimination or round robin. With double elimination, each team that loses two races is eliminated until only one team remains. In round robin, all teams play all rounds, and the team with the best record at the end of the day wins. Individual dogs accumulate points based on the accumulated times of their respective teams, earning them titles ranging from Flyball Dog (20 points) to Flyball Grand Champion (30,000 points). A game of speed and accuracy, flyball calls for dogs with single-minded determination.

Although ball-craziness is, of course, essential, it also is imperative that your dog gets along well with others in this team sport. A dog who is overly possessive of toys or aggressive toward other dogs will not be able to work in this team environment. If your dog loves canine camaraderie and loves balls even more, however, flyball may be the sport for her! Contact the North American Flyball Association for more information.

Border Collies also are naturals at playing with Frisbees, whether just for exercise in the yard or at national Frisbee competitions. Mark Miller, of Jacksonville, Florida, has found Frisbee to be the perfect outlet for his Border Collie's energy. "Boomer has a great deal of prey drive, which we have successfully channeled into playing Frisbee, ball, agility, and other activities. However, he loves to play Frisbee more than anything else in the world. I could have a steak in one hand and a Frisbee in the other and he would want the Frisbee. He started catching Frisbees in the air in our backyard when he was about five to six months old. He competed in his first canine Frisbee competition when he was seven months old. And last year, in his second full season competing, Boomer and I made it to the world finals with 15 other human/canine teams from around the country. We wound up finishing in tenth place. We have performed at professional football, baseball, and soccer games in front of some very large crowds, and Boomer has always remained focused on the Frisbee."

Frisbee certainly is a wonderful sport to keep your dog fit and trim and provide lots of fun, too. Train your dog slowly, however, and be careful not to ask a newcomer to the sport to perform intricate twists and turns in the air, which can lead to serious spinal damage.

Border Collies also can be trained to track, which is another great way to exercise your dog's mind. Tracking measures a dog's ability to follow a scent and to find one or more scented articles along the trail. Progressive levels of tracking competition steadily increase the challenge by aging the scented trail for one to several hours and by laying the track over increasingly difficult terrain, such as concrete or gravel. The AKC and UKC both offer tracking titles.

If your dog truly excels at tracking, and if you would like to work side by side with her in a volunteer position, you may want to check out search-and-rescue work. Although not a sport, search-and-rescue (a charitable pursuit, similar to volunteer firefighting) builds skills and provides great exercise for your pet, not to mention the thrill of providing such an important service to people in need. Search-and-rescue teams endure intense training and must be ready at any moment to help search for missing children or victims of disasters, such as earthquakes and tornadoes. You and your dog should not enter into this pursuit lightly. However, if you can dedicate yourself to the effort and want to help others, you and your Border Collie may be perfect for the job. For more information, contact the National Association for Search and Rescue.

If you really want to choose a sport for which the Border Collie was bred, there is no better choice than herding. Nothing can compare to the sight of a working Border Collie, hunkered down in front of her flock, anticipating every move of the sheep and controlling them with an unblinking eye. The AKC offers herding instinct tests and herding trials for dogs registered with the organization. For those who wish to pursue sheepdog trialing on a more advanced level, the United States Border Collie Handlers Association runs trials for serious competitors. The USBCHA is the sanctioning body for sheepdog trials throughout the United States and Canada. Each year, one Border Collie champion is determined. This is the dog or bitch who wins the National Handlers Finals sheepdog trial, sponsored jointly by the USBCHA and the American Border Collie Association registry.

Indeed, herding may provide the ultimate bonding experience between an owner and his sheepdog. If you are interested in pursuing this sport, go watch a few sheepdog trials and find an experienced handler who can serve as your mentor. Clinics, seminars,

Although not a sport, search-and-rescue (a charitable pursuit, similar to volunteer firefighting) builds skills and provides great exercise for your pet.

and classes are given all over the country to teach amateurs this sport, which requires the cooperation of human, dog, and the unpredictable third element—livestock. Although Border Collies are more often associated with sheep herding, cattle dog trials are another potential outlet for your dog's talents.

Some Border Collies also participate in sports that don't necessarily come to mind when you think of this breed. One example is sledding. Border Collie dogsled teams have actually proven themselves quite competitive in middle-distance races.

> Herding may provide the ultimate bonding experience between an owner and his sheepdog.

Liz Phares, of New Canaan, Connecticut, has two Border Collies that are sled-crazy. "The favorite sport of my Border Collies is dogsledding. When I pull the harnesses and equipment off the hooks, Duncan and Fly begin to spin in circles and howl in anticipation. By the time I pull into the park, they are frantic with excitement and can hardly contain themselves. Their greatest joy is sprinting down the trails at full speed. I own a sled and a cart so that we can go out no matter what the weather. It only took me a few days to train them to pull the sled and follow all the commands. When I bought my cart, they only looked back at me once, the first time I used the brakes, to see what all the noise was about. After that they loved the cart because it meant they could go sledding without snow."

Border Collies have even proven themselves in the sport of Schutzhund, which is more commonly associated with protection breeds such as German Shepherd Dogs and Rottweilers. Schutzhund offers three levels of competition, novice (SchH I), intermediate (SchH II) and advanced (SchH III), all of which test three areas of skill—tracking, obedience, and protection. While the tracking and obedience phases resemble those found in AKC trials, the protection aspect truly sets apart Schutzhund. During the protection phase, the dog searches six blinds for a planted "bad guy." The dog must not attack until the staged person attacks the dog or handler first; at that point the dog must execute a directed, but full-force attack on the helper's protective sleeve. When the handler issues the command "Out" (this command is sometimes given in German), the dog must immediately release the sleeve.

Although many people who don't understand the sport fear it, Schutzhund actually conditions a dog to have tremendous control and to attack only with provocation. Schutzhund not only teaches owners how to train, handle, and control their dogs, it also teaches dogs to understand human behavior as well as what does and does not constitute a threat. A Schutzhund-trained dog effectively poses much less of a threat to a person who means no harm than does an untrained dog of any breed. However, Schutzhund training cannot "correct" a poor temperament. Dogs who are aggressive or excessively shy will be unable to do the work required of this sport.

Although not a sport, therapy work provides another pastime option for your Border Collie. Therapy dogs visit nursing homes, hospitals, and other locations to provide companionship to elderly, ill, and disabled individuals. As much as Border Collies are motivated by work, they also are motivated by a love of people. Many Border Collies who are energetic hellions at home take this job seriously, exhibiting a careful, calm demeanor when brought into nursing homes or children's hospitals. Nothing is more heartwarming than seeing your pet bring out giggles of delight in an ill child, or a great big bear hug from a frail elderly person.

Anita Duhon, of Lake Charles, Louisiana, tells a wonderful story of how her dog touched the heart of a troubled little girl. "We were on our way out to the parking garage of the hospital and a young couple with two young children walked toward us. The young boy, maybe eight, stepped alongside his sister to shield her from Thor. The younger sister stopped and hesitated to pass us in the walkway. Thor and the girl stared at each other, then this Border Collie clown decided to act. He wanted to be petted and these kids were not petting him. He figured he must do something to earn that pet, so he stared at the kids, picked up a paw, and waved.

"The surprise on those faces was precious. I showed them the hand signals for sit, down, and wave, and Thor finally had his audience. He did whatever those little kids asked and then sat directly in front of the little girl and talked to her with his brown eyes. She petted him from ear to ear, head to tail, and he sat perfectly still.

"So where was the miracle in all of this? The mom then told me that the little girl had been attacked by a dog over a year ago, and had a metal plate in her head as a result. The brother had gotten very protective of his little sister, and both were very afraid of dogs. This was the first time they had petted a dog since the attack. Again, I saw the Border Collie magic displayed right in front of me. But therapy work is not always so spectacular. The magic may be so subtle you don't know it happened or it may be a glance of the eye, movement in crippled hands, or the memory of a forgotten past. But the magic is still there, the Border Collie magic, the magic of a therapy dog."

Pet therapy is becoming increasingly prevalent as doctors and health administrators realize the positive impact animals have on people of all ages. Not only do animals help patients mentally, they also can help patients in physical therapy to regain coordination through brushing a dog or holding a leash. If participating in therapy with your Border Collie interests you and you believe your dog has the proper temperament for the job, you can contact Therapy Dogs International, Therapy Dogs Incorporated, Delta Society, or other organizations that run pet therapy programs. You also can contact nearby hospitals and nursing homes for information on local therapy groups.

Playing Nicely with Children

Border Collies and children can make a wonderful mix, with each finding a pal and playmate for life. On the other hand, throwing a Border Collie and a child together without forethought and training can be a recipe for disaster.

First, if you have children or intend to have them down the road, it is important that you choose a Border Collie who shows signs of being receptive to children. Unless your dog is going to be a working stock dog, choose a family dog from a breeding line that is more laid back. Also, ask the breeder for help in choosing a puppy with a more mellow, accommodating personality. A workaholic Border Collie is not the best choice for a family with children.

Even if your puppy is on the less-intense side, you need to train him from the beginning in how to interact with children. Socialization with children of all ages is vital if you want your dog to grow up to be stable and trustworthy around youngsters. If you don't have any children of your own, borrow nieces,

> **Did You Know?**
>
> In Homer's The Odyssey, the only one to recognize Odysseus when he arrived home disguised as a beggar after a 20-year absence was his dog Argos, who wagged his tail at his master and then died.

nephews, or neighborhood children. Take your puppy to parks and schoolyards to get him used to the high-pitched squeals and running of children.

Border Collies were bred to herd, and in their minds, that means to herd anything that moves. While children may find it fun to have a small puppy chase them around the yard, they won't enjoy the game anymore when a full-grown Border Collie is nipping at their heels or herding them into a corner and not allowing them to leave. From the beginning, you must teach your dog to respect children and curtail any herding behavior around them. A Border Collie who sees children as livestock will feel perfectly within his right to discipline an errant youth with a nip on the heels. You also must teach children not to encourage chasing on the part of your dog, or your training efforts won't do much good.

> Even if you have taught your Border Collie to respect children, it is imperative that you supervise all interactions between your dog and children.

Even if you have taught your Border Collie to respect children, it is imperative that you supervise all interactions between your dog and children. A small child may—intentionally or unintentionally—mistreat your dog. In some instances, dogs have launched seemingly unprovoked attacks on small children that actually resulted from the child shoving a pencil deep into the dog's ear or some other atrocity.

If you already have a Border Collie in your life and find you are expecting a new human addition to the family, it is important to get your dog used to the sights, sounds, and smells of an infant before the baby even comes home. Buy a realistic-looking baby doll and carry it around for several weeks before the real baby arrives. Let your dog sniff the doll, but tell him "Easy" or "Gentle"

Commonsense Rules
for Kids and Border Collies

○ Parents must supervise all inter-actions.

○ Never leave a baby or small child alone with any breed of dog.

○ Crate train your Border Collie, but children should be taught to never go into the dog's crate. Teach the child that the crate is the Border Collie's special, private room.

○ Never bother a dog when he's eat-ing or sleeping.

○ Never tease and always be gentle. No yelling, feet stomping, or arm swinging. Never let your Border Collie chase children.

○ Don't poke or pull eyes, ears, nose, tail.

○ Don't permit snack stealing from kids. Place the Border Collie in his crate or another room with his own doggie snack during little people snack time.

○ Don't allow kids to supervise your Border Collie. Parents must be in charge of doggie discipline.

and reward him only when he is calm. Once the baby is born, but before you bring her home from the hospital, a member of the family should bring home a piece of clothing with the baby's scent for the dog to examine.

After you've settled the new baby at home, make sure you take some time out of your hectic schedule to give your dog at-tention as well. It is fine for your Border Collie to stay by your side while you bathe, feed, and change your baby, but if you must leave the room for some reason, separate the dog and child with a baby gate or a closed door.

Your Border Collie must learn from early on to respect your child's authority. Although it may seem impossible to convince a full-grown dog that this teeny person is his alpha, it is not only possible, it is imperative. If you have an infant, practice obedience commands while holding your baby in your arms and facing the dog. In your Border Collie's eyes, you will share your alpha status with the baby. Later, you can instruct your toddler to give commands while you stand behind her.

As your child grows, start assigning age-appropriate dog-care duties to her. For example, toddlers can help fill the water dish, and school-age children can tell the dog to sit, then give him his dinner when he complies. Older children and teenagers can groom their Border Collie and walk him. However, keep in mind your dog's rambunctiousness and never let a child walk a dog she cannot control. Your older child might even bond so closely with the dog that she may decide to take up a sport, such as obedience or agility, with him. Junior Showmanship also offers a wonderful way for children and dogs to bond. This sport judges kids on their handling skills in a conformation show setting.

Now, it's time to cover training your children to treat your Border Collie with respect. Dogs should never be asked to endure abuse, even at the hands of an innocent child. Children must be taught from an early age to be gentle. Also teach your children never to run from a Border Collie, since running only entices him to chase and possibly nip. You must also forbid your children from ever roughhousing or playing tug-of-war with your dog, because these games will show your Border Collie that he is stronger than your child and place him in a dominant position. In addition, make sure your children's friends know how to behave around your dog. Playing fetch is an excellent icebreaker for introducing your dog to new children and showing the children and dog how to behave around each other.

Lesley Krimpenfort, of Phoenix, Arizona, wasn't sure how her Border Collies would adapt to a new baby when she found herself pregnant two years ago. "We were so nervous about how our three Border Collies would react to our child. I read books, consulted a behaviorist, and posted on the Web to dog forums for advice on how to make the transition from dog household to dog/child household. I tried to include my Border Collies in the pregnancy experience as much as possible. I let them rest their heads on my belly, hang out in the nursery as we decorated it, and sniff and inspect all of the baby's future clothes, blankets, and toys. Since it was the first time I had ever been pregnant, I'm not sure they knew what was coming. They did, however, sense something.

> Teach your children never to run from a Border Collie, since running only entices him to chase and possibly nip.

"Prior to bringing Evan home, my husband brought home baby items like a blanket and hat for the dogs to sniff. They were very interested in the items. Then we brought Evan home and introduced him to the dogs one at a time. They were so curious. They sniffed and sniffed him and clung to my side to investigate every move the baby or I made. I invited them to lie next to us as I fed Evan and I would pet them as they watched. I knew everything would go smoothly for a while since Evan was always in our arms, his swing, or his bassinet. I didn't want to wait until he was crawling for child-dog interactions to transpire, so I'd put Evan on the floor on a blanket and let the dogs lay near him. When Evan flinched or moved his extremities, the dogs would jump up and move away. They were very nervous, which made me nervous.

"Well, within two weeks I was shocked when I realized our one Border Collie, Niall, was putting his tennis ball in Evan's lap as he swung in his swing. He'd drop it in his lap and stare at him as if he really believed Evan could throw it like we do. He's so smart. He saw this tiny baby, with arms and legs like ours, and made the connection that Evan was just a little one of us. He'd wait and wait for Evan to throw the ball. He'd whine and even gently lay his paw on Evan's lap as if to say, 'Hello. You're supposed to throw it back.' Niall loves this baby to pieces. Our other Border Collies, Simon and Murphy, are still a little hesitant, but each day it gets better and better. Niall and Evan are going to be so close. As the months have rolled by, Niall was the one who provoked Evan's first belly laugh, our son's first word was doggie, and they now, finally, play ball. Niall gives it to him and Evan can roll it back to him or hand it to him. I can see such a special bond forming already!"

Kathy Morgan, of New South Wales, Australia, says her one Border Collie helped teach her son to walk. "He started walking early at eight months. He would hold onto her around her neck and together they would walk, with her taking tiny steps so he could keep up. She also would walk between him and the furniture, so if he fell he would fall on her. Now he is four, and Ziggy is always with my son; he tells everyone that she is his best friend.

"My other Border Collie is the guardian of my ten-year-old. I remember one day in particular when he was four. I was doing housework and my Border Collie came in, stared at me, and barked. She did this a few times until I realized that she actually wanted to show me something. I followed her out back and there was my child lighting matches and paper in a barrel. Honestly, the look on her face when she knew she had done the right thing was priceless, and the look on my son's face that he had been busted by the dog was even more so. Mind you, he no longer plays with matches, but she still follows him around everywhere, just to keep an eye on him, I think."

Nanette Bragg, of Alice Springs, Northern Territory, Australia, also experienced firsthand the Border Collie's protective instinct. "I was on the phone and didn't notice my youngest child, Michaela, go out of the shed. I heard my dogs give a very strange bark and I thought they had cornered a snake. I always got rid of the snakes, so I went to check. My youngest bitch was bounding on the veranda and ran off toward the back of the property as soon as I showed my face, so I followed her. As I got closer, I realized my other dogs were there too. My oldest male was standing in front of my youngest child and barking ferociously at her, and my oldest bitch had a very firm grip on her nappy. Not more than a meter behind them was the worst drop into the valley we had—unfenced. My heart was in my mouth. I picked her up and the dogs settled straightaway and wandered back to the house. If not for those unbelievably loyal and protective Border Collies, I dread to think of the consequences of my poor care at that time."

A Border Collie who has been taught to respect kids likely will be game for anything your child wants to do, from romping in the yard and playing fetch for hours to lying side by side on the sun-soaked grass watching the clouds go by. Dogs listen to your deepest secrets and never judge. If you properly train both your child and your dog, you can help ensure that they truly do become best friends.

Border Collies and Other Animals

While some dogs naturally accept certain pets better than others, you can surely help the process by introducing your Border Collie to all types of animals while he is a puppy. Take him to a puppy class, introduce him to the neighbor's dog-friendly cat, and volunteer to keep the hamster from your child's class over a weekend. If

Ten Great Games
Kids Can Play with a Border Collie

Children should avoid playing certain games with your Border Collie, such as tug-of-war or wrestling, which can put your dog in a position of power, or chase games, which can lead to your child getting nipped. Here are ten safe games your child and your Border Collie can enjoy together. Remember that an adult must supervise all play.

Hide-and-Seek: Start teaching this game with your child "hiding" in plain view across the room, then gradually make the game more difficult by having her hide behind furniture, in another room, etc. It helps for your dog to know your family members by name. For example, you can hold onto your dog while your child hides and then release him with an encouraging, "Go find Susie!" Susie can reward the dog's find with praise and/or treats.

Marco Polo: This game is hide-and-seek with audio clues. While your dog searches the house for your child, Susie can "bark" or make another noise to help your Border Collie find her. Many dogs will respond with a bark of their own, with the barking continuing back and forth until the dog finds the child. "Bark" when the dog is in another part of the house, otherwise, the game is too easy!

Freeze Tag: This game requires several children and one dog. The children call the dog using whatever verbal and body language they want, but they must freeze before the dog gets close enough to touch them. The child commands the dog to sit, then praises, and the game continues. The dog moves from child to child. Whereas younger children may not stand still when a dog chases them, they understand how to freeze in a game setting.

Fetch or Frisbee: These games give a dog a great workout and also teach him that he must give up the ball or Frisbee in order for the game to continue. Make sure your children play this game properly, with the dog actually retrieving the object rather than a game of Keep Away, which undermines your child's authority. Also, be careful to throw a Frisbee close to the ground so your dog doesn't need to jump completely off the ground to catch it. The leaps and twists of Frisbee-catching can lead to serious spinal injuries.

Tricks: Teaching tricks, from Shake to Play Dead and Roll Over, is a way for your child to bond with your dog and enforce your child's alpha position.

Chase the Flashlight/Bubbles/Hose: With this game, your child can wear out your dog while barely moving a muscle. When playing with a flashlight, the child shines the beam on the ground and quickly runs it back and forth, in circles, or in figure-eights while the dog chases it. Make sure your child lets your dog see her take out and put away this toy. Since flashlight beams have no smell, appear out of nowhere, and can never be caught, they can turn an intense Border Collie even more obsessive, with the dog constantly searching for the elusive beam, even when the game is over. The new variation of this game uses laser toys to the same effect. Take care never to shine the laser beam in his eyes. This chase game can also be played with blown bubbles or water streaming from a hose. If your dog gets too obsessive, try another game instead.

Find the Toy: Help your child teach your dog to know his toys by name and to retrieve them on command. You can do this by associating a name with each toy as your dog picks it up. For example, if your dog picks up his tennis ball, say, "Ball" and then praise him. When he picks up his stuffed mailman say, "Mailman," again followed with praise. If you tell him to get his mailman and he instead picks up his ball, say "Wrong. Get the mailman!" Reward a correct find.

Doggie Soccer: If your Border Collie loves balls, this may be the game for him. As mentioned, however, teach your dog a "Leave it" command or your dog may control the ball and not let anyone else play with it. And don't play this game with an extremely dominant Border Collie; it may bring out aggressive tendencies.

Backyard Agility: With a few homemade jumps, a fabric tunnel from a toy store, and garden stakes pushed into the ground to form weave poles, you can make your own mini agility course. Of course, always keep your dog's well-being in mind and make sure obstacles are sturdy and safe.

Red Light, Green Light: If your dog has learned to follow the obedience command "down" while he is moving, try this game, played with several children and your dog. One child turns her back and calls "Come," and then "Red light, green light, one, two, three." On the count of three, the child turns to face the rest of the players and commands "Down," at which point the children must all freeze and the dog must drop in place. The game continues until one of the children or the dog reaches the child who is "it."

your Border Collie has frequent, positive experiences with all types of pets from an early age, he will be much more likely to live peaceably with a menagerie of animals as he gets older. Since it is impossible to teach cats and other small animals not to run from a Border Collie, it is important that you keep your dog and other pets separated when you can't supervise. In the case of a cat, provide areas for the cat to escape to that your Border Collie can't reach.

Liz Phares says her Border Collies get along well with all types of animals, but it took some work. "Both of my dogs are great with other animals. I used to have a guinea pig that had the run of the house for several hours a day. 'Da boyz' never hurt him. They even helped me raise a litter of kittens by baby-sitting them. The little devils crawled all over both dogs without a problem. However, this behavior is a result of years of training and supervised interactions. My one dog, Duncan, killed and ate my pet mouse before I taught him that animals were not to be harassed. Remember that Border Collies are herding dogs in charge of helping the shepherd without injuring the sheep, but that this skill is based on prey drive and the instinct to kill."

Some Border Collies love playing with dogs of all breeds and sizes, while others are a little more standoffish. Many Border Collies get snappy or even fight with dogs who get in their space. They often get along best with other Border Collies who respect their need for respectful distance when playing. In a large crowd of dogs, you may find your Border Collie on the outside, circling the group to make sure no one escapes!

Making Your Border Collie a Good Neighbor

You've taught your dog how to behave with your family pets and your children. Now, let's make friends with the rest of the neighborhood!

Holiday Hazards: Keeping Your Border Collie Safe and Healthy

Your Border Collie is an important part of your family, and you no doubt will want him to join in holiday festivities. However, you must keep in mind that some of the very touches that make the holidays special for us, such as rich food and tinsel decorations, can spell disaster for your pet.

If you are diligent about watching what your dog eats on a day-to-day basis, don't let this diligence slip during the holidays. Many foods we indulge in at these special times are hazardous for your dog. Chocolate can kill your dog, as can turkey bones. Other holiday foods, such as rich sauces, gravies, and spicy meats, may not pose as much danger to your pet, but they can give him a pretty bad stomachache (not to mention messy stool). Warn children and guests about the dangers of these foods to ensure that no one sneaks your pet a hazardous treat when you aren't looking. If you want to treat your dog to special snacks around the holidays, pick up holiday treats at a pet-supply store or bake your own fun-shaped dog biscuits. Your Border Collie will appreciate one of these treats just as much as he would your table food, and they won't compromise his health.

Another danger, especially around Christmas, is holiday decorations. The sparkle and shine of tinsel, garland, and Christmas tree ornaments might entice a curious Border Collie. Tinsel and garland are not digestible and may cause serious intestinal blockage. Fragile glass ornaments can break and pierce your dog's paw, or mouth or intestine if eaten. Many dogs are attracted to the tree and like to chew on it or to drink the water from the tree stand, both of which can make him sick. Your best bet is to block your dog's access to these hazards by putting up dog gates or by placing electrically charged mats (available through pet-supply stores and catalogs) around the tree and other decorations.

The holidays are a fun, but hectic time for most people. Take some time out to go for a walk with your Border Collie or to just snuggle with him in front of the fire. You'll both appreciate the break!

First, think about what could potentially turn your dog into a bad neighbor. Excessive noise is one thing that can upset neighbors. A dog who whines, barks, or howls for hours at a time is certainly a nuisance. To avoid this problem, do not leave your dog outside for hours on end. Border Collies need plenty of physical and mental stimulation, and noise problems can arise when a dog grows bored after being isolated in the backyard for long periods of time.

If your dog barks in the house when you leave, she is probably exhibiting separation anxiety. You can avoid this by following several steps. First, you must analyze your behavior both when you leave the dog and when you come home. Do you hug and kiss your Border Collie and apologize for leaving, and then shower her with more guilty love when you return? If so, naturally your dog gets upset when you leave. It is like sandwiching a barren desert of loneliness between two oases of attention! Try instead to make your departures and reunions matter-of-fact. Give your Border Collie a special toy such as a Kong stuffed with treats when you are about to go out the door and don't even say goodbye; slip out while she is busy investigating her goodie. When you come home, ignore your dog for the first few minutes. Take off your coat, change into comfortable clothes, or busy yourself in some other way, then calmly greet your dog. This helps "take the edge off" and makes your absences easier for your dog to handle. Of course, if your dog still seems unduly anxious or you come home one day to a shredded couch, consult an animal behaviorist to deal with your Border Collie's anxiety.

> If your dog barks in the house when you leave, she is probably exhibiting separation anxiety.

Another habit that may cause tense relations with your neighbors is a dog's penchant for roaming the neighborhood. Any dog who is off-leash can seem like a threat. Your dog may be the gentlest canine on Earth, but a neighbor is wise to assume the worst of a stray. Your dog may damage neighboring flowerbeds, gardens, and other property, and herd neighborhood children if she has not been taught that this is unacceptable behavior. Keep your dog on-leash during walks, and confined behind a sturdy fence when in your backyard. Never chain your Border Collie in your yard. It will provoke aggression in your dog (a by-product of being constantly jerked back when she attempts to protect her property), which will surely contribute to your dog's "bad neighbor" status.

Being unruly on walks gives your neighbors another reason to cross your dog off the block party invitation list. A dog who barks or lunges at every passerby is unpleasant to be around. Teach your Border Collie to greet strangers calmly and to sit at corners to allow cars to pass by. Practicing obedience heeling, sits, and downs while on walks around the neighborhood can show people how well trained your dog really is.

Traveling with and Boarding Your Border Collie

A point will surely come when you will need to get away from it all and take a vacation. Now, here's the dilemma: Do you take your four-legged best friend with you and make it an all-inclusive family affair, or do you let your Border Collie take a vacation of his own, either at a boarding facility or at home with a sitter? Each of these options has its pros and cons, and each requires some investigating and forethought on your part.

First, let's look at the plus side of bringing your pet with you. If you're like some dog owners, a vacation just wouldn't be a vacation without your Border Collie at your side. Even if you breathe a sigh of relief at the thought of a week free of 6:00 A.M. dog walks, you may surprise yourself during vacation by waking at sunrise and taking a lonely early-morning stroll along the beach, all the while thinking how much your Border Collie would enjoy this! If your Border Collie is your constant companion, you may actually feel lost without him sleeping on the floor next to you or waking you up with enthusiastic kisses and a hearty tail wag. Dogs also are marvelous tools for meeting new people, which can provide lots of fun when you're visiting a place foreign to you. Another advantage to bringing your dog with you is that you won't have to deal with the problem of finding a suitable person to watch your Border Collie.

Now, let's look at the negatives of traveling with canines. You may genuinely want a week free of dog walking, dog feeding, dog poop-scooping, and all the other responsibilities that go with dog ownership. That is not to say you love your dog any less; you just need a break. Another factor to consider is whether you plan to visit places that do not allow dogs, such as historic sites or museums. You may decide your Border Collie would feel more relaxed and happier staying at home or in a boarding facility than being cooped up in a hotel room day after day (if the hotel will even allow it). Finally, travel itself can pose dangers to the health and safety of your pet, from overheating in a car stuck in holiday traffic to the myriad stresses and potential risks of air travel.

A good boarding facility is an excellent place to leave your pet while you're out of town. A well-run facility will provide your dog with his own living space, which may include both indoor and outdoor runs. Some facilities will walk your dog a number of times each day and will make sure your pet receives plenty of individual attention. Some of the more posh places that are cropping up around the country will even give your dog his own room, complete with a cozy bed, fun toys, soft music, or even dog videos to watch on TV!

The cons of boarding include the fact that you are entrusting your dog's care to complete strangers. If the boarding staff mistreats your dog in any way, he won't be able to tell you about it. If a facility isn't kept clean and sanitized, your dog could pick up parasites, kennel cough, or other health problems. In addition, some Border Collies just don't take well to kenneling and become depressed, refuse to eat, or pace endlessly until you return.

Dogs who don't thrive in a kennel situation are perfect candidates for the services of a pet sitter. This extends to puppies who are not yet fully vaccinated and to older dogs who don't adjust well to a change in routine. Of course, you might rely on neighbors, friends, and relatives to watch your dog. On the other hand, if you want a professional to take care of your Border Collie in your absence, you may find that a pet sitter is right for you. Pet sitters will come to your house a few times a day (some may even stay overnight if you request it and they are available) to feed, water, and exercise your dog, keeping with his normal routine. Pet sitters also may perform small household tasks such as taking in mail and turning lights on and off. These personal touches not only make things more pleasant for your dog, but they also give your house a lived-in look, which can discourage break-ins (as does the fact that your barking Border Collie is at home).

What are the cons of pet sitters? They tend to cost more than boarding facilities, and their costs typically increase with the

> Some of the more posh boarding facilities that are cropping up around the country will even give your dog his own room, complete with a cozy bed, fun toys, soft music, or even dog videos to watch on TV!

number of services you ask them to perform. In the case of a pet sitter, you're not only trusting a stranger to care for your dog, you're also giving a stranger access to your home. You should thoroughly check out a pet sitter before handing over a key. Finally, unless you've made plans for the sitter to stay at your house, your dog may spend many more hours alone than he is used to, which could be a problem for an energetic Border Collie.

Traveling with Your Dog

If you make the choice to bring your dog along on your trip, you should plan and prepare carefully in advance for your dog's travel needs.

Before You Leave   Teaching your dog to behave well on a trip shouldn't start on the day you leave. In fact, if you want your Border Collie to be a pleasurable travel companion, you must introduce him to travel when he is a puppy. First, you'll need to ensure he is crate trained. Crates provide the safest haven for your dog during car travel and are a necessity for air travel (unless a dog is a certified assistance dog for the blind or disabled).

Next, you'll want to gradually get him used to riding in a car. First, place him in the car in his crate or strapped in with a doggie seat belt. This keeps him safe in case of an accident, prevents him from climbing on you while you are trying to drive, and stops him from hanging his head out the window. Although a grinning Border Collie with tongue flapping in the breeze may look like the picture of contentment, your dog could get hurt or worse from flying debris or a jutting tree branch. Once you've put your dog in the vehicle, turn on the car and speak to him calmly and encouragingly. If he remains calm, reward him with praise and possibly a treat. Then, turn off the car and let your Border Collie out. Repeat this process for a few days. Once you're sure he is not frightened, take him for a short trip to a friend's house. Keep everything upbeat and fun. Continue taking him on lots of short trips around the neighborhood or while you run errands. Remember to never leave your dog alone in the car on a warm day. Even if the temperature is not threatening, don't leave a young or newly acquired dog alone for more than a few minutes, because he may become frightened. If that happens, you will take a few steps backward in your training and will need to gradually reacquaint him with the car. The more often you expose your dog to the car and the more fun you make car travel, the more willingly he'll accept longer trips later in life. The last thing you want is for every ride to be for "business purposes," that is, going to the vet!

Next, you'll need to plan your vacation. Although you may pride yourself on being spontaneous, when taking a trip with your dog, spontaneity is usually not the best course of action. There's nothing worse than driving around trying to find a hotel that allows pets when you are tired and in a strange area. Be smart and call ahead to find a hotel at your destination that accepts pets.

When traveling out of the country, find out from the U.S. Department of Agriculture Animal Plant Health Inspection Service whether the areas you're visiting impose any restrictions on importing animals. England and even Hawaii, for example, have a quarantine period that

Did You Know?

Chinese royalty considered their Pekingese dogs to be sacred and provided them with human wet nurses, servants, and guards to protect them from other dogs.

will probably convince you to leave your Border Collie home for the trip. And begin your research early; some countries require time-consuming tests, quarantines, and multiple health certificates. Traveling without these may result in your pet not being allowed to travel into a country and being stranded. If you land on foreign soil before discovering such a problem, your dog may not be allowed to return home with you.

Traveling by Car   Having a well-trained dog is important when traveling by car, but it is only one part of the equation. Before loading your Border Collie into the car for a trip, first pack all his necessities. Remember to bring the following items:

○ Your dog's crate
○ Your dog's leash
○ Travel bowls for food and water (Dog canteens are wonderful to bring on hikes as well as on car rides.)
○ A supply of your dog's food (in case it is not available where you are traveling)
○ A thermos of water from home (to mix with the water at the vacation destination to prevent stomach upset)
○ Proof of vaccination
○ Medication and health records (if your dog has a medical condition)
○ A health certificate (if you're driving across the border, for example, between Canada and the United States, or a foreign-travel certificate if you are leaving North America)
○ Lots of plastic baggies and towels (paper and cloth) for cleaning muddy paws and drying wet coats
○ A basic first-aid kit

Grooming supplies may come in handy, too. Also, make sure your Border Collie is wearing a flat buckle collar (rather than a choke or prong collar, which could catch on something and strangle him) with his ID and rabies tags attached. The last thing you want is for your dog to become separated from you in a strange town without any identification. It's also a good idea to prepare for the worst by making up some lost dog flyers with a blank space in which to insert the phone number where you are staying.

While driving, stop every couple of hours to let your dog stretch his legs and relieve himself. If you are traveling in warm weather, monitor your Border Collie to ensure he does not overheat, and use air conditioning if possible. Again—and this deserves repeating over and over—never leave a dog in a parked car during warm weather; the results could be fatal. If you are traveling during cold weather and want to leave your dog in the car for a short time, while you get something to eat, for instance, provide your Border Collie with a blanket to snuggle in. Never leave a Border Collie in an unheated car in sub-zero weather.

Traveling by Air Air travel is more complicated than traveling by car. Unfortunately, a Border Collie is too large to ride in the passenger compartment under the seat in front of you (which is an option for smaller dogs). Unless your dog is a certified assistance dog, he will have to travel as freight in the cargo hold. You should book your dog's flight as far ahead as possible, since the airline may limit the number of animals it will carry, and try to schedule a nonstop flight. As each individual airline has its own pet policies, ask for detailed information, in writing if possible. When calling airlines, inquire whether their cargo holds are temperature controlled. Temperatures in cargo bays can fluctuate to extremes, from the heat of sitting in the sun on the runway to the cold of flying tens of thousands of feet above the earth. Even if the temperature is controlled, try to avoid temperature stresses on your pet by planning summer flights for early morning or evening and winter flights for the afternoon.

Within ten days before flying, take your Border Collie to the veterinarian for a full examination and ask for a health certificate stating your dog is in good health and cleared to fly. If you are worried your dog will experience exceptional stress during the flight, ask your veterinarian if she recommends tranquilizers. She may advise against them, because individual dogs react differently to tranquilizers, making the results difficult to predict. Also, ask her whether your dog needs any special vaccinations to prevent diseases specific to your vacation destination, such as against Lyme disease if you're traveling to an area with a heavy tick population.

> As each individual airline has its own pet policies, ask for detailed information, in writing if possible.

Most vets recommend that you withhold food for four hours before a flight and withhold water for two (although you can substitute ice cubes).

Make sure your dog fully relieves himself before you put him in his crate. All airlines require that you use a sturdy, federally approved crate. The crate must latch securely, but without locks (in case airline personnel need to remove your dog from his kennel); allow enough room for your Border Collie to stand up, turn around, and lie down; and provide air flow on three sides (four for international travel). You must also label the crate "live animal" and mark it with your name, home address and phone number, and your contact information at your destination. You will need to attach empty food and water bowls to the inside of the crate (airline personnel will fill them, if necessary). You must also fasten a plastic baggie filled with your dog's food to the top of the crate (so your dog can't reach it).

As with car travel, your dog should wear a flat buckle collar with ID and rabies tags. For your own peace of mind, you may want to remind flight attendants that your dog is on board in case of an emergency.

Hotels and Campgrounds   When traveling to a hotel or campground, call ahead to confirm that the facility allows pets. Many travel books list pet-friendly hotels, motels, bed and breakfasts, and campgrounds. The Automobile Association of America (AAA) is another good resource. If the hotel doesn't have a definite policy on pets, news that your dog is obedience-trained or has a Canine Good Citizen certificate may help sway policy in your direction. Never try to sneak your pet into a hotel or other establishment that doesn't permit dogs. Not only will you spend a stressful vacation trying not to get caught, but also, if you are found out, your actions will probably guarantee that the no-pets policy will never change in your favor. If you and your dog are good ambassadors, showing that animals can be calm and well behaved in a hotel setting, you and others like you will help convince more hotels to allow dogs. If, on the other hand, your Border Collie barks incessantly, relieves himself on the carpet, or chews up the nightstand, you may convince a hotel not to allow pets ever again.

When staying in a hotel that allows pets, always follow the rules. If they state no animals on the furniture, make sure your Border Collie stays on the floor, whether or not that is your personal policy. Some hotels require you to crate your pet if you leave the room, while others stipulate that you must never leave pets alone in the room. This rule doesn't necessarily prevent you from participating in activities without your canine, however. Ask the hotel about local boarding kennels or doggie day care. Some attractions, such as Six Flags and certain Disney locations, also provide on-site kennels.

Some people prefer the personal attention of a bed and breakfast or the privacy of a rented condominium or vacation home. Again, call ahead to make sure the owner or manager allows pets. Some bed and breakfasts forbid pets altogether, whereas, on the opposite end of the spectrum, others offer free dog-walking services and other pet-friendly amenities. If they allow pets at all, rental units or houses often require a pet deposit and a written contract spelling out the pet owner's liability for potential damage to the condominium or house.

Campgrounds usually allow dogs, but it is still best to call ahead to avoid disappointment. Those that allow dogs typically require that owners leash their dogs, pick up after them, and keep them from barking excessively. Some campgrounds also demand that owners never leave their dogs alone at the site.

When camping, remember to bring along water from home to mix with local water, at least for the first few days, to prevent stomach upset. Also, check your Border Collie regularly for signs of fleas and/or ticks.

Boarding Your Dog

Don't feel guilty if you decide not to bring your Border Collie on vacation with you. If you make the right arrangements, your dog might have so much fun, he won't even notice you're gone!

You can board your dog at either a veterinary facility or a private kennel. Veterinary boarding facilities are ideal for dogs with medical conditions or for senior dogs whose health is a concern. If your dog is familiar with the staff at your veterinary clinic, he may feel more comfortable staying there than at an unfamiliar kennel. Veterinary boarding facilities are usually smaller than most private kennels, which is a plus if your dog is uncomfortable surrounded by a lot of dogs he doesn't know. Services at veterinary facilities run the gamut, from simple runs that dogs are expected to use for exercise and elimination to scheduled individual walks, playtime, or even grooming.

Private kennels, too, offer a wide range of services, depending on the individual facility. Some expect dogs to remain confined to their runs, while others offer dog walks and supervised playtime with other dogs, while still others feature private doggie rooms and jam-packed days filled with training classes, agility obstacle courses, grooming sessions, and dog-biscuit snack breaks! Whatever amenities you are looking for, your chances are good of finding a kennel out there that offers them.

> Whatever amenities you are looking for, your chances are good of finding a kennel out there that offers them.

To find a private kennel, ask your veterinarian or dog-owning friends and relatives for recommendations. You also can call the American Boarding Kennel Association (ABKA) for member kennels in your area. For contact information on the ABKA, which requires members to adhere to a code of ethics, see the Resources section at the end of this book.

Once you've found several kennels in the area that sound promising, make an appointment to visit them personally. You'll want to make sure the facility is clean and the staff seems friendly and attentive to the animals. The kennel staff should allow you to see the area where your dog will actually stay and not just a front waiting room. If the kennel staff refuses to let you fully inspect the premises, don't leave your dog there.

Whether dealing with a veterinary or private boarding facility, you should ask several questions before entrusting your dog to them. How often are the runs and other boarding areas sanitized? Can you provide your dog's own food to lessen the likelihood of stomach upset? Where will your dog spend his time? Will he remain confined to a run, or will he be taken for walks or given supervised playtime? Is the facility staffed 24 hours a day? What plans are in effect in case of an emergency? Does the facility work in conjunction with a local veterinarian in the event of medical emergencies? Regardless of the type of medical and emergency provisions the kennel provides, always leave your own veterinarian's number with the kennel. What are the facility's rates? Of course, you'll also need to ask whether an opening exists for the dates you are planning to be away. Kennels tend to book up quickly during holidays and peak summer vacation times, so make your reservations as far in advance as possible.

If you are impressed with the facility, it wouldn't hurt to leave your dog there overnight for a trial run. This will allow you to judge his reaction to kenneling and will ease your mind when you take him in for a longer stay. It's also a good idea to leave an article of clothing with your scent, such as a recently worn T-shirt or sweatshirt, to help your dog feel more comfortable.

Hiring a Pet Sitter

If you decide your dog doesn't take well to kenneling, or if you just want the personal touch and extra services a pet sitter provides, this is an excellent option. But don't choose just anyone. Remember, this person will have access to your house so you need to use extra caution.

Again, ask your veterinarian or dog-owning friends for recommendations. The National Association of Professional Pet Sitters and Pet Sitters International also can help you in your search (see the Resources section at the back of the book). Check to make sure any professional pet sitter you consider is licensed, bonded, and insured. During your initial phone call, explain what you are looking for and ask if the pet sitter offers these services. Virtually all pet sitters will feed, water, walk, and play with your dog, but some also will water your plants, feed your goldfish, and perform other small tasks. Ask the sitter about her background and experience. Also ask for several personal references and call these people to ask about their experiences with the pet sitter.

Once you pick out a candidate, invite her over to meet your dog. Watch how the sitter interacts with your pet. Let her take your Border Collie for a walk around the block and play with him in the yard. You will want to find a sitter who understands the special exercise needs of a Border Collie before booking her to care for your pet.

> Check to make sure any professional pet sitter you consider is licensed, bonded, and insured.

Your sitter should offer a contract that clearly states the services rendered. She should display a friendly demeanor and an obvious love of animals. The sitter should have a working relationship with a local veterinarian in case of emergencies (although you should also provide your veterinarian's number). Also make sure the sitter has worked out a contingency plan in case she cannot attend to your pet because of illness or another personal matter.

Take the sitter through your house and show her where you keep the dog food, cleaning supplies, treats, toys, and other pet necessities. Explain any peculiarities in your dog's behavior (for example, he walks on your right side instead of heeling on the left, or he is afraid of thunder). On the day you leave for vacation, make sure your house is fully stocked with dog food, treats, any medication your pet needs, cleaning supplies, and other essentials. Also, leave your veterinarian's number and contact numbers for your destination in a prominent place. It's a good idea to arrange for the sitter to arrive just as you are leaving, so you can make sure your dog doesn't consider her an intruder. Then, walk out the door and enjoy your vacation. Don't hesitate to call once or twice (or more) during your trip—your pet sitter won't mind and you'll feel better hearing how well your dog is doing without you!

Neighbors and Friends and Relatives, Oh My!

Although these people are not professionals, they can make good dog sitters—or not. If you are considering asking a neighbor, friend, or relative to watch your pet, confirm that she has experience with dogs (another dog owner is preferable), is responsible, and gets along well with your Border Collie. You'll want to use someone who will treat watching your pet as seriously as a professional would. Payment can consist of whatever is mutually agreeable, from money to a dinner out or reciprocal dog watching when the other person goes on vacation.

As with a professional pet sitter, leave phone numbers for your veterinarian and your destination in a prominent place, as well as general care instructions and an ample supply of food and other necessities.

9

A Lifetime of Love and Good Health

In This Chapter

❍ Your Aging Border Collie—What to Expect
❍ How to Keep Your Older Border Collie Comfortable
❍ Saying Goodbye

Your Border Collie has always lived life on the run. Her boundless energy and tireless companionship have made the days pass quickly, always filled with new canine adventures. But, suddenly, you realize many days have slipped by since your Border Collie was an awkward little puppy, trying to herd fallen leaves skittering across the backyard. Perhaps her ball retrieving is not quite as rapid as it used to be, and her eyes, while still intense, are slightly clouded. A few gray hairs may even grace her grinning muzzle. You feel a tug at your heart—your dog is getting older.

Since we usually outlive our dogs, we may have several dogs come and go in our lifetime. However, you can do everything within your power to ensure that your dog receives the best nutrition, exercise, and veterinary care throughout her life and, most importantly, knows how much you love her each and every day. And when the time comes, your dog will need you to have the courage to say goodbye.

Your Aging Border Collie—What to Expect

Border Collies live to an average of 13 years. They seem to have a short period of old age, staying active for many years. Still, no matter how young and puppyish your Border Collie continues to look and act, changes are going on in her body that prove time is marching on. Learning what to expect as your dog ages better equips you for keeping her healthy and content in her sunset years.

Age-Related Disorders

A number of health problems can occur with advanced age. As with all health issues, it is important to educate yourself about these disorders ahead of time, so you know what signs to look for and what to do to keep your dog as comfortable as possible.

Arthritis

Virtually all elderly dogs develop stiffness in their joints. As a result, your aging Border Collie may struggle to get up from a nap, stumble and fall occasionally, or just seem to experience difficulty moving. Arthritis is a catchall term for a number of degenerative joint diseases. Other ailments, such as Lyme disease as well as kidney and liver problems may also make a dog sore, sluggish, and reluctant to move. Don't assume that your dog has arthritis if he shows these symptoms. Let your veterinarian make a diagnosis at the onset of these signs. If it is arthritis, your dog can begin treatment immediately. If it is another problem, the early diagnosis may be a lifesaver.

Some recent advances have made all the difference in dogs' lives, allowing some dogs to more comfortably live out many more years, whereas a short time ago, they might have been euthanized. Ask your veterinarian about these new pharmaceuticals and nutraceuticals (foods with health benefits) and whether any of them might be a good option for your dog if he is diagnosed with arthritis. As with many medications, some of the new drugs present side effects that, unfortunately, may offset their benefits. For some dogs, however, these medications (or supplements) truly are miracles. Many owners choose alternative medicines, such as acupuncture and chiropractic medicine, to treat their pet's arthritis in conjunction with or in place of conventional medicine.

> No matter how young and puppyish your Border Collie continues to look and act, changes are going on in her body that prove time is marching on.

In addition to treating the arthritis medically, you'll want to make some adjustments to your Border Collie's environment to offset the effects of aging, such as ensuring he doesn't catch drafts and making sure he eats a high-quality, well-balanced diet. While exercise is still vital, it should be toned down to reflect your older Border Collie's slower pace.

Obesity

In general, older dogs require fewer calories. They tend to exercise less than younger dogs. If they continue to eat the same type and quantity of food as they did in their prime, they usually gain weight. Obesity in a Border Collie not only is unattractive, it also can predispose your dog to heart disease, cancer, musculoskeletal problems, and diabetes.

There are many excellent lower-calorie senior-formula dog foods on the market that will provide your dog with the proper nutrition, yet allow you to continue feeding the same amount of food so that your dog doesn't suspect he is on a diet. You also can try splitting your Border Collie's food into several smaller meals during the day, just as you did when he was a puppy, to ease his digestion.

Again, exercise is important, but should not be overdone. While your dog may not be able to run all day like he used to, frequent walks and swimming, which place less stress on limbs and joints, are good options. Ask your veterinarian for more suggestions on how best to exercise your older Border Collie.

Diabetes Mellitus

With this condition, the body's cells are unable to metabolize sugar in the blood due to a deficiency of insulin or the cells' lack of response to insulin. Diabetes is a serious disease that can result in death if left untreated.

Symptoms of diabetes include increased drinking and urination, dehydration, and weight loss. Blood and urine tests can confirm a diagnosis by measuring for elevated sugar levels and abnormally high or low insulin levels. The causes of diabetes range from genetic disorders to obesity and a poor diet.

If your Border Collie is diagnosed with diabetes mellitus, he may require insulin injections for the rest of his life. Many owners find it easier to learn to give their pet insulin shots than to constantly take their

Senior Health Care

Many veterinarians recommend a geriatric screening for your dog at the appropriate age. A geriatric screening usually includes a physical exam, blood tests, and an electrocardiogram or specialized tests for your dog's specific health conditions. Diseases of older dogs that are not usually seen in young dogs include arthritis, diabetes, Cushing's disease (obesity and muscular weakness caused by malfunction of the adrenal or pituitary glands), cancer, and kidney, heart, and liver disease. Your veterinarian will perform blood tests during a geriatric visit to screen for many of these diseases.

Since dogs of different sizes age at different rates, screening begins at different ages:

Up to 15 pounds

Begin geriatric screening at age nine to eleven

16 to 50 pounds

Begin geriatric screening at age seven to nine

51 to 80 pounds

Begin geriatric screening at age six to eight

Over 80 pounds

Begin geriatric screening at age four to six

Your veterinarian may recommend semiannual visits once your dog becomes a senior. Between visits, be alert to changes in your Border Collie that could indicate serious illness and require immediate veterinary attention:

❍ Sudden loss of weight

❍ Serious loss of appetite

❍ Increase in appetite without increase in weight

❍ Diarrhea or vomiting

❍ Increased thirst without a change in activity level and increased urination

❍ Excessive fatigue

❍ Extreme limited mobility

❍ Coughing and excessive panting

pet to the veterinarian for injections. In addition, the Border Collie's diet must be carefully controlled and the obese dog must be slowly trimmed down, under a veterinarian's supervision.

Cancer

Cancer is as dreaded of a disease in canines as it is in humans. Ask your breeder about any types of cancer that may run in your dog's family tree and then pass along this information to your veterinarian, so she can look out for anything suspicious. Also continue to check your dog's entire body at least once a week for lumps or sores that don't seem to be healing. This body check becomes even more vital as your dog ages, since early detection can dramatically improve your Border Collie's chances of survival.

In the past, many dogs diagnosed with cancer were euthanized as a matter of course. Today, cancer treatments, such as surgery, radiation, chemotherapy, and even gene therapy, are giving many dogs a new lease on life. Unfortunately, the high cost of some of these procedures still prohibits many owners from taking advantage of these life-prolonging options.

Some of the holistic methods of treating cancer include nutritional, herbal and antioxidant therapies, organic diets, and stress reduction. Always consult with your veterinarian before embarking on any treatment plan.

Kidney and Liver Failure

Older dogs often suffer from kidney and/or liver dysfunction, which, like diabetes, may first be suspected due to increased thirst and urination, and dehydration. Luckily, special prescription diets are available that can help these organs to function properly. Your veterinarian will run tests on your dog's kidneys and/or liver and plot a course of action.

Cushing's Disease

Either a pituitary tumor or an adrenal lesion, leading to an abnormally high output of corticosteroid hormones, can cause this disease. Symptoms include weakness; muscle loss; thin, wrinkled skin; high blood sugar; and decreased resistance to infection. Cushing's disease is usually treated with drug therapy.

Heart Disease

Heart problems can show up in previously healthy dogs as they age, just as older humans can develop similar disorders. If your dog seems weak, won't eat, coughs, and cannot tolerate his normal amount of exercise, take him to the veterinarian to check for possible heart problems.

Deafness

Many older dogs develop hearing loss. If your dog seems to ignore you lately or to startle easily when you come up behind him, he may be going deaf. First, ask your veterinarian to check his ears to rule out infection or an excessive buildup of wax. If his ears are clear, you'll have to accept that your dog is hard of hearing and make certain adjustments to better communicate with him and keep him safe (see the section to follow, How to Keep Your Older Dog Comfortable).

> If your dog seems to ignore you lately or to startle easily when you come up behind him, he may be going deaf.

Eye Disorders

The most common eye problems in older dogs are glaucoma and cataracts. Glaucoma is caused by increased pressure in the eye due to a physiological malfunction. The first sign of glaucoma is usually a mild reddening of the white of the eye. If left untreated, the eye(s) may begin to bulge. At this advanced stage, the dog will likely go blind. If you notice any abnormality in your Border Collie's eyes, don't risk permanent damage by taking a wait-and-see approach—take your dog to your veterinarian right away.

Cataracts appear as a cloudiness inside a dog's eye(s). They are actually a clouding of the lens of the eye, which prevents a dog from having normal vision. Your veterinarian may prescribe a topical medication. These medications allow the eye to dilate, so the dog can see around the clouded lens, but they do not treat the cataract itself. Surgery is highly successful and can prevent blindness. Many owners opt to do nothing, however, since most dogs have little trouble coping with a gradual loss of sight (see How to Keep Your Older Dog Comfortable).

Lenticular sclerosis, a natural aging and clouding of the lens, can appear to the untrained eye to be cataracts. This condition is different from cataracts, however, because it does not cause blindness, just a mild clouding that the dog sees through well. Your veterinarian will be able to tell the difference.

> Even relatively healthy elderly dogs commonly leak urine occasionally, particularly females and especially while sleeping.

Urinary Incontinence

Owners who are unaware of this potential old-age condition may wonder why their housetrained dog suddenly starts to have accidents. A number of medical conditions can cause incontinence, including a bladder infection or a weakened bladder sphincter muscle. If your dog becomes incontinent, take him to a veterinarian for a thorough examination and to obtain treatment for any medical problems detected.

Even relatively healthy elderly dogs commonly leak urine occasionally, particularly females and especially while sleeping. An inexpensive medication, phenopropanolamine, can usually stop or at least minimize this leakage. If medication doesn't solve the problem, you may need to take your Border Collie outside to eliminate during the night. In addition, you may want to place a rubber-backed mat or a plastic tarp covered by an old quilt in your dog's sleeping area to protect your floor and carpet. Doggie diapers can also provide somewhat of a solution. Most important, don't punish your dog for behaviors she can't control. She most likely is as upset as you are. She needs love and understanding at this stage of her life, not scolding and disapproval.

How to Keep Your Older Border Collie Comfortable

You can do a number of things to keep your dog content and comfortable in his older years. The most important thing is to pay close attention to and understand your dog's needs. If he seems sore, massage his aching muscles. If he shivers, cover him with a blanket. If he wakes up one day and seems to have forgotten where he is, reassure him with your voice and touch that he is home and he is loved.

Exercise

Being a Border Collie, your dog most likely will resist the notion of growing old. There may be days when he seems

Did You Know?

The old rule of multiplying a dog's age by seven to find the equivalent human age is inaccurate. A better measure is to count the first year as 15, the second year as ten, and each year after that as five.

to think he's a pup again, dashing around the yard with pep and vigor. Then, there may be days when he lies in his bed and doesn't seem to want to get up. If your dog shows a sudden decrease in energy, make an appointment with your veterinarian right away. If the doctor rules out medical problems, he may just need a little extra attention and some incentive to get moving. Although older dogs naturally slow down, they still need daily exercise. Modify your Border Collie's exercise to fit his age and physical condition. Frequent, leisurely walks will get your dog's blood pumping and lift his spirits. Keep in mind that older dogs, especially, must warm up before and cool down after any exercise more strenuous than a stroll around the block. A game of hide-and-seek or find the hidden toy can also work your dog's mind and body without overtaxing him.

All dogs love routine, but older dogs especially rely on set patterns during their day. Try to pick certain times to exercise your pet and stick with the schedule. Your dog will naturally want to spend more time with you as he senses advancing age, and will look forward to these special moments of one-on-one companionship.

> If your dog shows a sudden decrease in energy, make an appointment with your veterinarian right away.

Although routine is important, a little excitement now and then can add spice to your Border Collie's day. Take an impromptu ride to the park or a trip to the beach or a lake. Your dog might even enjoy a dip in calm, soothing waters. If you are at the beach, however, don't let him romp any farther than the water's edge; he may swim out into the surf only to find he's not strong enough to swim back in. Swimming in a lake or pond (not a flowing river) provides great, low-stress exercise for your dog. Remember to thoroughly dry him off when he comes out of the water, so he doesn't get chilled.

Be aware of any sensitivity your dog may develop to heat and/or cold. If you take him out on a warm day, allow your dog plenty of rest in shaded areas and bring along a canteen of cool water. Remember that your pet will need more frequent stops to catch his breath than he did as a youngster.

Your dog may also need special accommodations when joining you on a wintry walk in the woods. While a Border Collie's coat in most cases is enough to keep him warm, you may want to invest in some canine booties to protect his feet. He won't care if he looks a little silly—he'll just be happy that he's toasty warm and can still accompany you on your journey.

Bedding and Sleeping Area

If your dog has always slept on the floor or even a thin blanket, now is the time to get something a little cushier. You can purchase a special orthopedic dog bed or buy egg-carton foam and cover it with blankets or fake sheepskin for a do-it-yourself doggie de-stressor. If your dog has trouble walking up stairs, you may need to move his bed from an upstairs room to a downstairs area.

While your dog will continue to enjoy some time in the yard, he most likely will spend more and more time lounging in the house by your side. His extra sensitivity to hot and cold weather makes the climate-controlled atmosphere of your home even more appealing. Enjoy this extra time with your pet. You will treasure these memories in the years to come.

Grooming

As mentioned earlier, checking your dog from head to toe is even more important as he ages. Look for any signs of odd lumps or bumps and brush your

Border Collie thoroughly to keep him looking and feeling his best. Older dogs can experience dry skin, but frequent brushing distributes natural oils over the coat and helps keep this problem in check.

Since your dog now gets less intense exercise than he used to, chances are his nails will need more frequent trimming. Don't neglect this important grooming ritual, or your dog's mobility may suffer.

If you traditionally used a grooming table, you may want to switch to grooming your Border Collie on the floor. He probably will feel more comfortable there, and you won't have to worry about him losing his balance and falling.

Dental health is also essential as your dog ages. If you've faithfully brushed your pet's teeth and taken him for regular teeth cleanings over the years, your Border Collie's teeth should remain in pretty good shape. If you notice that he has difficulty crunching his dry kibble, however, you may want to soak it in water to soften it or switch to a canned variety. If he still seems to experience pain when he eats, he may need some dental work. Putting a dog under anesthesia is always an anxious decision for owners, regardless of the dog's age. You may harbor special concerns about your senior Border Collie undergoing anesthesia. Your veterinarian can run a battery of tests beforehand to rule out any potential complications. It is important that you follow any pre-procedure instructions to the letter. For example, feeding a dog before anesthesia can result in your dog choking while he is under. If you have any questions about the instructions, talk about them with your veterinarian, so you can give your dog the best care possible.

Veterinary Visits

Your veterinarian might recommend that you switch your dog to a semiannual veterinary visit, rather than just coming in once a year. The more often she sees your dog, the more likely she will be able to spot any problems early on. As your dog ages, discuss preventive care with your veterinarian. She may want to run a number of tests on your dog to establish a baseline that will provide a comparison should your dog become sick. A typical senior exam includes a urinalysis, stool exam, and complete blood count. Liver and kidney function tests, chest x rays, and an electrocardiogram may also be included.

Nutrition

As discussed previously, obesity can pose serious complications in the older dog. Monitor your dog's weight to keep him trim and fit. Feed a balanced diet and keep your treat-giving in check. If your dog seems to be eating too little and has lost interest in his food, try mixing in some canned food with his kibble or stir in some water or unsalted chicken broth and slightly heat the mixture to make a gravy. Make sure the mixture cools down sufficiently before giving it to your dog.

> Talk to your veterinarian to determine which supplements, if any, she recommends for your Border Collie.

Dehydration in an older dog can be disastrous. If your dog seems to "forget" to drink, you may want to add extra water bowls around the house, so he happens upon fresh water frequently. With a particularly forgetful Border Collie, you might also want to issue an occasional command to "get a drink."

What about supplements? Dogs with reduced kidney function tend to lose B vitamins in their excess urine and might benefit from a supplement. Adding calcium and phosphorus can help prevent softening of bones; however, this practice can be dangerous if your dog is experiencing kidney failure. Remember to guard against over-supplementation, which can be hazardous. Talk to your veterinarian to determine which supplements, if any, she recommends for your Border Collie.

Communication

You can help a dog who is losing his sight and/or hearing in several ways. If your dog's eyesight starts to wane, he will actually memorize where things are placed in your home. He may get around so well you occasionally forget he can't see. Avoid rearranging the furniture, as this may cause your dog to bump into things, which can throw off his confidence and produce panic. Also, talk to your Border Collie when you approach him, so you don't startle your pet. Never let your dog off-leash in an unfenced area; he could easily wander into a dangerous situation that he doesn't see coming.

If your Border Collie is losing his hearing, you'll also want to make some adjustments. If he knows obedience hand signals for commands such as "Sit" or "Down," make sure to use those now. But if he doesn't know hand signals, don't despair; you can teach an old dog new tricks. Hand signals come in handy in a number of situations, such as if you are trying to call your hard-of-hearing dog back into the house from across the yard. As with a vision-impaired dog, never let a deaf dog off-leash.

Older dogs tend to get forgetful, irritable, and cranky. Practice patience and communicate to your dog how much you care about him through daily petting and nightly hugs.

Getting Your Dog a Companion

As their dog ages, many people entertain the idea of getting a puppy. They think it will put some spark in their older dog's life, and they also secretly hope it will ease their pain when their elder dog passes. But think long and hard before rushing out to buy a pup. Some older dogs, especially those who are still relatively healthy and active and have socialized well with other dogs throughout their lives, will love a new companion. They may rise to the challenge of keeping up with a youngster and the experience may even add years to their life. On the other hand, an infirm senior or a dog who has had little contact with other canines may resent a newcomer and withdraw. His health may even fade more quickly. Before adding a new pet to the family, carefully consider your dog's disposition and all aspects of the situation.

Saying Goodbye

Like all meaningful relationships in our lives, saying goodbye to our cherished pets is the most difficult part of being a dog owner. It is important that we accept this duty with courage and compassion, and make parting as easy as possible for our loyal companions.

How to Know When to Let Go

It's never easy to decide when to end your best friend's time on this earth. The decision is made for some lucky owners, whose dogs die peacefully in their sleep. Unfortunately for the rest of us, a time may come when we'll have to decide when our dog's life is no longer worth living. This is an extremely personal decision that you and you alone must

Did You Know?

The oldest dog ever documented was an Australian Cattle Dog named Bluey, who was put to sleep at the age of 29 years and five months.

make. Some owners will do anything to extend their dog's life by a few months or even a few weeks, no matter what the cost. Others, whether because of financial considerations or their personal belief that they would rather not extend their dog's suffering, will not go to extreme measures to treat their dogs. Many owners decide that when their pet loses her appetite for food, water, and for life itself, it is time to let go. Again, no one can make that decision but you.

What to Expect

When you decide it is time to alleviate your dog's suffering, call your veterinarian. Some doctors will make house calls for euthanasia, whereas others will ask you to bring in your dog. Make sure the clinic staff knows the reason for your visit. Most veterinary practices will let you move immediately into an exam room upon your arrival, where you can be alone with your dog, rather than spending your last moments together in a crowded waiting room.

> Don't feel you need to hold back your tears. Your doctor realizes what a difficult time this is and understands the flood of emotions that comes with the death of a beloved pet.

Your veterinarian will describe the procedure to you and answer any questions you have. Don't feel you need to hold back your tears. Your doctor realizes what a difficult time this is and understands the flood of emotions that comes with the death of a beloved pet. Talk to your Border Collie. Stroke her head and tell her how much you love her. We don't know what animals can understand in a situation like this, but your pet surely will feel comforted by your soothing voice and your presence.

Rainbow Bridge

Just this side of Heaven is a place called Rainbow Bridge. When an animal dies that has been especially close to someone here, that pet goes to Rainbow Bridge. There are meadows and hills for all our special friends so they can run and play together. There is plenty of food, water, and sunshine, and our friends are warm and comfortable. All the animals who had been ill or old are restored to health and vigor; those who were hurt or maimed are made whole and strong again, just as we remember them in our dreams of days gone by. The animals are happy and content, except for one small thing; they each miss someone very special to them who had to be left behind.

They all run and play together, but the day comes when one suddenly stops and looks into the distance. His bright eyes are intent; his eager body quivers. Suddenly he begins to run from the group, flying over the green grass, his legs carrying him faster and faster. You have been spotted, and when you and your special friend finally meet, you cling to each other in joyous reunion, never to be parted again. The happy kisses rain upon your face, your hands again caress the beloved head, and you look once more into the trusting eyes of your pet, so long gone from your life but never absent from your heart.

Then you cross Rainbow Bridge together.

—Author unknown

The Rainbow Bridge web site (www.rainbowbridge.tierranet.com/bridge.htm) includes this story, written by an unknown animal lover. The site includes tributes to and photos of deceased pets, a message board, and grief support. For owners who are sad after the loss of a pet, from dogs to guinea pigs, "the Bridge" is the place to go for understanding, sympathy, and help. If you've recently lost a beloved pet friend, be sure to check out this very popular web site, run by Kathie Maffit and a host of volunteers.

If you feel you absolutely cannot be in the room with your dog during her last moments, don't feel guilty. Each person handles saying goodbye to a pet differently. There is no right or wrong way to face death. Know that your need to distance yourself from your dog's final passing will not wipe away or diminish years of loving care.

After your veterinarian has explained the procedure and answered any questions, he may sedate your pet. He then will inject a drug into your dog's bloodstream that causes unconsciousness and heart failure. Your dog may appear to gasp for breath and may lose control of her bladder. These are physiological reactions to the drug—your dog will experience no pain.

Remembering Your Pet

Once you say goodbye, you can ask your veterinarian to take care of your dog's remains. Other owners ask to have their dogs cremated and request the ashes. A burial, either in your backyard (if local ordinances allow) or in a pet cemetery, is another option. For some, a favorite toy buried under a backyard tree provides the perfect memorial, while others choose to give a donation to an animal charity in their dog's honor. Whatever you choose, make sure you do what feels right for you and your family. The most important thing to remember is that emotional pain and grief are natural and must be experienced before the healing can begin.

Stages of Grief

Immediately after losing a pet, you'll probably feel numb; this often accompanies shock and denial. This first stage usually lasts longer for those whose pet's death was unexpected. The death of a senior dog who seemed fine one day, then rapidly declined, may leave her owner feeling like this couldn't possibly have happened.

Veterinary Teaching Hospital Grief Hotlines

○ University of California, Davis, California, (530) 752-4200, 6:30–9:30 P.M. PST, Monday through Friday

○ Colorado State University, Fort Collins, Colorado, (970) 491-1242

○ University of Florida, Gainesville, Florida, (352) 392-4700 (ext. 4080), takes messages 24 hours a day; someone will call back between 7:00 and 9:00 P.M. EST

○ Michigan State University, East Lansing, Michigan, (517) 432-2696, 6:30–9:30 P.M. EST, Tuesday, Wednesday, and Thursday

○ Ohio State University, Columbus, Ohio, (614) 292-1823, takes messages 6:30–9:30 P.M. EST, Monday, Wednesday, and Friday

○ University of Pennsylvania, Philadelphia, Pennsylvania, (215) 898-4529

○ Tufts University, North Grafton, Massachusetts, (508) 839-7966, 6:00–9:00 P.M. EST, Monday through Friday

○ Virginia-Maryland Regional College of Veterinary Medicine, Blacksburg, Virginia, (540) 231-8038, 6:00–9:00 P.M. EST, Tuesday and Thursday

○ Washington State University, Pullman, Washington, (509) 335-4569

During the middle stage of grief, you'll likely be filled with depression and anger. You may wake up in the morning expecting to find your Border Collie at your feet, only to be hit with a rush of emotion as you remember your dog is no longer with you. You may think you hear the sound of clicking nails in the kitchen or the jingle of dog tags down the hallway. You may feel guilty for not trying an experimental procedure, or you may feel angry with the veterinarian for not being able to cure your dog. You may find it difficult to make it through the day without crying, and you may have a hard time concentrating at work. It is important at this time to surround yourself with other pet lovers

Leaving Your Pet in Your Will

Who will care for your pet if you die before she does? Many people neglect to think this could happen, with the result of their beloved pet being placed in an animal shelter after their death. Talk with family and friends and find someone who is truly willing and able to take care of your Border Collie if you should pass. Then speak with your lawyer and include your pet in your will. You may also want to specify a certain amount of money to go to the person caring for your dog to offset the costs of food, veterinary care, and other pet-related expenses.

who will understand your grief and not criticize, wondering how you could be so upset over the death of an animal.

The final stage of grief is acceptance. At that point, you'll believe and understand the death of your pet, and the pain may begin to fade. Still, a tug at your heart may accompany memories of your Border Collie.

If you experience difficulty reaching this final stage, you may need to seek outside help. Several veterinary schools across the nation offer grief-counseling hotlines. You also can check with your veterinarian for the phone numbers of local pet-loss counseling services, which humane societies often offer. Books and Internet sites on dealing with the death of a pet can also offer some solace.

Many owners feel they need time to grieve before they can think of getting another pet, while others rush out to buy a puppy to help ease the pain. Whatever you do, realize that a new pet is an individual and can never fully replace your lost Border Collie. Appreciate your new pet for the wonderful dog she is and remember your first pet for what she was—the first Border Collie love of your life.

Appendix: Resources

Boarding, Pet Sitting, Traveling

books

Dog Lover's Companion series
Guides on traveling with dogs
 for several states and cities
Foghorn Press
P.O. Box 2036
Santa Rosa, CA 95405-0036
(800) FOGHORN

*Take Your Pet Too!: Fun
 Things to Do!*, Heather
 MacLean Walters
M.C.E. Publishing
P.O. Box 84
Chester, NJ 07930-0084

Take Your Pet USA, Arthur
 Frank
Artco Publishing
12 Channel St.
Boston, MA 02210

*Traveling with Your Pet 1999:
 The AAA Petbook*, Greg
 Weeks, Editor
Guide to pet-friendly lodging
 in the U.S. and Canada

Vacationing With Your Pet!,
 Eileen Barish
Pet-Friendly Publications
P.O. Box 8459
Scottsdale, AZ 85252
(800) 496-2665

...other resources

The American Boarding Kennels Association
4575 Galley Road, Suite 400-A
Colorado Springs, CO 80915
(719) 591-1113
www.abka.com

Independent Pet and Animal Transportation Association
5521 Greenville Ave., Ste. 104-310
Dallas, TX 75206
(903) 769-2267
www.ipata.com

National Association of Professional Pet Sitters
1200 G St. N.W., Suite 760
Washington, DC 20005
(800) 286-PETS
www.petsitters.org

Pet Sitters International
418 East King Street
King, NC 27021-9163
(336) 983-9222
www.petsit.com

U.S. Department of Agriculture
Animal and Plant Health Inspection Service
Import/Export rules, forms, and news
www.aphis.usda.gov/NCIE/

Breed Information, Clubs, Registries

American-International Border Collie Registry (AIBC)
www.aibc-registry.org/

American Kennel Club
5580 Centerview Drive
Raleigh, NC 27606-3390
(919) 233-9769
www.akc.org/

Border Collie Society of America (BCSA)
www.duke.edu/~awho/bc/bcsa.htm

United States Border Collie Club
12813 Maple Street
Silver Spring, MD 20904
www.bordercollie.org

Canadian Kennel Club
Commerce Park
89 Skyway Ave., Suite 100
Etobicoke, Ontario, Canada M9W 6R4
(416) 675-5511
www.ckc.ca

InfoPet
P.O. Box 716
Agoura Hills, CA 91376
(800) 858-0248

The Kennel Club
(British equivalent to the American Kennel Club)
1-5 Clarges Street
Piccadilly
London W1Y 8AB
ENGLAND
www.the-kennel-club.org.uk/

National Dog Registry
Box 116
Woodstock, NY 12498
(800) 637-3647
www.natldogregistry.com/

North American Sheep Dog Society
    (NASDS)
Route 3
McLeansboro, IL 62859
(618) 757-2238

Tatoo-A-Pet
6571 S.W. 20th Court
Ft. Lauderdale, FL 33317
(800) 828-8667
www.tattoo-a-pet.com

United Kennel Club
100 East Kilgore Rd.
Kalamazoo, MI 49001-5598
(616) 343-9020
www.ukccdogs.com

Dog Publications

AKC Gazette and AKC Events Calendar
51 Madison Avenue
New York, NY 10010
Subscriptions: (919) 233-9767
www.akc.org/gazet.htm
www.akc.org/event.htm

American Border Collie
218 Stagecoach Lane
Crawford, TX 76638-2911
(254) 486-2693
www.stockdog.com/abc/abc.htm

Direct Book Service
(800) 776-2665
www.dogandcatbooks.com/direct-
    book

Dog Fancy
P.O. Box 6050
Mission Viejo, CA 92690
(949) 855-8822
www.dogfancy.com

DogGone
P.O. Box 651155
Vero Beach Florida 32965-1155
(561) 569-8424
www.doggonefun.com/

Dog World
500 N. Dearborn, Suite 1100
Chicago, IL 60610
(312) 396-0600
www.dogworldmag.com/

The Ranch Dog Trainer
P.O. Box 599
Ellendale, TN 38029
(901) 383-7371

The Shepherd's Dogge
51 Farewell Road
Tyngsboro, MA 01879-1007
www.gis.net/~shepdog/Shep_Dogge/

The Working Border Collie
14933 Kirkwood Road
Sidney, OH 45365
(937) 492-2215
www.working-border-collie.com/

Working Sheepdog News
5 Vale Crescent
Bishop Walton
York, England
YO42 1SU
http://k9netuk.users.netlink.co.uk/ne
ws/wsn/index.html

Fun, Grooming, Obedience, Training

books
The Complete Idiot's Guide to Fun and Tricks with Your Dog,
Sarah Hodgson
Alpha Books

Dogs and Kids, Parenting Tips, Bardi McLennan
Howell Book House

How to Raise a Puppy You Can Live With,
Clarice Rutherford and David H. Neil, MRCVS
Alpine Publications

Old Dogs, Old Friends: Enjoying Your Older Dog,
Bonnie Wilcox, Chris Walkowitz
IDG Books Worldwide

Pet Care on a Budget, Virginia Parker Guidry
Howell Book House

Surviving Your Dog's Adolescence, Carol Lea Benjamin
Howell Book House

...other resources
American Dog Trainers Network
161 W. 4th Street
New York, NY 10014
(212) 727-7257
www.inch.com/~dogs/index.html

American Herding Breed Association
1548 Victoria Way
Pacifica, CA 94044
www.primenet.com/~joell/abba/main.htm

American Kennel Club (tracking, agility, obedience, herding)
Performance Events Dept.
5580 Centerview Drive
Raleigh, NC 27606
(919) 854-0199
www.akc.org/

American Pet Dog Trainers
P.O. Box 385
Davis, CA 95617
(800) PET-DOGS

Animal Behavior Society
Susan Foster
Department of Biology
Clark University
950 Main Street
Worcester, MA 01610-1477

Association of Pet Dog Trainers
P.O. Box 385
Davis, CA 95617
(800) PET-DOGS
www.apdt.com/

The Dog Agility Page
www.dogpatch.org/agility/

Intergroom
76 Carol Drive
Dedham, MA 02026
www.intergroom.com

National Association of Dog Obedience Instructors
PMB #369
729 Grapevine Highway
Hurst, TX 76054-2085
www.nadoi.org/

National Dog Groomers Association of America
P.O. Box 101
Clark, PA 16113
(724) 962-2711

North American Dog Agility Council
HCR 2 Box 277
St. Maries, ID 83861
www.nadac.com

North American Flyball Association
1400 W. Devon Ave, #512
Chicago, IL 60660
(309) 688-9840
www.muskie.fishnet.com/~flyball/

Pet Warehouse
P.O. Box 752138
Dayton, OH 45475-2138
(800) 443-1160

PETsMART
www.petsmart.com

U.S. Border Collie Handler's
    Association
2915 Anderson Lane
Crawford, TX 76638
254-486-2500 (phone)
254-486-2271 (fax)
www.bordercollie.org/usbcha.html

United States Canine Combined
    Training Association
2755 Old Thompson Mill Road
Buford, GA 30519
(770) 932-8604
www.siriusweb.com/USCCTA/

U.S. Dog Agility Association, Inc.
P.O. Box 850955
Richardson, Texas 75085-0955
(972) 231-9700
www.usdaa.com/

Grief Support

books
*Preparing for the Loss of Your Pet:
    Saying Goodbye With Love, Dig-
    nity and
Peace of Mind,* Myrna M. Milani,
    D.V.M.
Prima Publishing

...other resources
Chicago Veterinary Medical
    Association
(630) 603-3994

Cornell University
(607) 253-3932

International Association of Pet
    Cemeteries
P.O. Box 163
5055 Route 11
Ellenburg Depot, NY 12935
(518) 594-3000
www.iaopc.com

Michigan State University
College of Veterinary Medicine
(517) 432-2696

Petloss.com
Ed Williams
P. O. Box 571
Roseland, NJ 07068
www.petloss.com

Tufts University (Massachusetts)
School of Veterinary Medicine
(508) 839-7966

University of California, Davis
(530) 752-4200

University of Florida at Gainesville
College of Veterinary Medicine
(352) 392-4700

Virginia-Maryland Regional College
of Veterinary Medicine
(540) 231-8038

Washington State University
College of Veterinary Medicine
(509) 335-5704

Humane Organizations and Rescue Groups

American Humane Association
63 Inverness Drive E
Englewood, CO 80112-5117
(800) 227-4645
www.americanhumane.org

American Society for the Prevention
of Cruelty to Animals (ASPCA)
424 East 92nd Street
New York, NY 10128-6804
(212) 876-7700
www.aspca.org

Animal Protection Institute of America
P.O. Box 22505
Sacramento, CA 95822
(916) 731-5521

Humane Society of the United States
2100 L St. NW
Washington, DC 20037
(301) 258-3072, (202) 452-1100
www.hsus.org/

Massachusetts Society for the Prevention of Cruelty to Animals
350 South Huntington Avenue
Boston, MA 02130
(617) 522-7400
www.mspca.org/

SPAY/USA
14 Vanderventer Avenue
Port Washington, NY 11050
(516) 944-5025, (203) 377-1116 in
Connecticut
(800) 248-SPAY
www.spayusa.org/

Medical and Emergency Information

books
The Allergy Solution for Dogs,
Shawn Messonnier, D.V.M.
Prima Publishing 2000
3000 Lava Ridge Court
Roseville, CA 95661
(800) 632-8676
www.primalifestyles.com

The Arthritis Solution for Dogs,
Shawn Messonnier, D.V.M.
Prima Publishing

Dr. Pitcairn's Complete Guide to Natural Health for Dogs and Cats,
Richard H. Pitcairn, D.V.M., PhD, and Susan Hubble Pitcairn
Rodale Press, Inc. 1995

Dog Owner's Home Veterinary Handbook,
Dr. Delbert Carlson and Dr. James Griffin
Howell Book House

Pet First Aid: Cats and Dogs, by Bobbi Mammato, D.V.M.
Mosby Year Book

Skin Diseases of Dogs and Cats: A Guide for Pet Owners and Professionals,
Dr. Steven A. Melman
Dermapet, Inc.
P.O. Box 59713
Potomac, MD 20859

...other resources
American Academy on Veterinary Disaster Medicine
4304 Tenthouse Court
West River, MD 20778

American Animal Hospital Association
P.O. Box 150899
Denver, CO 80215-0899
(800) 252-2242
www.healthypet.com

American Holistic Veterinary Medicine Association
2214 Old Emmorton Road
Bel Air, MD 21015
(410) 569-2346
www.altvetmed.com

American Kennel Club Canine Health Foundation
251 West Garfield Road, Suite 160
Aurora, OH 44202
(888) 682-9696
www.akcchf.org/main.htm

American Veterinary Medical Association
1931 North Meacham Road, Suite 100
Schaumburg, IL 60173-4360
(800) 248-2862
www.avma.org/

Canine Eye Registration Foundation, Inc. (CERF)
Veterinary Medical Data Program
South Campus Courts, Building C
Purdue University
West Lafayette, IN 47907
(765) 494-8179
www.vet.purdue.edu/~yshen/cerf.html

Centers for Disease Control and
Prevention
1600 Clifton Road NE
Atlanta, GA 30333
(404) 639-3311 (CDC Operator)
(800) 311-3435 (CDC Public In-
quiries)
www.cdc.gov

National Animal Poison Control
Center
1717 S. Philo, Suite 36
Urbana, IL 61802
(888) 426-4435, $45 per case,
with as many follow-up calls as
necessary included. Have
name, address, phone number,
dog's breed, age, sex, and type
of poison ingested, if known,
available.
www.napcc.aspca.org

Orthopedic Foundation for
Animals (OFA)
2300 E. Nifong Blvd.
Columbia, MO 65201-3856.
(573) 442-0418
www.offa.org/

PennHip
c/o Synbiotics
11011 Via Frontera
San Diego, CA 92127
(800) 228-4305

U.S. Pharmacopeia
vaccine reactions: (800) 487-7776
customer service: (800) 227-8772
www.usp.org

United Animal Nations
5892 South Land Park Drive
P.O. Box 188890
Sacramento, CA 95818
Phone: (916) 429-2457
www.uan.org

Veterinary Medical Database/
Canine Eye Registration Foun-
dation
Department of Veterinary Clini-
cal Science
School of Veterinary Medicine
Purdue University
West Lafayette, IN 47907
(765) 494-8179
www.vet.purdue.edu/~yshen/

Veterinary Pet Insurance (VPI)
4175 E. La Palma Ave., #100
Anaheim, CA 92807-1846
(714) 996-2311
(800) USA PETS, (877) PET
HEALTH in Texas
www.petplan.net/home.htm

Nutrition and Natural Foods

books

Dog Treats, Kim Campbell Thornton
Main Street Books 1996

Home Prepared Dog and Cat Diets, Donald R. Strombeck
Iowa State University Press
(515) 292-0140

...other resources

American College of Veterinary Nutrition
Department of Large Animal Clinical Sciences
Virginia-Maryland Regional College of Veterinary Medicine
Blacksburg, VA 24061-0442
(540) 231-3956
www.acvn.vetmed.vt.edu/

California Natural, Natural Pet Products
P.O. Box 271
Santa Clara, CA 95052
(800) 532-7261
www.naturapet.com

PHD Products Inc.
P.O. Box 8313
White Plains, NY 10602
(800) 863-3403
www.phdproducts.net/

Sensible Choice, Pet Products Plus
5600 Mexico Road
St. Peters, MO 63376
(800) 592-6687
www.sensiblechoice.com/

Search and Rescue Dogs

National Association for Search and Rescue
4500 Southgate Place, Suite 100
Chantilly, VA 20151-1714
(703) 622-6283
www.nasar.org/

National Disaster Search Dog Foundation
323 East Matilija Avenue, #110-245
Ojai, CA 93023-2740
www.west.net/~rescue/

Service and Working Dogs

Canine Companions for
　　Independence
P.O. Box 446
Santa Rosa, CA 95402-0446
(800) 572-2275
www.caninecompanions.org/

Delta Society National Service Dog
　　Center
289 Perimeter Road East
Renton, WA 98055-1329
(800) 869-6898
www.petsforum.com/deltasociety/dsb
　　000.htm

Guiding Eyes for the Blind
611 Granite Springs Road
Yorktown Heights, NY 10598
www.guiding-eyes.org/

The National Education for Assis-
　　tance Dog Services, Inc.
P.O. Box 213
West Boylston, MA 01583
(508) 422-9064
www.chamber.worcester.ma.us/neads
　　/INDEX.HTM

North American Working Dog
　　Association
Southeast Kreisgruppe
P.O. Box 833
Brunswick, GA 31521

The Seeing Eye
P.O. Box 375
Morristown, NJ 07963-0375
(973) 539-4425
www.seeingeye.org/

Therapy Dogs Incorporated
2416 E. Fox Farm Road
Cheyenne, WY 82007
(877) 843-7364
www.therapydogs.com

Therapy Dogs International
6 Hilltop Road
Mendham, NJ 07945
(973) 252-9800
www.tdi-dog.org/

United Schutzhund Clubs of America
3704 Lemay Ferry Road
St. Louis, MO 63125

Index

Meet Your Border Collie Care Experts

Author **Kim D.R. Dearth** is a native New Yorker who graduated from the University of North Carolina at Chapel Hill. A frequent contributor to *Dog World* magazine, Kim is a member of both the Dog Writers Association of America (DWAA) and the Cat Writers' Association (CWA). She has won DWAA awards for writing on the topic of grooming and for editing *Puppy Guide*, *Dog World's* annual edition. The author of Prima's *Your Rottweiler's Life* and *Your Boxer's Life,* Kim teaches classes in puppy preschool, puppy kindergarten, companion obedience, and agility with her able assistant, Rio, a Shetland Sheepdog. In addition, she is the editor of five local special-interest newspapers in Madison, Wisconsin, where she lives with her husband, Dave, their Sheltie, two cats, and new baby.

Trainer **Liz Palika** has been teaching classes for dogs and their owners for over twenty years. Her goal is to help people understand why their dogs do what they do so that dogs and owners can live together successfully. Liz says, "If, in each training class, I can increase understanding and ease frustration so that the dog doesn't end up in the local shelter because the owner has given up, then I have accomplished my goal!" She is the author of 23 books and has won awards from both the Dog Writers Association of America and the ASPCA. Liz and her husband, Paul, share their home with three Australian Shepherds: Dax, Kes, and Riker.

Series Editor **Joanne Howl, D.V.M.,** is a graduate of the University of Tennessee College of Veterinary Medicine and has practiced animal medicine for over ten years. She currently serves as president of the Maryland Veterinary Medical Association and secretary/treasurer of the American Academy on Veterinary Disaster Medicine. Her columns and articles have appeared in a variety of animal-related publications. Dr. Howl presently divides her time between family, small-animal medicine, writing, and the company of her two dogs and six cats.

Prima's YOUR PET'S LIFE® Series

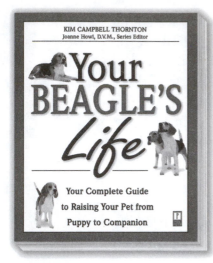

ISBN 0-7615-2050-3

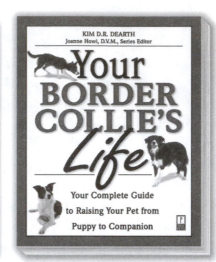

ISBN 0-7615-2536-X

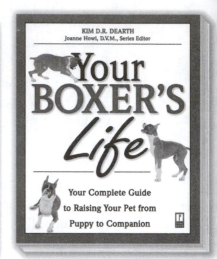

ISBN 0-7615-2048-1

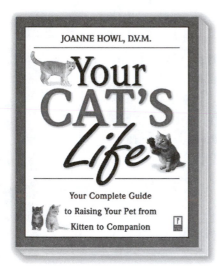

ISBN 0-7615-1361-2

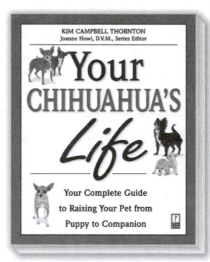

ISBN 0-7615-2051-1

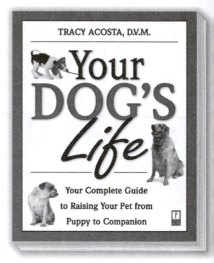

ISBN 0-7615-1543-7

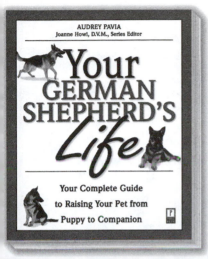

AUDREY PAVIA
Joanne Howl, D.V.M., Series Editor

Your **GERMAN SHEPHERD'S** *Life*

Your Complete Guide to Raising Your Pet from Puppy to Companion

ISBN 0-7615-2052-X

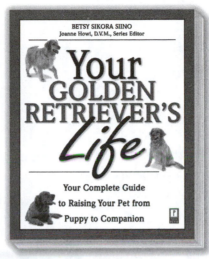

BETSY SIKORA SIINO
Joanne Howl, D.V.M., Series Editor

Your **GOLDEN RETRIEVER'S** *Life*

Your Complete Guide to Raising Your Pet from Puppy to Companion

ISBN 0-7615-2047-3

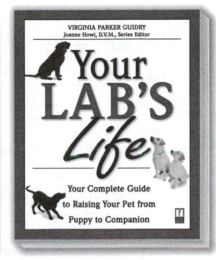

VIRGINIA PARKER GUIDRY
Joanne Howl, D.V.M., Series Editor

Your **LAB'S** *Life*

Your Complete Guide to Raising Your Pet from Puppy to Companion

ISBN 0-7615-2046-5

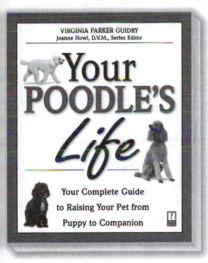

VIRGINIA PARKER GUIDRY
Joanne Howl, D.V.M., Series Editor

Your **POODLE'S** *Life*

Your Complete Guide to Raising Your Pet from Puppy to Companion

ISBN 0-7615-2537-8

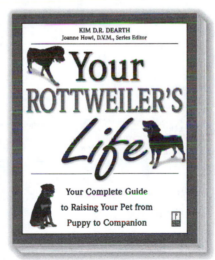

KIM D.R. DEARTH
Joanne Howl, D.V.M., Series Editor

Your **ROTTWEILER'S** *Life*

Your Complete Guide to Raising Your Pet from Puppy to Companion

ISBN 0-7615-2049-X

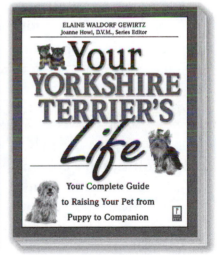

ELAINE WALDORF GEWIRTZ
Joanne Howl, D.V.M., Series Editor

Your **YORKSHIRE TERRIER'S** *Life*

Your Complete Guide to Raising Your Pet from Puppy to Companion

ISBN 0-7615-2535-1

YOUR PET'S LIFE® series is written with one purpose in mind—to give owners the most up-to-date information and guidance they need about the health, nutrition, training, and care of their pet.

A Heartwarming Look at the Emotional Power of Animals

A dog swallows a lit firecracker to protect a child in strife-torn Belfast. A pet pig steers his human family to safety before a propane gas explosion. A horse keeps vigil over an elderly woman until help arrives.

With dozens of touching, true-life stories like these, this heartwarming book gathers compelling proof of the intense love that animals feel for humans.

"Nobody writes about animals better than Kristin von Kreisler."
—CHRIS WILLCOX, editor-in-chief, *Reader's Digest*

"These wonderful stories show once again how close we are to our evolutionary cousins."
—From the foreword by JEFFREY MOUSAIEFF MASSON, coauthor of *When Elephants Weep*

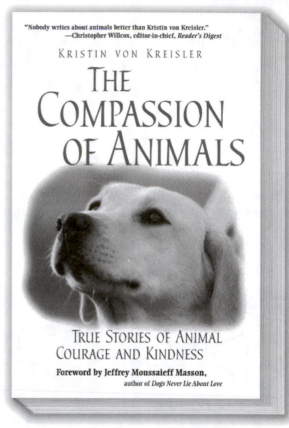

"Nobody writes about animals better than Kristin von Kreisler."
—Christopher Willcox, editor-in-chief, *Reader's Digest*

KRISTIN VON KREISLER

THE COMPASSION OF ANIMALS

TRUE STORIES OF ANIMAL COURAGE AND KINDNESS

Foreword by Jeffrey Moussaieff Masson, author of *Dogs Never Lie About Love*

ISBN 0-7615-1808-8 / Paperback / 288 pages
U.S. $14.95 / Can. $22.95

PRIMA

Available everywhere books are sold.
Visit us online at www.primapublishing.com

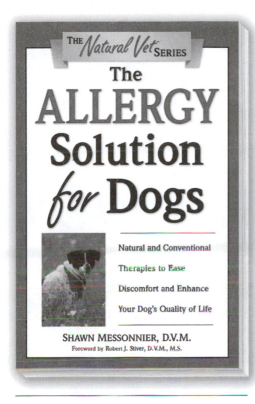
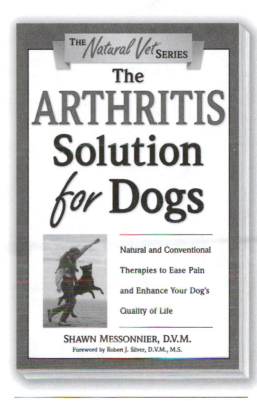